Contemporary Black Theatre and Performance

Methuen Drama Agitations: Text, Politics and Performances

Theatre has always offered immediate responses to political, social, economic, and cultural crisis events that are local, national, and global in dimension, establishing itself as a prime medium of engagement. Methuen Drama Agitations interrogates these manifold intersections between theatre and the contemporary: What is the relationship between theatre and reality? Which functions does the theatre perform in public life? Where does the radical potential of the theatre reside and how is it untapped?

Methuen Drama Agitations addresses issues from across a number of spectrums, including contemporary politics, environmental concerns, issues of gender and race, and the challenges of globalization. The series focuses on text as much as performance, on theory as much as practice. It investigates the lively dialogues between theatre and contemporary lived experience.

Theater of Lockdown: Digital and Distanced Performance in a Time of Pandemic
Barbara Fuchs

Theater in a Post-Truth World: Texts, Politics, and Performance
Edited by William C. Boles

Performing Statecraft: The Postdiplomatic Theatre of Sovereigns, Citizens, and States
Edited by James R. Ball III

Forthcoming Titles

Performing Left Populism: Performance, Politics and the People
Edited by Théo Aiolfi and Goran Petrović-Lotina

Theatre and its Audiences: Reimagining the Relationship in Times of Crisis
Kate Craddock and Helen Freshwater

Performing the Queer Past: Bodies Possessed
Fintan Walsh

Contemporary Black Theatre and Performance

Acts of Rebellion, Activism, and Solidarity

Edited by
DeRon S. Williams, Khalid Y. Long,
and Martine Kei Green-Rogers

methuen | drama
LONDON • NEW YORK • OXFORD • NEW DELHI • SYDNEY

METHUEN DRAMA
Bloomsbury Publishing Plc
50 Bedford Square, London, WC1B 3DP, UK
1385 Broadway, New York, NY 10018, USA
29 Earlsfort Terrace, Dublin 2, Ireland

BLOOMSBURY, METHUEN DRAMA and the Methuen Drama logo are trademarks of Bloomsbury Publishing Plc

First published in Great Britain 2023

Series design by Ben Anslow
Cover images: Red and Black Lit Match Poster (© serazetdinov / Shutterstock); Painted Red Color Background (© fotograzia / Getty Images); Mid adult woman leading a demonstration using a megaphone (© FG Trade / Getty Images)

A catalogue record for this book is available from the British Library.

A catalog record for this book is available from the Library of Congress.

ISBN: HB: 978-1-3502-5292-9
PB: 978-1-3502-5291-2
ePDF: 978-1-3502-5293-6
eBook: 978-1-3502-5294-3

Series: Methuen Drama Agitations: Text, Politics and Performances

Typeset by Integra Software Services Pvt. Ltd.
Printed and bound in Great Britain

To find out more about our authors and books visit www.bloomsbury.com and sign up for our newsletters.

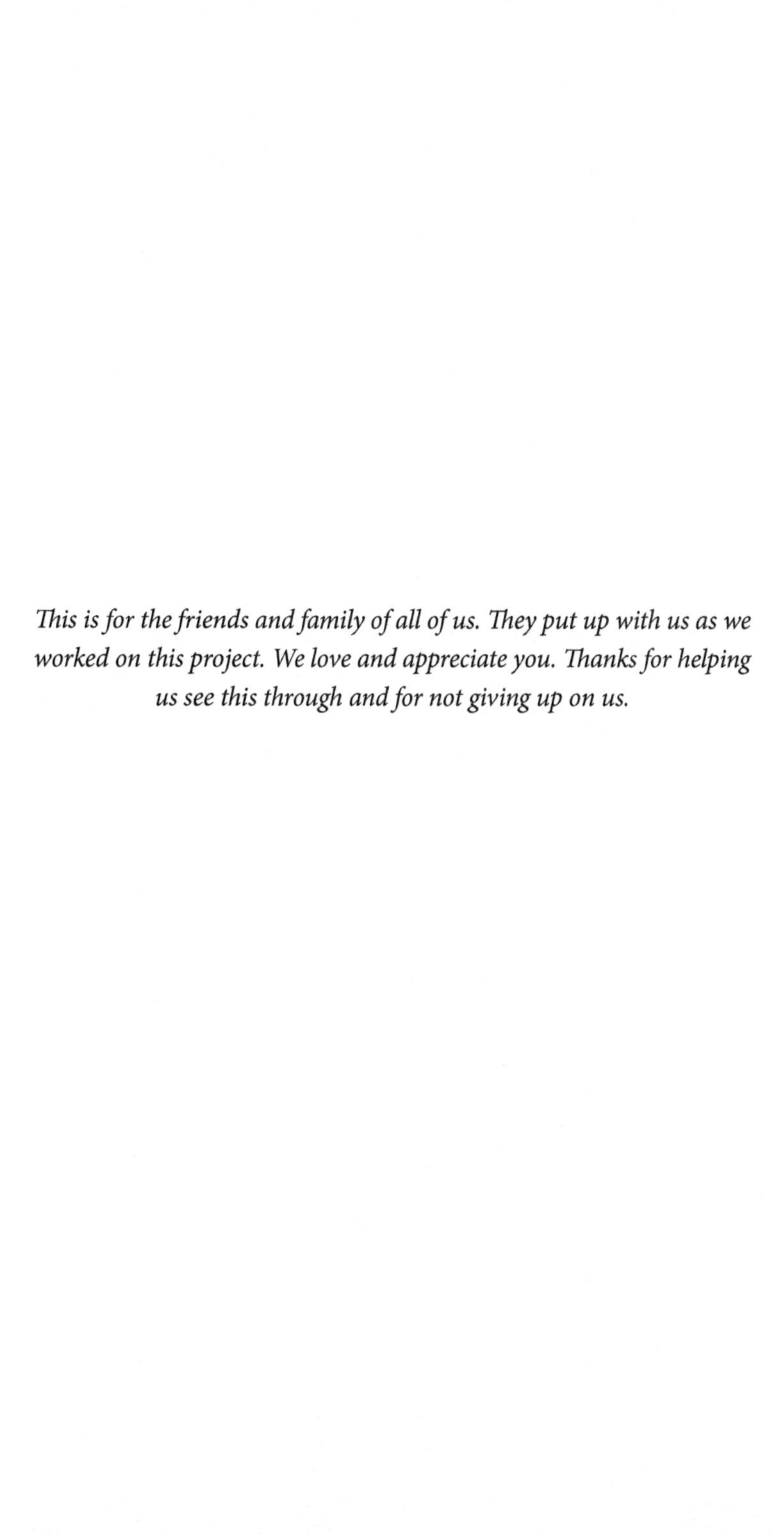

This is for the friends and family of all of us. They put up with us as we worked on this project. We love and appreciate you. Thanks for helping us see this through and for not giving up on us.

Contents

List of Illustrations

Notes on Contributors

Editors

DeRon S. Williams is an Assistant Professor of Theatre in the Department of Fine and Performing Arts at Loyola University Chicago and a freelance director and dramaturg. He has published in *The Journal of American Drama and Theatre* and *Continuum: The Journal of African Diaspora Drama*. His directing credits include both new and canonical works, including Tarell Alvin McCraney's *The Brothers Size*, Regina Taylor's *Crowns*, Bruce Norris's *Clybourne Park*, and *Africa to America: A Celebration of Who We Are*, an interdisciplinary performance written by Wendy R. Coleman.

Khalid Y. Long is an Assistant Professor in the Department of Theatre and Film Studies and the Institute for African American Studies at the University of Georgia. Khalid has published work in the *Journal of American Drama and Theatre*, *The Routledge Companion to African American Theatre & Performance*, and *Continuum: The Journal of African Diaspora Drama, Theatre and Performance*, and is a regular contributor to *Black Masks*. His dramaturgical credits include the world premiere of Tyla Abercrumbie's *Relentless*, *Sunset Baby* by Dominique Morisseau, *Milk Like Sugar* by Kirsten Greenidge, *Mom, How Did You Meet the Beatles?* by Adrienne Kennedy and Adam Kennedy, and *Kill Move Paradise* by James Ijames. Khalid is currently completing his manuscript on Black feminist theatre artist Glenda Dickerson.

Martine Kei Green-Rogers is the Dean of The Theatre School at DePaul University, freelance dramaturg, and Past-President of the Literary Managers and Dramaturgs of the Americas (LMDA). Her publications include "Talkbacks for 'Sensitive Subject Matter' Productions: The Theory and Practice" in *The Routledge Companion to Dramaturgy* and

"A New Noble Kinsmen: The Play On! Project and Making New Plays Out of Old" in *Theatre History Studies*.

Contributors

Quenna L. Barrett is an Educational Theatre EdD candidate at NYU Steinhardt and a Chicago-based theatre artist + practitioner, developing programs to amplify teen + community voices and hold space to rehearse, tell, and change the stories of their lives. She is a company member of ICAH's For Youth Inquiry company, an Associate Artist with Pivot Arts, a member of the Center for Performance and Civic Practice leadership circle, and serves as the Associate Director of Education at the Goodman Theatre.

Loretta L. C. Brady is a Professor in the Department of Psychology at Saint Anselm College and a psychologist. She is also the Director of the Community Resilience and Social Equity Lab, a dynamic research center and consultancy which translates social equity research into practices that make organizations resilient and result in equitable community impact. She co-hosts the podcast *Traumaturgy* (2020–2, Anchor) with Suzanne Delle. Her work engages game and play stories—like theatre—to transform lives and communities experiencing adversity. Her forthcoming book *Technology Touchpoints Parenting in the Digital Dystopia* (2022, Rowman & Littlefield) features research on human development and technology's impact on individuals and families.

Jocelyn L. Buckner is an Associate Professor of Theatre at Chapman University. As a dramaturg, she has supported productions, new play development, and audience engagement at theatres, including South Coast Repertory Theatre, Center Theatre Group, Native Voices at the Autry, and Chance Theater. Her research and publications focus on representations of intersectional identities, materialism, and affect in nineteenth- to twenty-first-century US theatre and popular entertainment. Dr. Buckner is the Editor of the peer-reviewed journal *Theatre History Studies* and President of the American Theatre and Drama Society. She is the Editor of *A Critical Companion to Lynn Nottage* (2016).

s. e. callender, also known as Esi, is a poet, playwright, and producer, completing an Erasmus Mundus European Interdisciplinary Masters in African Studies. Their collective, Sort of Productions, experiments with ways of being together that resist oppression; credits include *bite your tongue* (2018), *ineffable* (2019), and *Wine & Halva* (2020). Esi created the *Hyper Real: Black History Month Exhibition and Event Series* at the VAV Gallery in November (2018). An occasional performer, they appeared as a stage kitten in *Afro Drag* (2019–20).

Suzanne Delle is an Associate Professor of Theatre at York College of PA. She has written about her experience producing "Every 28 Hours" for a Notes from the Field contribution in the July 2018 issue of Theatre Topics and presented it at the Arts and Society Conference in Paris in 2017. Suzanne is the co-host of the podcast *Traumaturgy* with Dr. Loretta Brady and has worked on using theatre in-game creation to help first responders deal with PTSD. She has also presented their work at the 2022 College of English Association and Association of Theatre in Higher Education conferences.

Jenny Henderson is a PhD student in the Department of Theatre and Performance Studies at Tufts University. In 2021, she successfully defended her master's thesis, which examined the US highway as a route to freedom and a site of violence for Black Americans. Her research focuses on the intersections between geography, performance, transit, protest, and public memory.

Maya Johnson graduated from Loyola Marymount University with a major in Communication Studies, with an emphasis in Media, and minors in African American Studies and Theatre Arts in 2021. She is currently a Director's Assistant, having previously worked for Management 360 as a Literary/Talent Assistant. While at LMU, she worked as an administrative assistant in LMU's Office of Ethnic and Intercultural Services and became a Rains Research Assistant, working alongside Dr. Daphnie Sicre and Karl O'Brian Williams on projects covering anti-racist approaches to theatre pedagogy. Outside of LMU, Maya produced films and other creative content at Uni-Colors Entertainment.

Aviva Helena Neff is the Director of Youth and Community Learning at Columbus College of Art and Design and an adjunct faculty member with Otterbein University Department of Theatre and Dance. She is a rustbelt artist-scholar-educator with expertise in diversity, equity, and inclusion in the arts. Dr. Neff enjoys working in devised theatre and theatre for social change with participants aged 1–100. She is an ensemble member with Teatro Travieso, which premiered her solo performance, *Blood, Earth, Water*.

Jocelyn Prince is a Principal at ALJP Consulting, a Lecturer in the Performance Studies Department at Northwestern University, and an Associate Member of Beehive Dramaturg Studio NYC. She has worked with theatres across the country, including Steppenwolf Theatre Company, The Public Theater, Court Theatre, Woolly Mammoth Theatre Company, Cleveland Play House, and Yale Repertory Theatre. Jocelyn is a frequent staffer and volunteer with the Democratic Party, including the 2008 Obama for America, 2016 Hillary for America, and 2020 Kamala Harris for the People campaigns. She has written for *Nonprofit Quarterly*, *African American Review*, *The Chicago Reporter*, and *TimeOut New York*, among other publications. She is a graduate of Bradley University and Northwestern University.

John "Ray" Proctor is an Assistant Professor of Theatre at Tulane University, Department of Theatre and Dance. Proctor holds a BA (Literature) from Webster University, an MFA (Acting) from West

Virginia University, and a PhD (Theatre Research) from the University of Wisconsin-Madison. He has played Mercutio in *Romeo and Juliet (Organic Theatre/Chicago)*, Alonzo in *The Tempest* (New Orleans Shakespeare Festival), *Peter* in Lorraine Hansberry's *Les Blancs* (Madison), *Shylock* in *The Merchant of Venice* (Arizona Repertory Theatre), and the title role in *Othello* (The Greenbriar). In New Orleans, Ray has appeared on the Southern Rep stage in *Airline Highway* and *Father Come Home from the Wars*. He is also an essayist in the forthcoming collection *Romeo and Juliet: Adaptation and the Arts*.

Leticia Ridley is an Assistant Professor of Theatre History and Performance Studies at Santa Clara University. Her primary teaching and research areas include African American theatre and performance, Black feminisms, Black performance theory, and popular culture. She has published scholarly essays in *Frontiers: A Journal of Women's Studies*, the *August Wilson Journal*, *Routledge Anthology of Sports Plays*, and *Journal of American Theatre and Drama*. Leticia is also the co-producer and co-host of *Daughters of Lorraine*, a Black feminist theatre podcast supported by HowlRound Theatre Commons and is a recurring co-host on *On Tap: A Theatre & Performance Studies Podcast*.

Daphnie Sicre teaches Theatre at Loyola Marymount University, where she shares a deep passion for Black and Latinx perspectives in theatre. Engaging in anti-racist and culturally competent theatre practices, she facilitates workshops to teach about EDI theatre pedagogy. When she is not teaching, writing, conducting seminars, or researching AfroLatinidad on stage, she can be found directing or serving as a dramaturg professionally. She has recently published in the *Theatre Symposium—Theatre & Race* journal and a chapter in *The Routledge Companion to African American Theatre and Performance*. Other publications include book chapters in *Black Acting Methods* and the forthcoming *Dynamic Bodies, Emerging Voices*. Daphnie is the resident dramaturg at the Robey Theatre, where she runs the Playwright's Lab and is a culture consultant for Nickelodeon.

Karl O'Brian Williams is the Artistic Director of Braata Productions and coordinates the Theatre Program at BMCC/CUNY. He is an Adjunct Professor at NYU and a Mentor with the Arthur Miller Foundation. He is an award-winning actor and playwright whose work has been produced regionally, Off-Off-Broadway, in the Caribbean, and the UK. His play, *Signs of Friendship*, is part of the anthology "We're Not Neutral: Reset Series 2020 Collected Short Plays" (2021), showcasing BIPOC artists addressing systemic racism, police brutality, and the Covid-19 pandemic.

Isaiah Matthew Wooden is an Assistant Professor of Theater at Swarthmore College. He has published widely on contemporary African American art, drama, and performance in scholarly and popular publications. Wooden is currently working on a monograph that explores the interplay of race and time in contemporary Black expressive culture and co-edited *Tarell Alvin McCraney: Theater, Performance, and Collaboration* (2020).

Harvey Young is the Dean of the College of Fine Arts at Boston University. He has published widely on the performance and experience of race in academic journals, profiled in *The New Yorker*, the *Wall Street Journal*, and *The Chronicle of Higher Education*. He has published seven books, including *Embodying Black Experience* (2010), winner of "Book of the Year" awards from the National Communication Association and the American Society for Theatre Research. Harvey has also appeared on CNN, 20/20, and Good Morning America and within the pages of the *New York Times, Vanity Fair*, and *People* as a popular culture commentator.

Preface

This is a book for, and of, our ancestors. They are the ones who came before—who made and paved the way for us to document the revolution. That revolution is born of their resistance and made of their blood. This book is also for, and of, us. The ones who remain and the ones who continue to ask the world around us to be better and do better. We continue the revolution with our blood, sweat, tears, minds, and art. We are scholars who are practitioners who want to push our industry through documentation, theory, practice, and criticism.

We set on this journey as a triumvirate because it made sense to us as three Black people who value thinking about the practice of theatre just as much as we value making art to puzzle through the question of "who and where are we now?" and find those amongst us who were asking the same question.

This project took several years with starts and stops—as a global pandemic will do with any project—written for a publisher or produced on a stage. We felt the spirit of this book needed to extend grace to ourselves as well as the many collaborators you will find in this book. Self-care is the nemesis of white supremacy and urgency is a tool of capitalism to keep those who have lives sans privilege out of action and discourse. It felt right as editors of a book focusing on rebellion, activism, and solidarity to remember that as an action throughout this process and not just abstract ideas to be cultivated and discussed within the pages. As such, we (as well as our collaborators) changed jobs, went up for tenure, searched for jobs with varying outcomes, etc., and still endured to bring all the information found within this text.

We hope this inspires you to keep rebelling, that this fosters activism, and results in solidarity as we move our field of study, inquiry, and practice forward.

Acknowledgments

First and foremost, we would like to acknowledge the present and omnipresent ancestors who paved the way to create this book because of their vigorous resistance to second-class citizenship, multifaceted activism for equity, and devotion to building solidarity and collective voice through performance, storytelling, and community formation. We give all the glory and gratitude to the trails they have cleared, blazed, and prepared for all of us to do this most important work.

With deep gratitude, we acknowledge and thank the panelists—Sharell D. Luckett, Kashi Johnson, Jonathan Lassiter, and DeRon S. Williams—for creating the "Okkuurrr! Still Woke and Still Engaged in Black Rebellion and Intersectional Solidarities" panel for the 2019 American Studies Association Conference. At this moment the universe began to orchestrate this project, laying the groundwork for this book. Thank you to Mark Dungeon for recognizing the project's significance and shepherding us through the proposal process. We sincerely appreciate William C. Boles and Anja Hartl, our editors, Ella Wilson, Editorial Assistant, and the Methuen Drama Imprint team for their patience, grace, and support throughout the project.

Thank you to all contributors for your brilliance, insight, and attentiveness. Your ability to work through two pandemics—Covid and Social Injustice—has not gone unnoticed. We recognize the mental and physical challenges you have had to navigate to make this project come to fruition.

As in life, it takes a village to raise a child. Therefore, we would like to thank our respective villages for lending their ears, opening their hearts, and embracing this project as if it were theirs.

DeRon would like to thank Khalid and Martine for a collaboration made from heaven, joining the project with great enthusiasm, devotion, and thoughtfulness. He thanks his parents, George Williams and Shirley

Scott, sister, Shalira Williams, and nephews, JaVeon Brigham and Anthony Nasir Watson, because their love, support, and willingness to take this journey have helped make it a bit easier. He sends his love and appreciation to his family as they understood the assignment and provided the space, time, and support necessary to make it come to light. DeRon also would like to thank his community of encouragers, givers, and supporters (in no particular order): Julius B. Fleming Jr., Wendy R. Coleman, La Marr Jurrelle Bruce, Isaiah Matthew Wooden, Don Gagnon, Kevin Lawrence Henry Jr., Jawan Jackson, Chase Sullivan, Jeffrey Ambroise, La Donness Belle Peterson, Renee Jones, Isabel Logan, Sharrell D. Luckett, Joshua Sumrell, Michael Rouleau, Ta'Varis Wilson, and Amar Atkinson. He would like to thank the New England Board of Higher Education (NEBHE), North Star Collective Fellowship Program, Eastern Connecticut State University, his colleagues, and students for supporting him throughout the process, with special thanks to Kristen Morgan and the Assistants to the Editors Shalaine McCall and Karis Burke. And though this project began in 2019, DeRon would like to extend thanks to his new colleagues at Loyola University Chicago for their encouragement and continued support.

Khalid would like to thank DeRon and Martine for being fantastic and fun collaborators and friends. Khalid thanks his family and friends for their support and encouragement, especially his grandmother (his favorite girl in the world) Myra "Nonnie" White, the White family, the Long family, the Harper family, and the Taylor family. Khalid would also like to thank his chosen family: Shiraya Soto, Timea Webster, Wayne Cooper, Markeytah Garrett, Chase Sullivan, Isaiah M. Wooden, Tia Dolet, Jazmin Pichardo, Tatiana Benjamin, MK Abadoo, Nana Brantuo, Robert Jiles, Donelle Boose, Darius Bost, The McGuires, The Drakes, Victor Slaughter, Trent Williams, Floyd Hardin III, and Shaeeda Ama. Khalid gives thanks to his former professors, mentors, and colleagues, especially Faedra Chatard Carpenter, James Harding, Scot Reese, Esther Kim Lee, Sandra G. Shannon, Ann Elizabeth Armstrong, Psyche Williams-Forson, Julius Fleming, La Marr Jurrelle Bruce, Dawn Renee Jones, Justin Brill, and Jesse Carlo. Khalid would also like to thank his colleagues at the University of Georgia for supporting the completion of this collection. Khalid gives praise to the ancestors who've guided him over the past few years, especially Paul Bryant-Jackson, Chris C. White, Hasan Long, Steve Long, and Edythe Scott Bagley. Khalid dedicates his work in the collection to his husband, Robert Davison-Long, and their fur baby, DaLo, for reminding him daily of why he studies, teaches, and creates Black theatre: that is, to materialize a world where all folks are free and liberated.

Martine would like to thank DeRon for keeping us in line and Khalid for being the stable rock he is. She would also like to thank Shane, my colleagues and students at SUNY New Paltz, UNCSA, and her new colleagues and students at DePaul (yes, that much change happened over the course of this book!) for supporting her as she figured out how to make the time and space for this project.

Last but not least, we want to thank you for sharing this knowledge with us.

Introduction

DeRon S. Williams, Khalid Y. Long, and
Martine Kei Green-Rogers

When we first began working on this collection, we were inspired by two edited collections that took up the politics and the possibilities of Black theatre and performance. The first was *The Theatre of Black Americans: A Collection of Critical Essays,* edited by Errol Hill. In particular, Hill's introduction to the collection inspired us to think about how artist-activists today are employing Black theatre to respond to the social crises plaguing Black America. Hill writes,

> Theatre is both an art and an industry; an expression of culture and a source of livelihood for artists and craftsmen; a medium of instruction and a purveyor of entertainment. The essays collected in this book attempt to view Black theatre in all aspects, but the exercise goes beyond the purely academic. There is a sense of urgency that informs our inquiry. Black Americans today recognize, perhaps more clearly than at any other time in their history, that theatre as an institution can have a significant impact on the relentless struggle of a deprived racial minority for full equality and on the need for spiritual well-being of a people divorced from their ancestral heritage through centuries of degrading slavery.[1]

Hill's assertion about the necessity of Black theatre could easily be employed to consider the landscape of Black theatre and performance today. What stood out, in particular, is Hill's notion about the "sense of urgency"[2] that informed the chapters within the collection. *Contemporary Black Theatre: Acts of Rebellion, Activism, and Solidarity,* too, is motivated by the same sense of urgency; thus, we recognize, like Hill, "the theatre's potential for changing, healing, and restoring."[3] We further acknowledge that for change to happen, artists/activists must first ignite the rebellious flame of Black art, that is, to push beyond the confines of what is deemed permissible and appropriate and to insert/assert an identity and a politic that is not limiting through the prism of performance. We also contend that healing and restoring are both foundations of activism that are best achieved through solidarity efforts for a more transgressive and peaceful world. In total, we maintain that the theatre and performance have played and continue to play a significant role in the fight for social justice and civic engagement.

The second text to inspire this collection was Harry J. Elam, Jr. and David Krasner's *African American Performance and Theater History: A Critical Reader*. Like Errol Hill, Elam and Krasner's text pushed us to think about how contemporary dramatic works, theatrical events, and social performances have been regarded as a means to combat social ills. In the introduction, for instance, Elam writes "Accordingly, the social and historical contexts of production can critically affect theatrical performances of blackness and their meanings. At the same time, theatrical representations and performances have profoundly impacted African American cultural, social, and political struggles."[4] At the heart of Elam's statement is the notion that Black theatre and performance are subversive and thus have served as a radical means of "social protest" and "revolt in order to change black lives and fight oppressive conditions."[5]

What can be gleaned from both texts mentioned above is that acts of rebellion, activism, and solidarity form the roots of Black theatre and performance. And the reverse must also be noted: the affective qualities of Black theatre and performance practices are core tenets for acts of rebellion, activism, and solidarity. Whereas the history and experiences of Black people are deeply entrenched in years of enslavement, oppression, and abuse, performance and theatricality have served as a linchpin in the reckoning for social justice. From William Alexander Brown's opening of the African Grove Theatre in New York

City in 1821 and Sojourner Truth's "Ain't I a Woman" speech at the 1851 Women's Rights Convention in Akron, Ohio, to more contemporary examples such as Aretha Franklin singing "My Country' Tis of Thee" at President Barack Obama's inauguration and Idris Goodwin's Free Play: Open Source Scripts toward an Antiracist Tomorrow inspired by the marches and protests around the killing of unarmed Black men and women such as Breonna Taylor, Ahmaud Arbery, and George Floyd, Black folks have always employed performance and performative modes to advocate for a more peaceful world. Even more, artists-activists are using theatre and performance today to address social issues that have still not received much attention in the mainstream theatre and performance world, such as HIV and queer love.

And so, with *Contemporary Black Theatre: Acts of Rebellion, Activism, and Solidarity*, we set out to document the ways in which Black artists/activists have used theatre and performance—from scripted performances, street protests, and other popular culture/public displays of Black performance—to negotiate racialized terrains while also advocating for a more utopian world. Like feminist theatre scholar Jill Dolan, we, the editors and the contributors, "believe that theatre and performance can articulate a common future, one that's more just and equitable, one in which we can all participate more equally, with more chances to live fully and contribute to the making of culture."[6] Thus, we believe deeply in the power of "performance as a tool for making the world better, to use performance to incite people to profound responses that shake their consciousness of themselves in the world."[7]

Additionally, this anthology considers performance in the way that Black feminist cultural critic and now ancestor bell hooks has laid out in her essay, "Performance Practice as a Site of Opposition," denoting that performance can "serve as critical intervention, as site of resistance"; thus, performance "has been crucial in the struggle for liberation."[8] Hooks further writes, "Whenever we choose performance as a site to build communities of resistance, we must be able to shift paradigms and styles of performance in a manner that centralizes the decolonization of black minds and imaginations, even if we include everyone else in the process."[9] This collection aims to record in print form the various ways artists have taken up this mantle, subsequently offering a mix of critical scholarship, meditations, and blueprints for surviving and thriving throughout the continuation of social unrest that has been particularly harmful to Black people. The chapters in this compendium seek to push the boundaries of Black cultural performance and discuss how Black artists, activists, and pedagogues find themselves at the nexus of rebellion, activism, and solidarity, further impacting Black cultural, social, and political struggles. Just as well, these chapters prove that theatre and performance are cathartic, transformative, powerful, and necessary.

We hope this text will inspire readers while igniting their curiosity to examine, create, and/or document the various ways in which they use theatre to accentuate activist movements, empower sociopolitical resistance, and establish communal bonds that facilitate healing, growth, and understanding. As such, we offer a breakdown of the book's three sections: stage as a site of radical possibilities, performance in the making, and performance and/*as* protest.

Part I: Stage as a Site of Radical Possibilities

We begin this book by examining text from two Black contemporary playwrights and investigating dramatic structures' impact on audiences. Jocelyn L. Buckner's chapter, "*Sweat* Equity: Lynn Nottage's Dramaturgy of Deindustrialization," investigates the more radical aspects of Lynn Nottage's labor as a leading Black playwright dedicated to challenging traditional Eurocentric forms of storytelling while simultaneously privileging underrepresented voices and communal forms of playwriting, narrative development, and production. To dramaturgically shift perspective and narrative, the next chapter, "Those Songs Were More than Just: Spirituals, Queer Reckonings, and Tarell Alvin McCraney's *Choir Boy*," by Isaiah Matthew Wooden, examines the ways in which playwright Tarell Alvin McCraney shrewdly incorporates songs from the African American spiritual tradition in his coming-of-age drama *Choir Boy* to explore connections between the Black past and present. In their chapter, "Trauma, Truth, and Turning the Lens: Black Theatre Artists and White Theatre Audiences," Suzanne Delle and Loretta L. C. Brady ask us to ponder the dramatic structures found in works in the American Theatre (and the previous chapters) as a form of "traumaturgy" and its ultimate audience impact. Rounding out this section is an interview with Christina Anderson facilitated by co-editor DeRon S. Williams. Their discussion touches upon the ways in which Anderson wrote the plays—*How to Catch a Creation* and *Blacktop Sky*—to disrupt society's limited understanding of Black women and reveal the depth and breadth of how they live and love. More significantly, Anderson sheds light on her work's intentionality to empower Black women and create a world where they can live and love without the need to explain their feelings.

Part II: Performance in the Making

This section of the book interrogates the possibilities around performance-making processes and pedagogy as a site for activism and solidarity. Beginning with "*Re-writing the Declaration*: Healing in Theatre from a Black, Queer, Feminist Lens" by Quenna L. Barrett, this chapter offers an analysis of the possibility of the (virtual) theatre site as an active space of social transformation and reflects how a theatrical process attempts to address and disrupt power and oppression internally with the theatre-makers themselves and externally to its audiences. The section then moves to "*ineffable* Dramaturgies: Experiments in Black Queer and Trans Theatre" by s. e. callender. This chapter charts the development of *ineffable: a play in process* which was established in an open-ended process of intercultural collaboration. Through an understanding of its creation process and the local context in which it appeared, this chapter discusses the process as a subversion of how a play is made, centering on Black queer and trans lives. "Reconsidering and Recasting" by John "Ray" Proctor seeks to think through how casting practices concerning race have the potential to undermine the very issue it is meant to open for BIPOC artists. Pushing us to think further about performance and how it manifests in the classroom is the impetus for "Reflecting on 'The Work' of *We Are the Canon*: AntiRacist Theatre Pedagogy Workshops" by Maya Johnson, Daphnie Sicre, and Karl O'Brian Williams. This chapter lays out the history of the pedagogical work the three accomplished together and discusses. What does the anti-racist classroom look like? How do you revise your syllabus with a revisionist anti-racist approach? How do we deconstruct the meaning of "the canon" and include the missing voices, especially Black voices? How do we rethink teaching theatre courses and creating inclusive curricula? This section culminates with an interview of Donja R. Love facilitated by co-editor Martine Kei Green-Rogers. In this interview, Love discusses how he used playwriting as a place of liberation after his HIV diagnosis. He also discusses his *Love Plays* that center on queerness in the Jim Crow South and on Civil War plantations.

Part III: Performance and/as Protest

Lastly, this section delves into the varying ways in which performance either is the protest or lives as documentation of protest. Jenny Henderson starts with "(W)Right of Way: Black Geographies and American Interstates," which situates the highway as a route of freedom and a site of violence for Black Americans. Next, we move on to "Honk for Justice Chicago" by Jocelyn Prince and Harvey Young. This chapter spotlights social and performance-based activism in Chicago by examining the Honk for Justice Chicago Protests, created by Democratic Party activist Jocelyn Prince in conversation with the performance art of Tricia Hersey and damali ayo. "Grunt Work: Serena Williams' Black Sound Acts as Resistance" by Leticia Ridley focuses on the grunting of Serena Williams during her tennis matches. Situating the "grunt" as a sonic disruption, this chapter offers Williams's sonic expressions as performances of her refusal to articulate in ways deemed acceptable by the white hegemonic space of tennis. Aviva Helen Neff's chapter "Black Squares, White Faces: Cancel Culture and Protest in the Age of Digital Blackface," explores how acts of solidarity such as "calling out" instances of racism are intertwined with allegations of cancel culture across social media and how accountability is rendered in/tangible online. Additionally, it chronicles the ways in which social media has evolved as a space for solidarity, racial performance, and subversion through comedy, protest, and so-called cancel culture. Last but not least, this journey ends with co-editor Khalid Y. Long's discussion with Willa J. Taylor, Director of Education and Community Engagement at the Goodman Theatre (Chicago), on how institutions such as the Goodman Theatre have pushed the boundaries with efforts to be more diverse, inclusive, and equitable.

Notes

1 Errol Hill, *The Theater of Black Americans: A Collection of Critical Essays* (New York: Applause, 1987), 1.

2 Ibid., 1.

3 Ibid., 1.

4 Harry Justin Elam and David Krasner, *African-American Performance and Theater History a Critical Reader* (Oxford [England]: Oxford University Press, 2001), 3.

5 Ibid., 6.

6 Jill Dolan, "Performance, Utopia, and the 'Utopian Performative,'" *Theatre Journal* 53, no. 3 (2001): 455. http://www.jstor.org/stable/25068953

7 Ibid., 456.

8 bell hooks, "Performance Practice as a Site of Opposition," in *Let's Get It On: The Politics of Black Performance*, ed. Catherine Ugwu, 210–19 (Seattle: Bay View Press, 1995), 211.

9 Ibid., 217.

Part One

Stage as a Site of Radical Possibilities

1

Sweat Equity: Lynn Nottage's Dramaturgy of Deindustrialization

Jocelyn L. Buckner

Lynn Nottage has devoted her career to researching and telling stories of Black individuals and communities with expressed interest in laborers, advocating for their agency, humanity, and legacy. In her second Pulitzer Prize-winning play, *Sweat*, Nottage dramatizes more recent US history, illuminating the lives of workers marginalized by the deindustrialization of the Rust Belt in the early 2000s. *Sweat* is emblematic of Nottage's sustained effort to deploy playwriting as activism and stand in solidarity with those whose stories she chooses to tell. As a constant theme in her works, Lynn Nottage's stories align with marginalized workers' efforts and histories, connecting the pride of the factory employees in *Sweat* with the dignity of Mama Nadi in *Ruined*, the resourcefulness of the women and men in *Intimate Apparel*, the resilience and tenacity of Undine Barnes in *Fabulation*, and the determination of the titular character in *By the Way, Meet Vera Stark*. These fellow laborers all demonstrate an intent to survive amid dire circumstances and diminishing resources. *Sweat* is another act of rebellion designed to advocate for workers' lives and meet changemakers on their own turf, advocating for a compassionate conversation about and action to alleviate the human cost of the economic policies of the past quarter-century.

Nottage's writings, in many ways, serve as a documentation of history. In *Sweat*, Nottage reflects on events precipitating the Great Recession, including the prolonged economic strain of the North American Free

Trade Agreement (NAFTA) on US factory workers and the stock market collapse of September 2008. But perhaps more presciently, she anticipates the (inter)national focus on American deindustrialization and the disenfranchised working-class spotlighted in the historic 2016 US presidential election. The extreme sense of governmental neglect felt by laborers, and particularly by the white working class, became evident as many aligned with Trump's backward-looking, nostalgia-laced promise to "Make America Great Again," a slogan lifted directly from Ronald Reagan's own 1980 presidential campaign and encouraging associations with an earlier celebrity President. Nottage has stated the play is not about the election: "The play is not about Donald Trump's America .... I think that that's one way for people who feel guilty for not being more alert interpret it. This play was written before Donald Trump was even on the landscape, and it takes place in 2000 and 2008."[1] Yet she also notes the importance of the play's political context, explaining, "Absolutely I was considering politically what was happening, and it's part of why we wanted the play to be produced just before the election. I knew exactly."[2] Nottage's depiction of workers' displacement in an economy that no longer values their contributions to an industry or company to which their families have been loyal for generations anticipates and captures the zeitgeist of the era immediately preceding and surrounding *Sweat.*

The press response to the play's premiere (2015), Broadway run (2017), and Pulitzer Prize win (2017) often focused on its significance and sociopolitical themes. This chapter investigates Nottage's dedication to re-imagining traditionally white-centered, Aristotelian, Western forms of storytelling while simultaneously privileging underrepresented voices and communal forms of playwriting, narrative development, and production such as ethnography, docudrama, devising, and complementary community arts programming. Her efforts to represent the context and implications of manufacturing and (inter)national economic policy of the last two decades, and her investigations of forgotten archives of embodied, lived experience yield a dramatization of the dangers of economic monopoly and shrinking markets. Nottage foregrounds this in production through layering multimedia evidence and supertitles that historically grid the play's action. She practices a collaborative development process with creative team members and the citizens of Reading, PA, to capture their stories in production. As supplemental programming, she also developed a separate transmedia, site-specific production called *This Is Reading*, a celebration of the community with and for residents. She also coordinated outreach performances of *Sweat* for Rust Belt communities supported by The Public Theater's Mobile Unit National program. Finally, her sculpting of multigenerational, multiracial characters pushes audiences to confront the history Americans are currently living. These combined dramaturgical efforts reframe evidence, remember the disenfranchised, and refocus conversations about our collective post-industrial future.

Reframing Evidence

Beyond the play's charged premiere amidst the 2016 election campaign, *Sweat* reflects several defining moments from recent history: the contentious 2000 millennial moment, the transition period between the two-term Clinton/Gore administration and the controversial election of Bush/Cheney, the 2008 historic election of Barack Obama which coincided with the surge in economic prosperity on the verge of a bursting financial bubble, and the pending Great Recession. Both acts begin in 2008, highlighting two young men, Jason (white American of German descent) and Chris (African American).[3] After eight years, the two have just been released from incarceration and struggle to reunite with their families and re-enter their community, which are worse off than when they went to prison. The play ends in 2008, with the characters fighting to rebuild their lives and hoping for change.

Most of the play occurs over the course of eleven months in 2000 and is informed by international economic policy and diplomatic negotiations begun a decade earlier. For example, Nottage provides historical and political context to the circumstances of the Reading community by referencing trade policies such as the North American Free Trade Agreement (NAFTA) between Mexico, Canada, and the United States. NAFTA negotiations began in 1990 under President George H. W. Bush. The agreement was then ratified in 1994 under newly elected President William (Bill) Clinton, who stated, NAFTA "means greater productivity, lower unemployment, greater worker efficiency, and higher wages and greater security for our people .... Good jobs, rewarding careers, broadened horizons for middle class Americans can only be secured by expanding exports and global growth."[4] Some herald NAFTA as a jobs creator, securing a tariff-free market and creating one of the largest markets for US exports between Mexico. Yet the outsourcing of US manufacturing led to economic collapse in states where manufacturing long served as the primary source of employment.

In conjunction with increased automation in manufacturing, NAFTA's rollout adversely affected the town of Reading, PA, precipitating factory closures and a subsequent rise in unemployment. In 2011, the US Census Bureau named Reading the poorest city in the nation, prompting Nottage to question what led this once-profitable railroad town to the point of demise and eventually inspiring *Sweat*.[5] The play focuses on the careers and families of three women who have worked in the same factory for decades—Tracey (white American of German descent and Jason's mother), Cynthia (African American and Chris's mother), and Jessie (Italian-American)—whose close-knit, inter-racial friendship is destroyed by the deindustrialization of their town. Throughout the play, the women gather in their favorite bar run by a former mill worker, Stan (white American of German descent), and a Colombian-American barkeep named Oscar. When Cynthia earns a promotion ahead of a plant lockout, followed by Spanish-speaking laborers crossing the union picket line to gain nonunion employment, rifts between the women surface, dissolving their relationships along racial lines. This dissolution reflects Nottage's observations about workers' frustrations in Reading, which she witnessed during more than two years of visiting the town, engaging with community members, and gathering research for the play. She notes, "There are powers that be that are invested in us remaining divided along racial lines, along economic lines. And so at the heart of my play, what I was looking at is the way in which economics fracture people along racial lines."[6] As circumstances in the play become increasingly desperate, micro-aggressions about the precarity of wages and inequities based on race, gender, age, and citizenship morph into full-blown hate speech and physical violence, with dire consequences.[7]

Nottage introduces each scene with a date and the Fahrenheit temperature, followed by events of the day that locate the action chronologically, economically, and seasonally and outline the scene's temporal, sociopolitical, and physical cartography. She carefully constructs what Elinor Fuchs would term the "small planet" of Reading, creating a microcosm of US deindustrialization and inviting audiences to engage intimately with one community's experience of this widespread crisis. She codes the play with sensorial touchpoints and cultural references, encouraging resonance with viewers' own memories of the not-so-distant past. In production, this translates into a multi-sensory onslaught of archival news feeds, soundbites, music, and supertitles, framing the action and transporting viewers to a specific moment. As each scene begins, the uncertainty of the turn of the millennium in 2000 and the tensions of the economic freefall and political landscape of 2008 became more apparent in what Courtney Elkin Mohler, borrowing from Linda Hutcheon, describes as an "ironic nostalgia." The flood of footage showing presidential elections, housing bubbles, stock market highs and crashes, trade, unemployment, war, all of the "wrenching, grim scenes that take place in the scenes occurring in 2008 beg us to examine our feelings of nostalgia for those moments in 2000 when we did not yet realize the extent to which the neoliberal project would turn America's industrial cities into economic ghost towns."[8] Nottage evokes these images intentionally, crafting an affective cocktail of irony, remembrance, and anxiety that positions viewers to intellectually and emotionally understand the magnitude of the sociopolitical and historical moment the characters are navigating while remaining transfixed by their interpersonal dramas.

This transmedia montage is evocative of the "ripped from the headlines" approach of docudramas and Living Newspaper performances of the 1930s. It is coupled with Brechtian elements such as supertitles, music, and exposed scene changes to underscore the characters' shifting circumstances. Nottage's use of media in production creates an "immersive but estranging and disintegrative environment of postdramatic theatre; 'a space between realities'" that distances but also encourages critical consideration.[9] In the Oregon Shakespeare Festival, Center Theatre Group (Los Angeles), and Donmar Warehouse (London) productions of *Sweat* I have experienced, media was a lure into the world of the play, permeating the fourth wall and blending the onstage reality with my own lived experience and memories of these moments. Nottage's radical use of media and spectacle reframes archival evidence of the socioeconomic history of the not-so-distant past, juxtaposing seismic political and financial paradigm shifts with changes in the material conditions of individual workers' lives. This approach to reframing the recent past is a radical act intended to advocate for workers such as the residents of Reading, who are not often featured in news headlines, yet whose lives and livelihoods are impacted by the sociopolitical events of the day.

Remembering the Disenfranchised

Nottage was accompanied on her ethnographic research visits to Reading by a team of assistants and her long-time collaborator director Kate Whoriskey, enabling them to spend significant amounts of time with residents to develop an understanding of the complicated social fabric of the town, as well as a shared vocabulary for aesthetically rendering the community. Nottage spoke with a wide range of individuals. Their stories enabled her to re-member the disenfranchised citizens of Reading into composite characters, giving voice to forgotten American workers reflected yet anonymized in bleak unemployment figures and marginalized by the legacy of NAFTA and the Great Recession.[10] *Sweat* dramatizes Nottage's research in a humane and impactful form, drawing attention to the community's circumstances and the larger crisis of deindustrialization.

After working in the same factory since high school, Tracey and Cynthia, now in their mid-forties, have been joined in the plant by their twenty-one-year-old sons Jason and Chris and are concerned about possible cutbacks at the facility. Cynthia dismisses the rumors, to which the bartender Stan, retired from the plant after twenty-eight years due to an injury, replies, "You could wake up tomorrow and all your jobs are in Mexico, whatever, it's this NAFTA bullshit-" to which Tracey retorts, "Sounds like a laxative. NAFTA."[11] Her laughter reveals a simultaneous bitter acceptance and resistant, willful ignorance of their circumstances in the face of imminent threats of job loss and unfair treatment.

Cynthia views the rumor of a management shakeup at the plant as an opportunity to move off the assembly line floor and into a position more forgiving of a body prematurely aged by a quarter-century of physical labor. When Tracey dismisses her chances of a promotion, Cynthia counters, "Don't know about you, but I can feel my body slowing down, a little every day."[12] Cynthia's concerns reveal the human costs of such labor and the detachment between the material realities of the white-collar executives overseeing the plant and the blue-collar workers reporting every day, decade after decade, on the factory line. Stan also doubts Cynthia's ability to make the leap from factory floor to administrative office, noting that the new generation of management is even further removed than previous ones from the labor occurring in the factory: "The problem is they don't wanna get their feet dirty, their diplomas soiled with sweat … or understand the real cost, the human cost of making their shitty product."[13] The disconnect between management and workers and their respective views on the value of education versus labor further manifests the dissonance between politicians' economic legislation and citizens' lived realities.

When Cynthia does earn the promotion off the floor, her distinct experience as a Black woman working in the plant becomes even more apparent. After her promotion, the plant stages a lockout, forcing workers off the line and causing rifts between friends and co-workers.

Tracey and Jessie pressure Cynthia to fight for union negotiations; yet, Cynthia struggles to stand with her friends while maintaining her new position. As she explains to Stan, "Not many of us folks worked there .... I wonder if they gave me this job on purpose. Pin a target on me so they can stay in their air-conditioned offices."[14] Cynthia's experience of "us folks" (Black workers) versus "them" (white managers of the plant) frames her worldview and her ultimate decision to protect her promotion rather than striking with her colleagues. She explains to Tracey and Jessie: "I've stood on that line, same line since I was nineteen .... I don't think you get it, but if I walk away, I'm giving up more than a job, I'm giving up all the time I spent standing on line waiting for one damn opportunity."[15] Aligning with generations of workers marginalized, passed over, and racially discriminated against, Cynthia's refusal to turn down the promotion to stand in solidarity with her white co-workers is an act of rebellion that underscores her need to advocate for herself distinct from the needs of her colleagues. Tracey's inability to recognize Cynthia's double disenfranchisement as a Black woman in the factory results in an irrevocable rift in their relationship and erodes the workers' collective ability to resist oppression from plant management.

When Cynthia shares her plans to apply for promotion, Tracey considers applying for the job too, but tempers her expectations by reasoning, "none of us *girls* are gonna get it, right?"[16] Her comments reveal her internalized sexism, reinforced by decades of working for exploitative managers. Later, Tracey further describes the blatant gender discrimination and sexual harassment she experienced from supervisors in the workplace while also revealing her own racial bias toward workers of color. While celebrating Cynthia's promotion, Tracey takes a smoke break outside the bar and encounters Oscar, the Colombian-American barkeep. Tracey begins to question how Cynthia earned the job and shares her own job insecurity explaining "the only reason I didn't get the job is because Butz tried to fuck me and I wouldn't let him ... And, I betcha they wanted a minority. I'm not prejudice, [*sic*] but that's how things are going these days."[17] Tracey's revelation of her own sexual harassment, coupled with her racist perspective on

Cynthia's hiring and those she assumes are immigrants (like the other characters, Oscar was born in Berks County, PA), again highlights the dis-ease of white, blue-collar workers. Her perspective points to the fact, as Michelle Alexander observes, that race is "a powerful wedge, breaking up what had been a solid liberal coalition based on economic interests of the poor and the working and lower-middle classes."[18] Nottage, in turn, notes that "when people become desperate, they begin to cannibalize the people who are closest to them .... rather than uniting as a group, what they choose to do is become even more fractured."[19]

Tracey's resistance toward a diversified workforce anticipates the backward-facing nostalgia evoked by so many voters during the 2016 US presidential election. As economic solidarity between workers fades, Tracey clings to her family's labor history and the sense of privilege and pride it evokes. She reminisces about her German immigrant grandfather. "It was back when if you worked with your hands people respected you for it. It was a gift. But now, there's nothing."[20] Tracey's memories echo Nottage's observations that Reading residents often described their town in the past tense, "Reading was ..., " prompting her to wonder how a community envisions a future when they cannot fully live in the present or plan for a tomorrow.

In contrast to Cynthia and Tracey, Jessie represents personal dreams deferred. While Jessie provides some of the play's hard-earned dark comedic relief through her boozy blackouts—manifestations of her unhappiness in her job and her personal life—she also reveals the hope and possibility she had when she started working at the factory. "I figured I'd be at Olstead's six to eight months max .... I guess, I wish ... I had gotten to see the world. You know, left Berks, if only for a year. That's what I regret. Not the work, I regret that for a little while it seemed like, I don't know, there was possibility."[21] The disparity between Jessie's dreams and her reality is a stark model of labor and sacrifice in a town where options are few.

Tracey, Cynthia, and Jessie's middle-aged concerns about job security and survival are triangulated to create a composite of the challenges of their circumstances in contrast with Jason and Chris, who represent a younger generation of workers weaned on the promise of union wages who must suddenly acquire more transferable skills, likely outside their hometown. Chris struggles with whether to continue working in the plant or go to college to become a teacher. His decision is financially complicated, noting, "Nobody tells you that no matter how hard you work there will never be enough money to rest."[22] Jason and Stan try to persuade him against it, arguing that teaching "don't pay jack shit," and "you leave, it'll be impossible to get back in. They'll be ten guys lining up for your fucking job," again underscoring the blue-collar community's emphasis on labor in favor of education as a means of advancement.[23] Chris responds unapologetically that he aspires to do something different than his parents. They are ultimately forced to leave the factory when the lockout ensues and mostly Latinx nonunion workers, such as Oscar, who leaves the bar for the promise of a better wage, cross the union protest line to work in the plant. The young men's anxieties and fears about their future, stoked by Tracey's growing frustration with her own circumstances and racist, anti-immigrant aggression, become the catalyst for the play's climax leading to their incarceration.

In comparison, Oscar has a much different perspective on Reading's opportunities for young workers. A silent but attentive fixture in the bar, his job is the only manual labor actually performed onstage. He quietly cleans, hustles inventory, and assists tipsy patrons, serving as a visual reminder that the leisure of some is always afforded by the labor of others. Oscar is also concerned about his livelihood, but his pathway to more profitable employment is hampered by xenophobia and a devaluation of service workers. As he considers crossing the picket line for a $3.00 increase to his hourly earnings he tells Stan, "my father, he swept up the floor in a factory like Olstead's—those fuckas wouldn't even give him a union card .... people come in here every day. They brush by me without seeing me, no: 'Hello, Oscar.' If they don't see me, I don't need to see them."[24] For Oscar, a factory job is critical to survival. For Jason and Chris, factory jobs are practically an inherited opportunity. As Tracey condescends to Oscar, "You gotta know somebody to get in. My dad worked there, I work there, and my son works there. It's that kinda shop. Always been."[25] Given Oscar's limited avenues for upward mobility and the kind of hostility he encounters from current factory workers, he jumps at the chance to improve his position during the union lockout, choosing survival over solidarity with the current factory workers. His act of rebellion against Stan and the nepotistic, racist hiring practices of the factory ultimately affords him the financial ability to create a space for himself and others by eventually taking control of the local bar and re-imagining it as a new location of community and connection building.

Through the ensemble of diverse characters, Nottage underscores the challenges of solidarity in moments of economic catastrophe. She reminds audiences of how interconnected we all are and yet how fragile those connections can be when stressed by systemic changes that threaten communal and individual survival. Nottage depicts worker frustrations from varying vantage points arguing that "everyone is focusing on the white middle class, but you forget that it's not just white people up on that stage. It's not about white people. It's about the way in which our culture, which is a multicultural culture, becomes fractured because of the way in which corporate greed chooses to divide us."[26] How each worker responds to their marginalization is influenced by capitalist forces and industry's attempts to benefit the bottom line. In Nottage's Reading, while individuals' experiences differ, there is equity in everybody's sweat, in their effort at preserving their dignity, and in their frustration over their financial precarity.

Refocusing on a Collective Future

In addition to connecting the world to Reading's residents, Nottage has also created transmedia opportunities for Reading to re-engage with itself. Co-produced by Labyrinth Theater Company, Project&, and Market Road Films, *This Is Reading* integrates live performance with film and projection to bring to life the exterior façade and interior walls of the historic Reading Railroad Station. *This Is Reading* "us[es] as its foundation, the hardships, challenges, and triumphs of people living in and around Reading, PA. *This is Reading* weaves their individual stories into one cohesive and compelling tale of the city."[27] For the spring 2017 installation, the aim was twofold: first, to engage the community in a dialogue about its past and its future. Second, the artistic team provided a model for how "traditional producing organizations can work together with artists to create socially engaged projects that defy the conventions of theatrical form and purpose, and to establish a fresh and visually-adventurous new mode of storytelling."[28] By reframing evidence of residents' lives across dance, spoken word, montage, music, mural, and immersion, Nottage and her collaborators reflected the community back to itself, refocusing Reading's self-awareness and reimagining the community's future. The piece "took a deep dive into what a nostalgic city was holding onto, and set the worthwhile parts back into motion," asking, "What if our country could forge more of these personal connections—ones that can reconnect the places once linked by railroad stations?"[29]

In 2018, Nottage partnered with The Public Theater to create the inaugural production of the Mobile Unit, a radical revisiting of Joseph Papp's original 1957 Mobile Theater project. The Public's Artistic Director Oskar Eustis noted, "The *Sweat* Mobile National Tour is our most dramatic attempt to break out of our New York bubble and speak to those who the non-profit theatre has largely ignored: the rural communities of the upper Midwest."[30] Touring *Sweat* to eighteen Rust Belt communities throughout Michigan, Ohio, Pennsylvania, Minnesota, and Wisconsin represents another form of activism through performance, rebelling against the commercial theatre industry's production constraints and financial expectations. The tour extended a dialogue about workers' lives and futures to more post-industrial communities by sharing the universal need for hope represented in the dialectic of *Sweat*'s characters and by inviting audiences to engage with these representations of their own lived truths and each other through talkbacks with the artists (including Nottage herself), community-centered art projects, and workshops.

Sweat and its affiliate projects represent the activism of Nottage's canon, designed to engage leaders and policymakers and encourage them to recognize the human toll of political and economic policies of the past quarter-century. *Sweat* also offers solidarity with working-class individuals who have lived the recent history of deindustrialization and are now struggling to navigate the post-industrial landscape of the United States. Nottage challenges government and corporate officials to hear the message and respond with tools and resources for workers in need of retraining, education, and health care. Likewise, she encourages fellow laborers to attend to their communities and take care of each other. Because, as Oscar notes at the end of the play, "that's how it oughta be."[31]

Notes

1 June Thomas, "Lynn Nottage on Her Broadway-Bound Play, *Sweat*, and Why She's Wary of 'Poverty Porn,'" *Slate Magazine*, last modified December 6, 2016, https://slate.com/culture/2016/12/lynn-nottage-on-her-broadway-bound-play-sweat-and-why-shes-wary-of-poverty-porn.html

2 Victoria Myers, "Lynn Nottage on the Music and Images of Writing 'Sweat,'" *The Interval*, last Modified December 6, 2016, https://www.theintervalny.com/featurettes/2016/12/lynn-nottage-on-the-music-and-images-of-writing-sweat/

3 Character identities are listed in Lynn Nottage, *Sweat* (New York: Theatre Communications Group, 2018), 1.

4 William Clinton, "Remarks on Signing of NAFTA," Presidential Speeches, Miller Center, UVA. 8 Dec. 1993.

5 Nottage began writing *Sweat* after receiving a letter from an out-of-work friend and reading Sabrina Tavernise, "Reading PA Knew It Was Poor. Now It Knows How Poor," *The New York Times*, September 26, 2011, https://www.nytimes.com/2011/09/27/us/reading-pa-tops-list-poverty-list-census-shows.html?searchResultPosition=1

6 Thomas, "Poverty Porn."

7 As Michelle Alexander notes in *The New Jim Crow: Mass Incarceration in the Age of Colorblindness* (New York: The New Press, 2010), there is a

long history of factioning efforts by white elites leveraging racial loyalty among the white working class to prevent class alignment with Black laborers.

8 Courtney Elkin Mohler, Christina McMahon, and David Román, "Three Readings of Reading, Pennsylvania: Approaching Lynn Nottage's *Sweat* and Douglas Carter Beane's *Shows for Days*," *Theatre Journal* 68, no. 1 (March 2016): 79–94.

9 Bill Blake, *Theatre and the Digital* (New York: Palgrave MacMillan, 2014), 14.

10 See Lynn Nottage, "Extracting Art from a Downfall," *The New York* Times, 30 July 2015.

11 Nottage, *Sweat*, 20.

12 Ibid., 25.

13 Ibid., 26.

14 Ibid., 77.

15 Ibid., 83.

16 Ibid., 25, emphasis added.

17 Ibid., 48.

18 Alexander, *The New Jim Crow*, 47.

19 Thomas, "Poverty Porn."

20 Nottage, *Sweat*, 49.

21 Ibid., 55–6.

22 Ibid., 29.

23 Ibid., 30–1.

24 Ibid., 92.

25 Ibid., 48.

26 Thomas, "Poverty Porn."

27 "This Is Reading," *Lynn Nottage*, accessed June 17, 2022, http://www.lynnnottage.com/this-is-reading.html

28 "This Is Reading," *Project &*, accessed June 17, 2022, https://projectand.org/project/this-is-reading/

29 Considine, "This Is Reading."

30 Olivia Clement, "The Public to Bring Free Performances of Lynn Nottage's *Sweat* to the Midwest," *Playbill*, August 2, 2018, https://playbill.com/article/the-public-to-bring-free-performances-of-lynn-nottages-sweat-to-the-midwest

31 Nottage, *Sweat*, 112.

2

"Those Songs Were More than Just": Spirituals, Queer Reckonings, and Tarell Alvin McCraney's *Choir Boy*

Isaiah Matthew Wooden

Tracing their roots to the brutal conditions of chattel slavery in the US South, African American spirituals have long been recognized and heralded for their capacity to index and reflect the will and determination of the people to persevere in the face of unrelenting violence, terror, and oppression. In his ground-breaking collection of essays, *The Souls of Black Folk*, scholar-activist W. E. B. Du Bois, for example, described these "sorrow songs" as "the most beautiful expression of human experience born this side the seas" and "as the singular spiritual heritage of the nation and the greatest gift of the Negro people."[1] James Weldon Johnson, a contemporary of Du Bois and an important contributor to and anthologist of Black music, similarly insisted that spirituals were "unsurpassed among the folk songs of the world and, in the poignancy of their beauty, unequalled!"[2] Du Bois and Johnson were certainly not alone in their categorical praise and admiration for this rich musical tradition. Indeed, countless generations of African Americans have understood and engaged spirituals as powerful resources for manifesting joy, registering grief, expressing faith, inspiring hope, and making sense and meaning.

For the prep school protagonists in Tarell Alvin McCraney's *Choir Boy*, performing spirituals serves both as a means to participate in and extend this vital musical legacy and to reckon with some of the existential questions and concerns that Black youth often face while transitioning from adolescence to adulthood.[3] Premiering at London's

Royal Court Theatre in 2012 with subsequent productions at various theatres throughout the United States, *Choir Boy*, at its core, is a coming-of-age story. The show primarily centers on Pharus Jonathan Young, a student enrolled at the fictional Charles R. Drew Prep School for Boys with an immense passion for singing and devising lush acapella vocal arrangements. Described in the stage directions as "an effeminate young man of color," Pharus stands out in his boarding school environment, where the performance of Black masculinity and sexuality is highly surveilled and regulated. Stewarding Drew's storied choir is one of the few things that endows Pharus with a sense of purpose. However, taking on the leadership role does not protect him from the ongoing efforts by several of his peers to harass and demean him: most notably, Robert "Bobby" Marrow III, a Drew legacy student and nephew of the school's headmaster, along with his obsequious sidekick Junior "JR" Davis. It also does not shield him from coming to terms with the implications of the multiple identities he embodies, including the discoveries he makes about his sexuality.

This chapter explores how McCraney shrewdly integrates and mobilizes the African American spiritual tradition in *Choir Boy* to explore connections between the Black past and present and inspire reckonings with what it means to embody and pursue queer ways of knowing and being. As Shana Redmond reminds, music accrues its power, in part, from the ways that it "allows us to do and imagine things that may otherwise be unimaginable or seem impossible."[4] For Black people, in particular, music has consistently served as a powerful "method of rebellion, revolution, and future visions," Redmond adds.[5] This chapter reveals how spirituals become significant sites of possibility in McCraney's dramaturgy, catalyzing both *Choir Boy*'s characters and its audiences to confront and perhaps embrace the unimaginable. By incorporating spirituals into the storytelling, McCraney, I argue, at once enables new visions and forms of belonging while also opening important space to acknowledge and affirm those experiences and expressions of difference that too frequently go unrecognized or unremarked upon in narratives about contemporary Black life.

My analysis in this chapter grows out of a robust body of work by scholars of African American theatre and drama that speaks to the influence of music in shaping the "Black dramaturgical imagination."[6] In his discussion of August Wilson's "bluesology," Harry J. Elam, Jr., for example, calls attention to the ways Black dramatists have exploited the possibilities of music "to negotiate relationships of power, to transcend and illuminate the meanings of the present, to impact, as well as establish, community" in their work.[7] Elam suggests that playwrights like Wilson have been drawn to music because it "contains the potentiality for regeneration, for reaffirmation, and for … 'reconsideration of narrative cause and consequence.'"[8] McCraney notably served as Wilson's assistant on the premiere production of *Radio Golf* at Yale Repertory Theatre in 2005. The experience proved quite formative for him as a young playwriting student, affirming the fresh possibilities that integrating music—and, surely, other expressive forms—into his dramaturgy could enable. Much like the suffusion of the blues throughout Wilson's work, the inclusion of spirituals in *Choir Boy* is both strategic and purposeful. Significantly, it provides a crucial means by which to dramatize and wrestle with the "pleasure and pain, struggle and survival, [and] the complexities and contradictions inherent in African American experience."[9]

Past and Present Refrains

McCraney introduces vocal music as a significant vehicle for recalling and honoring the past while prompting considerations of its impact on the present early in *Choir Boy*. Having been chosen to serve as the choir's lead during his senior year, which also marks Drew's fiftieth anniversary, Pharus is granted the privilege and responsibility of singing the school's anthem during its forty-ninth Commencement ceremony, an event that holds particular significance for the school community as a signal coming-of-age ritual. Though Pharus begins his rendition of the classic hymn "Trust and Obey" confidently, offering a vocal performance that evokes the tone and feeling of spirituals, he eventually stops singing before completing the chorus. The cause for the unplanned pause is Bobby, who, from the shadows, attempts to distract his peer by taunting him with homophobic slurs. The tense exchange sets the scene for several clashes between Pharus and his classmate throughout *Choir Boy*. It also establishes McCraney's investments in re-presenting particular African American histories and cultural traditions in the show as a way to contend with and comment on some of the politics and themes affecting contemporary Black life, including issues of race, gender, sexuality, and coming of age.

Participating in Drew's choir necessitates that Pharus and his fellow choristers—who, in addition to Bobby and JR, include Anthony Justin "AJ" James and David Heard—carry history and tradition forward reverentially. Pharus' perceived breach of school tradition during the commencement ceremony, accordingly, exposes him to harsh rebukes. Headmaster Marrow is especially incensed by what he interprets as the teen's intentional efforts to embarrass him and mar a cherished school ritual. "Why, after I asked you not to, told you you couldn't, made you understand the tradition, pointed out its potency, did you get up there at the senior's graduation, a day that should afford them every rite and ritual of the ceremony, and mess up their moment, Why?" he barks (13). Pharus' transgression is so egregious to him—and to the school's Board, who, Headmaster Marrow intimates, was already dubious about the youth's ability to lead—that he threatens to strip him of his scholarship, thereby expelling him from Drew. Obeying the Headmaster's forceful demands that Pharus provide an explanation for his offense will mean further breaching school tradition. Crucial to "being" and "acting" as a Drew man is abiding by a code—passed down between generations of students—to never implicate another classmate in any wrongdoing. The code insists and instructs that "a Drew man doesn't tell on his brother, he allows him the honor to confess himself" (18). While Pharus remains steadfast in his commitment to this code throughout *Choir Boy*, despite being threatened with severe consequences for doing so, he is nevertheless accused of "snitching" by Bobby, who presents this charge as yet another reason why he should be deposed and rejected.

Bobby renders and rejects Pharus as a counterfeit example of a "Drew man," a bogus imitation of the Black masculine ideal that he believes only he and other "legacy" students—that is, those who have family members who previously attended the school—can properly embody and appreciate. In so doing, he recalls the ways that the "arbitrariness and politics of authenticity" too often informs hegemonic conceptions of Blackness and constructions of Black masculinity.[10] Black authenticity, E. Patrick Johnson observes, "has increasingly become linked to masculinity in its most patriarchal significations."[11] A crucial effect of this linkage is the active disavowal of anyone or anything perceived as failing to uphold and reify heteronormativity and heteropatriarchy by the self-appointed arbiters of "authentic Blackness." As both Headmaster Marrow and Bobby's admonishments of Pharus highlight, these arbiters are particularly antagonistic to Black male expressions and embodiments of effeminacy, which they often regard as one of "the most damaging thing[s] one can be in the fight against oppression."[12] Expressions and embodiments of queerness are likewise dismissed as a perversion of and corruption to what these self-appointed arbiters come to propagate as "authentic Blackness."

Significantly, along with what Bobby perceives as flagrant violations of the school's masculine and heteronormative norms and breaches to its long-standing "no-snitching" codes, he considers what he deems as an insufficiently deferential approach to and engagement with the spirituals as further evidence of Pharus' fraudulence. Correspondingly, he bristles when, at the first choir rehearsal of senior year, Pharus reveals that he has created new, more contemporary vocal arrangements for the choir's repertoire. When Pharus rejoins that it is his "prerogative as choir lead" to generate and teach new arrangements, Bobby derides him, remarking, "Eh, don't be pushing dem kinda rights up in here" (24). The thinly veiled homophobic retort is not only meant to put Pharus in his place but also to remind him of why, at least in Bobby's mind, he cannot be trusted to steward the Drew legacy responsibly. According to Bobby's logic, a "real" Drew man would know and understand that spirituals do not require any alteration. Pharus' efforts to make the spirituals "more modern" (24), coupled with his presumed penchant for snitching, serve as confirmation for Bobby of his peer's queerness and his "inauthentic Blackness."

Bobby's disavowals of Pharus reanimate a broader set of concerns that have recurred throughout African American history about meaningful ways to acknowledge and demonstrate the significance of certain Black cultural traditions in the present. McCraney explores the tensions produced by these concerns most saliently in a crucial exchange that sees the dispute between Pharus and Bobby reach a boiling point. To help bolster the students' readiness for college, Headmaster Marrow convinces a former teacher at Drew, Mr. Pendleton, to come out of semi-retirement and lead a class on creative thinking. The first assignment he gives the class, which includes all the choir members, is to choose and challenge a well-known theory. While David elects to explore "The Rise of Capitalism and the Atlantic Slave Trade" (53) and AJ chooses to examine the Battle of Tours, Pharus opts to take on a subject of great importance to him and his fellow chorister: spirituals. "When I was little my grandmother would sing songs to me that she told me freed slaves. Not physically but spiritually. She said sangin these songs deep in the night here helped teach and coax other slaves, runaway and free, into peace, serenity, let them know God was with them everywhere they went, gave them strength and spiritual nourishment. Thus, we call them 'Negro Spirituals,'" he begins his presentation (56). Pharus prompts his classmates to reconsider the belief that spirituals contained coded messages for the enslaved about pursuing and achieving liberation.

This theory is documented in some of the earliest writings on spirituals. Frederick Douglass, for example, suggested in his 1845 memoir that "every tone" of the slave songs he heard while growing up "was a testimony against slavery, and a prayer to God for deliverance from chains."[13] As Bernice Johnson Reagon writes, "The African American oral tradition is full of stories about the use of spirituals like 'I Couldn't Hear Nobody Pray,' 'Wade in the Water,' 'Steal Away,' and 'Run Mourner Run' as signal songs of escape in general or, more specifically, with the efforts of those working the Underground Railroad."[14] She adds, "These stories tell of how the songs and the singing serve the survival of the community. Spirituals were songs created as leverage, as salve, as voice, as bridge over troubles one could not endure without the flight of song and singing."[15] Even while acknowledging the important role that the stories Johnson cites have played in African American life, history, and culture, Pharus presses his classmates to contemplate whether spirituals maintain their value and significance without them. "There is no substantive proof that spirituals contain coded secret passageways to freedom," he insists, adding "All the proof is hearsay and guestimations" (57–8). He proposes that instead of speculating about whether spirituals functioned as "Slave Escape 007 plans" or "a strategic map guiding slaves North" (61), his peers should consider the ways they "prove true that hope and love can live, thrive, and even sing" (57). The central contention of Pharus' presentation, which he aptly titles "Spirituals: Solely Songs for the Spirit" (56), is that, as in the present, spirituals were for the enslaved a significant vehicle for imagining and experiencing the world otherwise. Rather than theorizing about the ways they were "more than just" (61) songs that uplifted the people who composed, performed, and relished in them, Pharus encourages his peers to attend more closely to the ways that spirituals "were and are Sweet Honey in the Rock that didn't just help the slaves but help us now, this day" (61).

What is striking about Pharus' presentation are the ways that it draws attention to some of the themes animating debates about the connections between the Black past and present. While the obsession with tradition at Drew leads many of his peers to view that relationship as linear and unidirectional, Pharus, through his take on the history and meaning of the spirituals, suggests that it is perhaps much more symbiotic and reciprocal. In so doing, he demonstrates how the present can help inform understandings of the past just as much as the past can help deepen understandings of the present. It follows for Pharus that, if the performance of spirituals elicits such intense emotional responses from people like him and the supporters of the choir in the present, then the narratives about how the music served and functioned for people in the past demand reconsideration. The present notably provides an occasion to re-evaluate the past, and this re-evaluation, in turn, opens space to reckon further with the conditions of the present. Of course, bound up in these re-evaluations and reckonings are broader concerns about the meanings of identity and belonging.

Queer Reckonings

McCraney centers identity and belonging as themes throughout much of his body of work. Indeed, as in *Choir Boy*, several of his theatrical texts—*Marcus; or the Secret of Sweet* and *Wig Out!*, for example—and film and television projects—*Moonlight* and *David Makes Man*—feature youthful protagonists who feel out of joint culturally and struggle to meet societal expectations to develop and articulate a coherent sense of who they are and how they fit in with prevailing racial, gender, and sexual norms. That these characters do not completely align with the roles prescribed for them or fail to adhere to the bounds of dominant orthodoxies marks them as "other" and, correspondingly, subjects them to significant consequences, including, as Pharus' journey through Drew illuminates, relentless efforts to discipline and punish them. One of the potent ways McCraney troubles culturally sanctioned expectations and norms is by endowing his central characters with attributes, aspirations, and desires that function to expose the tenuousness of the narratives and ideologies undergirding them.

Music is an important medium for enacting and enabling refusal, resistance, and transgression in the worlds McCraney creates. The titular character in *Marcus; or the Secret of Sweet*, for example, appeals to Dr. Buzzard's Original Savannah Band's oft-sampled 1976 song, "Sunshower," to explore and reckon with the meanings and possibilities of his same-sex desire and non-normative sexual identity in "A Dream of Drag" with his two best friends, Shaunta Iyun and Osha. The members of the legendary drag/ballroom houses at the center of *Wig Out!* likewise turn to music by popular groups like Soul for Real and Destiny's Child to express agency and autonomy while participating in acts of queer worldmaking. What undoubtedly distinguishes *Choir Boy* from some of these other works are the ways it draws on "sacred" music, in particular, to confront and challenge hegemonic beliefs about what constitutes "proper" identity. Likely because McCraney got to witness and experience firsthand the transformative performance practices and traditions of the Black church as the grandson of a Baptist minister, he embeds religious and spiritual elements throughout his dramaturgy.

The Black church, of course, is a site of tremendous contradiction. Although it frequently circulates in popular discourse as a space of restriction, limitation, and exclusion, such characterizations belie the multitude of ways that it emboldens waywardness and disobedience. Scholars like E. Patrick Johnson have been especially illustrative on this point, noting how the choir lofts of many Black churches have functioned as crucial sites for Black queer people to stake a claim for their racial and sexual identities and to cultivate a sense of belonging. For many Black gay men especially, the Black church is "a contradictory space, one that exploits the creative talents of its gay members even as it condemns their gayness, while also providing a nurturing space to hone those same talents," Johnson writes.[16] The sheer pleasure derived from making "a joyful noise"—and doing so while forging and participating in robust spiritual and creative community—can supplant, at least for a time, the discomfort or unease that some might otherwise feel and be forced to negotiate when hearing negative views about queerness or same-sex desire voiced from church pews or pulpits. While Pharus' day-to-day life unfolds in an ostensibly secular (rather than a religious) setting in *Choir Boy*, the character, in many ways, stands in for the countless Black queer youth who have found solace and refuge in the Black church despite its many antagonisms. His deep commitments to carrying forth the musical traditions of the church serve as a reminder of the ongoing relevance of the institution in Black social life.

McCraney also powerfully uses Pharus' commitments to invite consideration of some of the challenges that issues of sex and sexuality often present in both sacred and secular contexts. While, in many instances, the performance of spirituals gives rise to even more friction between Pharus and his adversaries at Drew, there are other moments wherein they become catalysts for transitioning to intimate conversations between the youth and the two roommates he's had at the school, AJ and David, about their personal, spiritual, and sexual growth. AJ is very much the opposite of Pharus. Indeed, he possesses many of the qualities that the school's administration and its supporters suggest are emblematic of a Drew man: namely, he is athletic and conventionally masculine. Despite the position that he occupies within the social hierarchy of Drew, AJ refuses to participate in any attempt to bully Pharus. He is, in fact, deeply protective of his roommate and expresses compassion for the singularity of the challenges he must navigate as a student at Drew.

Among the most important ways AJ manifests this compassion is by granting Pharus the necessary space to reckon with the complexities of his sexuality. While Pharus grows accustomed to asking his classmates about their romantic and sexual lives—and doing so without any expectation of reciprocity—AJ expresses genuine interest in knowing more about his roommate's sense of self as a sexual being. He asks Pharus about it directly in an exchange that takes place in the school's shower room just before bedtime and moments after the boys sing a stirring version of the spiritual "Motherless Child." The conversation features Pharus teasing AJ about the size of his endowment, which subsequently prompts the latter to point out Pharus' tendency to use "they" instead of "she" series pronouns when referring to future sexual partners. While

AJ's comment is more of an observation than a criticism, it provides an occasion for him to ask Pharus about his own sexual desires:

AJ Who you saving it for?

Pharus Oh me? Jesus.

AJ I don't think Jesus interested.

Pharus Well I'm here for whatever He needs.

AJ But what you need, Pharus? You need anything? (78–9)

Recognizing Pharus' efforts to deflect from risking too much of himself in the conversation by jocularly invoking Jesus, AJ opens space for him to be more vulnerable by reminding him of the importance of his own desires. AJ's questions are less about pressing Pharus to disclose something about his sexuality before he is ready to and, instead, about further demonstrating the emancipatory potential in embracing introspective questioning.

Whereas Pharus and AJ's relationship is marked by mutual trust and tenderness, Pharus' relationship with David is much more complicated. The source of this knottiness remains ambiguous for much of *Choir Boy*, but McCraney does embed a hint in the names that he gives the two characters.[17] Placing David alongside Jonathan, Pharus' middle name, calls to mind the Biblical story of King David and Jonathan, who, despite being groomed as rivals for the throne of Israel during their youth, ultimately develop a deeply intimate relationship. The question of how to interpret the Biblical duo's relationship—that is, whether to read it as platonic or romantic—is one that David grapples with in *Choir Boy*. David also struggles with how to reconcile his newfound fervency for his Christian faith with the sexual and romantic feelings he has developed for Pharus. It is this struggle that leads to *Choir Boy*'s violent climax.

Beginning with a spirituals-inflected rendition of "There is a Fountain Filled with Blood," a hymn whose refrain speaks to David's desire to "wash all [his] sins away," and ending with Pharus grasping his bloodied face after being attacked in the shower stalls, the scene throws into sharp relief the harms that sexual repression and homophobia produce. Pharus' assailant remains unseen during the bashing and, indeed, remains unknown until David ultimately confesses to carrying out the brutal attack. King David's assertion in Psalm 139 that "we are fearfully and marvelously made" serves as a catalyst for the teen to reveal his own surprise and confusion about " … who he really is" (115). He utters to Headmaster Marrow, "I had prayed over it. So many times, just praying on it. Every time it would happen," noting, "And the Lord was silent" (115). The "it" that David seeks divine intervention to rid himself of is his same-sex desire—his sexual longing for Pharus, in particular. The fear that another classmate might have witnessed him engaging in a sexual act with Pharus is what spurs him to assault his clandestine lover. The revelation that Pharus is not the only student at Drew negotiating same-sex desire helps bolster the invitation McCraney issues through *Choir Boy* to recognize and affirm experiences and expressions of difference. Concomitantly, it troubles the idea that Black youth must embrace and embody a sense of identity that is at once coherent and aligned with dominant norms and orthodoxies. Through the relationships he creates for Pharus and AJ and Pharus and David, McCraney lays bare the potency and possibilities of staging queer reckonings.

Troubling Categories

Undoubtedly, much is at stake in McCraney's thoughtful fusing of song and dance with spoken dialogue in *Choir Boy*, including the very terms we might use to describe and categorize the work. In his review of the 2013 MTC production, *New York Times* critic Charles Isherwood, for example, described it as "an ambitious new play."[18] Critic Sara Holdren called it "an undercover, and gorgeous, acapella musical" in her review of its Broadway run, while Manhattan Theatre

Club billed it as a "soaring music-filled work" in their promotional materials.[19] What the ambiguities about whether to classify the show as a play, an acapella musical, or a "music-filled" drama point to are the ways in which works by Black theatre-makers have often troubled the boundaries of dominant theatrical genres and categories. In her comprehensive discussion of the pioneering Black Broadway musical *In Dahomey* (1903), Daphne Brooks observes that "a single passion to experiment with form and a dedication to advancing the field of Black theatrical performance to new levels of innovation and imagination" is what often connects and motivates Black theatre artists.[20] To represent and reflect Blackness with nuance and complexity necessarily demands the development of new formal, dramaturgical, and performance strategies. And, since such strategies are often created in opposition to the delimited and delimiting representations of Blackness that the stage has been instrumental in producing and proliferating, they routinely register as anomalous.

Thus, even while *Choir Boy* is perhaps most often categorized as a play—McCraney himself usually refers to it as such, and it was nominated for Best New Play at the 2019 Tony Awards—it is worth taking stock in the ways the show forces us to re-evaluate the assumptions structuring our understandings of theatrical genres. The work's engagements with the lush legacy of the spiritual tradition, I suggest, invite us to experience McCraney's style, language, and plotting on its own terms, while also expanding our thinking in this regard. Reflecting on his decision to ground *Choir Boy* in this tradition, McCraney explains, "We used Negro spirituals because they have such a legacy of both spiritual and political importance. They are a treasure in the African American experience in this country. When we talk about our myths, our legends, our mythology, our gifts; these songs are a part of them."[21] Centering spirituals allows McCraney to pursue broader questions and themes about Black history, identity, and culture: "When we entrust [spirituals] into the hands of young people, what does that mean for us? How do we give them that responsibility without taking away their individuality? Is there a pressure put on them to be like we were or do we allow them to be their own selves and still carry the mantle of this incredible music?"[22] *Choir Boy*, of course, avoids supplying facile answers to such inquiries. Instead, the show examines and demonstrates what might perhaps be gleaned by fully pursuing and embracing questioning as a project. A primary concern of this chapter has been to analyze the ways the use of spirituals serves to enhance not only this project but also the efficacy of *Choir Boy*'s dramaturgy.

Notes

1 W. E. B. Du Bois, *The Souls of Black Folk*, edited with an introduction and notes by Brent Hayes Edwards (Oxford: Oxford University Press, 2007), 168.

2 James Weldon Johnson, "Preface" in *The Book of American Negro Spirituals*, ed. James Weldon Johnson and J. Rosamond Johnson (New York: Da Capo Press, 2002), 12.

3 Tarell Alvin McCraney, *Choir Boy* (New York: Theatre Communications Group, 2016). All subsequent references to the play are cited in the text parenthetically.

4 Shana L. Redmond, *Anthem: Social Movements and the Sound of Solidarity in the African Diaspora* (New York: New York University Press, 2014), 1.

5 Redmond, *Anthem*, 1.

6 See Harry J. Elam, Jr. and Douglas A. Jones, Jr., editors, *The Methuen Drama Book of Post-Black Plays* (London: Methuen Drama, 2013).

7 Harry J. Elam, Jr., *The Past as Present in the Drama of August Wilson* (Ann Arbor: University of Michigan Press, 2006), 55–6.

8 Elam, *The Past as Present*, 56.

9 Ibid., 30.

10 E. Patrick Johnson, *Appropriating Blackness: Performance and the Politics of Authenticity* (Durham: Duke University Press, 2003), 5.

11 Johnson, *Appropriating Blackness*, 48.

12 Ibid., 51.

13 Frederick Douglass, *Narrative of the Life of Frederick Douglass: An American Slave* (Oxford: Oxford University Press, 1999), 24.

14 Bernice Johnson Reagon, *If You Don't Go, Don't Hinder Me: The African American Sacred Song Tradition* (Lincoln: University of Nebraska Press, 2001), 74–5.

15 Johnson Reagon, *If You Don't Go, Don't Hinder Me*, 74–5.

16 E. Patrick Johnson, *Sweet Tea: Black Gay Men of the South* (Chapel Hill: University of North Carolina Press, 2011), 183.

17 McCraney provides an additional hint in the song that David chooses to sing for his classmates after Mr. Pendleton enlists each boy to perform a popular tune from his parents' childhoods to compensate for their disruptive behavior during choir rehearsals. David selects L.T.D.'s "Love Ballad" (1976), a song that also serves as the soundtrack for the first kiss shared between Raymond and Kelvin, the two central characters in Black gay writer E. Lynn Harris' 1991 debut novel, *Invisible Life*. A coming-of-age story that explores themes of sexual identity and discovery, the relationship between Raymond and Kelvin in *Invisible Life*, in many ways, anticipates the relationship between Pharus and David in *Choir Boy*. See E. Lynn Harris, *Invisible Life: A Novel* (New York: Anchor, 1994).

18 Charles Isherwood, "Hoping the Songs Lead Him to Freedom," *New York Times*, July 2, 2013, https://www.nytimes.com/2013/07/03/theater/reviews/in-tarell-mccraneys-choir-boy-spirituals-are-solace.html

19 Sara Holdren, "Theatre Review: Contemporary Northern Prep and Southern Gothic, in *Choir Boy* and *Blue Ridge*," *Vulture*, January 8, 2019, https://www.vulture.com/2019/01/theater-reviews-choir-boy-and-blue-ridge.html; Also, see the Manhattan Theatre Club's promotional site here: https://www.manhattantheatreclub.com/2018-19-season/choir-boy/

20 Daphne A. Brooks, *Bodies in Dissent: Spectacular Performances of Race and Freedom, 1850–1910* (Durham: Duke University Press, 2006), 222.

21 Nicole Granston, "Playwright & Oscar Winner Tarell Alvin McCraney on Why 'Choir Boy' Sings to Your Heart," *Blackfilm.com*, January 20, 2019, https://www.Blackfilm.com/read/2019/01/playwright-oscar-winner-tarell-alvin-mccraney-on-why-choir-boy-sings-to-your-heart/

22 Granston, "Why 'Choir Boy' Sings to Your Heart."

3

Trauma, Truth, and Turning the Lens: Black Theatre Artists and White Theatre Audiences

Loretta L. C. Brady and Suzanne Delle

If "the master's tools will never dismantle the master's house,"[1] then one might argue that playwrights of color cannot continue to follow Aristotelian structure when exposing trauma and healing on stage. The professional American theatre has been filled with the successes of white plays that, in structure and expectation, capture how white people see the world. In her 2021 essay for the National New Play Network (NNPN), current Artistic Associate at Cleveland Public Theatre, India Nicole Burton writes,

> As the American Theatre moves towards a more communal way of creating theatre (devised theatre), seeking marginalized stories, and finding a way to work with artists of color and also non-artists of color, you must understand that you have been indoctrinated, washed in the blood, doused in and put-upon, aka 'trained,' to believe that the 'right way' to do theatre is the way of the white patriarchal structure, created by European practitioners.[2]

Burton, who started her own African American theatre company directly after completing her undergraduate education, challenges all of us to rethink how plays are selected during season planning and if Black playwrights can even express themselves using Aristotelian structures. She is urging artists to engage in rebellious story-making in both their structural approaches and choice of subject. In this chapter, we outline ways that Black American theatre, from the years 2014 to 2021, reflected survival stories of Black people working and studying in the systems of American academia, white philanthropy circles and within their own family units.

Contemporary Black artists are actively trying to confront audiences with the discomfort, othering, pain, and—yes trauma—of their daily, and ancestral, experience. Using the research on trauma and PTSD by psychologist Judith Lewis Herman, we examine the work of Anna Deveare Smith, Claudia Rankine, Jackie Sibblies Drury, and other Black playwrights who are presenting forms of rebellion, examples of activism, and a means of creating solidarity (all in the form of cultural activism as described by sociologist Patricia Hill Collins). In their depictions of the trauma of racism, these playwrights utilize increasingly direct ways that demand techniques beyond the well-made play to delve into searing psychological and physiological realities often skirted in white American theatre.

In our review of Black work performed between the years 2014 and 2021, we saw rebellion stories, activism stories, and stories of solidarity. Often these racism survivor stories revealed American truths as Black playwrights, directors, and actors turned the audiences' lens away from the work on stage, out past the fourth wall and on to white faces sitting around them. For example, in the opening of Aleshea Harris' play *What to Send Up When It Goes Down*, a character, who has only been given the denomination of FOUR, breaks the fourth wall to welcome the audience. Harris does not name her characters in this play. Healing is offered to all by not specifying what the actors' bodies should be—though they all need to be Black. Claudia Rankine uses this same motif in her new play *Help* where each character is just called White Man #1–20. While Rankine does this to make the point that all white men are the same, Harris does it to invite difference in casting while allowing the actors and audience to feel solidarity through the theatrical expression they are experiencing. Harris is challenging the assumption of the intended audience, through the casting directives and non-naming, she clearly expresses who her intended audience is: "We are glad non-Black people are here. We welcome you but this piece was created and is expressed with Black folks in mind. If you are prepared to honor that through your respectful, conscientious presence, you are welcome to stay."[3] With this opening monologue, Harris establishes that she did not write this play for white people. In fact, in her author's note she writes, "This play uses parody and absurdity to confront, to affirm, to celebrate."[4] She is exposing Black grief and inviting us to a theatrical ritual to make peace with our history of race relations. The surprise for a white audience member is that the story is not told from their perspective or with a thought to how they might react. As Black playwrights engage what American Black Feminist theorist Patricia Hill Collins labels intellectual and cultural politics through their art, they shift white gaze and Black possibilities as to what can be expected on stage and who and how an artist can write for solidarity or rebellion.[5] In making meaning of each play it is helpful to look at their work through the pervasive anti-blackness that so permeates the psychological and physiological realities of Black American life.

Psychologists specializing in trauma and recovery underscore that survivors thrive when their anger, sense of betrayal, and mistrust can be personally understood, and their emotional energy can then be channeled into community change.[6] When survivors' energies are devoted to the creative destruction of systems or practices that cause or perpetuate harm, they are able to recreate new possibilities, and this promotes healing and recovery. Through such creative destruction, as can be seen in many stagings of Black American theatre this half-decade, there is transformation for the audience and for Black characters' relationship to racism and anti-blackness which elevates audience understanding, that makes what came before in shape or obfuscation now impossible to tolerate in performance, and that moves entire (white) communities into shared understanding of what must be done to stop the harm they can most immediately affect. For many of these playwrights, the transformation starts with, like Harris or Sibblies Drury, having characters specifically address white audiences explaining that the journey is not for them. For others, change for the audience happens through design choices and even theatrical devices like self-selecting in groups.

Black American playwrights are demanding the fullness of this potential in their work as they engage with the wealthy white audiences that populate regional and New York City theatre, and it can be argued that the recent displays of breaking the well-made play form in the work of contemporary playwrights represent an extended intergenerational trauma and recovery cycle, one that with each turn provides white America an opportunity to reconcile and repair its original and enduring harms. It is also posing core questions of tradition that challenge all audience members to reconcile their current emotional realities with their individual moral vision for plural communities born and constrained by white supremacy. As Jeremy O. Harris succinctly puts it in his 2019 *Guardian* interview, "You need to make black art for your black self."[7]

When Black artists and audiences enter predominantly white spaces, often there is an expectation that they will accept the current norms and not cause disruptions in their manner, their presentation, and most certainly, their tone. This is not by accident; it is by design. In her book, *The Reasonable Audience*, Kirsty Sedgman explores the history of theatre etiquette to look at how managers used these expectations to keep the space primarily white: "Today's theatre etiquette campaigns are still to some extent bound up with historical efforts to exclude the 'wrong kind' of theatergoer. This reimagined theatre contract was part of a coordinated (classist, racist, sexist) maneuver by the elite to separate themselves from the new mass society, just one way of delimiting hierarchical zones within public space more widely."[8] Racialized organizations like professional American theatre create environments where artists wishing to create will find it easier to shape work that looks like what came before it. As Wiletta, the practical Black actress in Alice Childress' 1955 play *Trouble in Mind* (which had its delayed Broadway opening in 2021), tells a younger performer as he gushes about the art of theatre, "*Show business*. It's just a business."[9] The expectations for revenue have the impact of forcing an artists' experience and their community-specific art into another community's general shapes, or else risk being passed on for production or funding, no matter the endowment size (ability to absorb risk) or community need (reparations for prior harms within a given community) for relevant and real programming. The American theatre recreates the marginalization Black theatre artists face in developing themselves enough to arrive at the stage.

In a March 2021 article in *The Atlantic* playwright Anna Deavere Smith describes her time in pursuing her education as one of the first Black students at an all-white college, and the expectation that she would fit in and be a "nice Negro girl."[10] Any deviation from these expectations came with a high social penalty, one that had academic and lifelong professional costs for Smith. She points to the universality and generational realities inherent in the Black experience of being Black in white dominant spaces, including theatre. Black rebellion in these spaces would surely be penalized and yet this is how a Black rebel is born, by living in and through injustice and trusting their experience as truth in the face of (white) denial. Today, in the most lauded productions written by Black playwrights which present as race conflict stories, we see that rather than be silenced, a new generation of Black playwrights is finding ways to turn their personal and historical trauma into important social and popular theatre. In doing so some bring up the lights on white audiences as part of the play to provide the possibility of provoking opportunities for transformation.

For example, in Claudia Rankine's *The White Card* as produced by American Repertory Theatre in early 2018, the audience is challenged to consider what art and which artists are lost in the face of white patronage, and patronizing stances toward the common flaws of being human in a resource scarce environment.[11] The white gaze is explicitly confronted as the house lights never truly come down and audiences stare at themselves as the alley stage design places them as witnesses to the tennis match of white supremacy and anti-blackness within the arts and philanthropic worlds while they are also witnessing each other and their reactions. Where can the predominantly white Cambridge, MA, audience look as a modern slave auction is enacted on stage? Do they dare look at each other or at the trauma unfolding on the stage in front of them? The mourning this provides for the audience, the commitment to change that the post-show discussion ritual processing provides, is a step in activating the identity and community that collective change requires. At the same time, it may not always provide mourning for those who need to mourn.

In our day-to-day lives, we must deal with both injustices and joy in real time—often without being able to think about the past or the future. When creating a theatrical landscape, playwrights have the luxury of crafting the world of the play and how their characters will respond to stimuli. What playwrights cannot control is how critics and audiences will respond to their work. However, unless the point is to place the audience out of their scripted role of observer, there is little that can engage an observer who does not want engagement. For this reason, playwrights traditionally used familiar forms in order to bring forth disruptive ideas and sentiments, such as the family drama nestled in a well-made play structure. This structure made popular with the post-Second World War living-room drama pushes the narrative that trauma requires truth in order to be survived.

Lorraine Hansberry, understanding the interconnectedness of family conflict and systemic injustice, sets her play *A Raisin in the Sun* in the nicest room of the home. This play looks like a traditional well-made, living room play though the stage directions state that "weariness has, in fact, won in this room." It is this slight-of-hand that Hansberry pulled off that keeps high school and college teachers assigning this play over sixty years after it premiered on Broadway. The play appears to be a family drama that instead of being led by a Willie Loman or Amanda Wingfield is overseen by Ruth Younger, but beyond one uncomfortable scene where clearly Karl Linder is the antagonist, most white audiences can see themselves and their family relationships as the Youngers strive for the American Dream. Imani Perry, the author of the seminal *Looking for Lorraine*, writes that the college-aged Hansberry was thinking "about race and racism, war, a general concern about the state of the world, and a desire to do something about it all. It was in college that her sense that art might enable her to do something meaningful for the world emerged."[12] It is interesting to wonder how many of those encountering *A Raisin in the Sun* for the first time in a classroom learn anything about Hansberry's Black nationalism and Civil Rights activism? She used the tricks learned from Ibsen and Strindberg's naturalism to disguise her own revolutionary story and exploited the structure of the well-made play to use her writing and ideas to reach traditional theatre audiences, and this was a lesson that others learned. August Wilson adopted this same framing for his Century Cycle of plays as his work almost exclusively focuses on the Black family by blood or creation, often in their home or their backyard, expressing the truth of racism but in ways that looks familiar to white play goers.

It wouldn't be until the filmed footage of police and vigilante killings affected Tamir Rice, Trayvon Martin, Eric Garner, Michael Brown, Alton Sterling, Sandra Bland, and more recently Ahmaud Arbery, Breonna Taylor, and George Floyd that white audiences became familiar (or white producers familiar enough) with Black realities that new forms were eagerly produced and promoted. In her 2016 winter Art of Poetry feature in *The Paris Review*, Claudia Rankine pinpoints the images of Hurricane Katrina in 2005, and the Black neglect and abandonment she witnessed through CNN's cameras, that prompted the first verses of her lyric *Citizen*.[13] Cameras and camera phones have become the tracker of traumas that had long been continuing and long since continue to persist for Black Americans. The phones, the images they bore, the messages they shared, all became pivotal to American theatre without needing to be centered in any of the plays we mention here. Temple University Professor Marc Lamont Hill writes, "The rush of public emotion that spilled into the streets after the killing of Michael Brown alerted the world to the existence of a multitude of other, competing truths. … There was not only Brown's shooting to consider; there was also the aftermath. There was Brown's body, left for hours on the hot pavement."[14] Theatre artists rushed to document this aftermath.

Taking a cue from the Federal Theatre Project and Tectonic Theatre Company's documentary style, rapid-response theatrical events are being utilized to harness the anger and sadness of the moment to "foster dialogue through performance."[15] Just two weeks after Michael Brown's murder, "five theatre artists, including Claudia Alick, Mica Cole, Katy Rubin, Danny Bryck, and Rebecca Martinez, traveled from different cities to Ferguson and St. Louis, where they engaged members of the local communities."[16] This project, eventually titled *The Every 28 Hours Plays*, is a good example of solidarity as it was truly collaborative as theatre artists from across the country, some with national name recognition and some only known locally, all volunteered their time and resources to create over seventy plays that clocked in at about one minute in length and addressed specific racial and societal themes around police violence. "With a modular framework and short-play dramaturgies, collective theatre action crosses boundaries and challenges our understanding of what theatre is, how it is made, who gets to participate, who it is for, where it is produced, and how we connect theatre to our future as engaged citizens."[17]

Aleshea Harris wrote *What to Send Up* specifically to reflect on the national news stories of Black people being killed by police officers with impunity.[18]

> The idea was to hold people accountable, be confrontational, let it be messy, let it be angry, and let it tread as absurdly as the idea that a Black person could be killed on camera unarmed and the person who killed them get away with it. That is an absurd reality. I wanted to mirror that absurdity in the form of the play.[19]

Responding to trauma with theatre is one action taken in American theatre, but making space in American theatre for Black trauma, and for white confrontation, was also the revolution that marked the artistic response to the unrelenting trauma of the rise of Trumpism, itself a white supremacist response to America's increasing diversification. Even as theatre was willing to accept stories of racist confrontation and morality lessons told to the Blue coastal audiences of the contemporary American theatre subscription and foundation funding model, Artistic Directors, notably some whose own trauma within theatre spaces was well documented, began creative destruction of their own. In these spaces emerge responsive, reflective, and revolutionary production moments where observing, emoting, and being stimulated are not enough of an audience response for the work presented. Action is the expectation and pathways to those actions are pointedly available.

In an interview for our podcast *Traumaturgy*, Joan Lipkin, one of the Euro American writers and producers of *The Every 28 Hour Plays*, indicated that one step she has personally taken in approaching work that engages the experience of communities victimized and oppressed is to listen, to be humble, and to amplify others. "Now is the time for white people to listen" she admonishes her peers.[20] Yet the forms that took shape beyond the community-grounded productions and into Broadway-produced spaces were asking even more of white audiences than to listen and be educated. They were demanded to talk, to feel, to bear witness; perhaps the most disarming demand.

In Boston this demand was often guided with a series of productions that included deliberate civic engaged dialogues and, in some cases, facilitated in-play audience breakouts. Anna Deavere Smith used community-engaged theatre interviews and her early-life traumas from being in white classroom spaces as the vehicle for her 2015 production of *Notes from the Field: Doing Time in Education*. Breakout groups were created and moderated during the performance, and resources to further support exchanges beyond the immediate performance were also offered. This familiar therapeutic structure is used to play with the audience, putting them directly into the drama of the story, demanding actions be voiced at least within the space of the show and asking them to have community-facilitated discussions. Safety emerges in this framing, grounding us in common facts and language, and providing a guide to increase awareness of others' needs so that they can be anticipated and responded to, and so that they can move into mourning and confronting.

The block that white supremacy makes is in blocking truth. Without reality there can be no confronting, no connecting, and certainly no recovery. Family estrangement based on this in micro is the central theme of family dramas. And in the past years, as white supremacy in American life continued its harrowing rise, it was Black playwrights who challenged the white American audience to see itself, its family's secrets of white supremacy and patriarchy, of exploitation and exclusion, and confront those increasingly comfortable audiences with the complicity that supports the dishonesty that upholds the lies of white supremacy. While this creative destruction and reconstruction is recovery, it does not mean it does not cost to create. There is enormous toll in the telling of truths. Truths that are so well-known as to be invisible are the hardest, and harshest, to tell, but, of course, what gets press is the hard viewing—the difficulty in white audience consumption, rather than the pain of creating such demanding and vulnerable work for consumption.

While a production like *The White Card* might make an audience squirm, some Black playwrights are taking the provocation further than just subject matter by literally turning on the house lights and forcing audiences to see themselves under a different kind of white gaze. By 2018 *Fairview* took on the familiar living room form and confronted it with exacting commentary on white gaze: its omnipresence, its insidiousness, its blindness, its power, its purpose. Playwright Jackie Sibblies Drury lulls the audience into a false sense of security as act one is a family dramedy that takes place in a kitchen in her 2019 Pulitzer Prize for Drama winning play.[21] While not a living room play in the strictest sense of the meaning, it follows all the tropes associated with naturalism as a Black family prepares for the matriarch's birthday party. However, in the second act of the play, we watch the Black family on stage re-enact the movement of act one without a voice. Again, carrots are cut, cheese is eaten, clothes are changed but now instead of hearing the original dialogue, the audience hears the commentary of non-Black viewers. These voyeurs discuss race, class, and OJ Simpson—all while the audience watches a Black family go through the motions of middle-class life on stage. Finally, the commentators discuss the real issue of their conversation:

Mack But that sounds … why is that racist?

Jimbo It's not, actually.

Suze Yes, it is.

Jimbo It's just that we think that everything black people had to do back in the day is racist now.

Suze That is because everything was racist back in the day.

Jimbo No, everything is racist now, which means that nothing is racist now.

Bets I am not racist.

Suze Yes, you kind of are.

Bets I am not.

Mack She is not.

Suze Everyone is racist.

Jimbo It's like if everything is racist, that means that nothing is racist.[22]

Then Sibblies Drury strips expectations again in act three where the white actors come on stage recreating stereotypes of Black people and the tension reaches such a crescendo that the actors engage in a food fight until "the set feels destroyed."[23] Contemporary plays will often rely on the shock of scenic elements falling or breaking[24] but Sibblies Drury doesn't stop there. If her audience still feels complacent or uninterested, what she has in store for them next will shake up their expectations. The actress who plays the Black teenage daughter suddenly stops the play, breaks the fourth wall, and calls white audience members up to the stage. The stage manager turns on the house lights and the actress implores, "Come up here folks who identify as white, you know who you are. You can choose to come up here to where I've always been, where my family has always been. Sit on the couch. Make yourself a plate. Look out from where I am."[25] As more and more white audience members leave their seats and walk to the stage, those who choose not to begin to feel more and more conspicuous until suddenly they are one of a handful of white bodies among people of color left seated in the house. Seeing what needs be seen is hard enough, but we argue the forced witness of physical experience is perhaps an even harsher demand Black playwrights are making, and we anchor this to the necessary mourning phase within trauma recovery. These portrayals of interpersonal interactions shaped by race, space, and place are not redemptive, but provocative so that moment and long after both white and Black audiences reflect on their own place in the theatre space and in the larger world.

In Anna Deveare Smith, Claudia Rankine, Aleshea Harris, and Jackie Sibblies Drury's work, we see the same challenged stories confronted by Hansberry and Wilson staged and performed in ways that put white audiences less in the patron seat and more in the seat of funding Patrice Cullors' Patreon and other Black artists who are using theatre as rebellion, activism, and solidarity. These artists urgently demand that white audiences commit to and know the difference between watching and knowing. Rankine's latest work, *Help*, excerpted in the Winter 2020 edition of *The Paris Review*, underscores the opportunity to now flip Black erasure and consolidation that occurs as a result of white specificity and turn that experience into an opportunity for engagement and understanding between specific people, represented by the dehumanized numeric white male characters she converses with. As "White Man 8" asks in the play, "When is someone going to see me for who I really am? When is someone going to ask me what I need?" we can appreciate the irony of Rankine putting those words into a nameless white man's mouth.[26] We, audiences both white, Black (both and neither), are left to experience this turning of the lens and to look within for the courage to address the external pervasive truths of classist, racialized, and gendered trauma. American theatre must embrace the power of truth telling in Black theatre, and theatres must work to connect their stages to the community's reconciliation stage: preparing a way for the beginnings of community action through the powerful intimate distance, and opening of action opportunities, that Black theatre makes possible.

Notes

1 Audre Lorde, "*The Master's Tools Will Never Dismantle the Master's House." 1984. Sister Outsider: Essays and Speeches* (Berkeley, CA: Crossing Press, 2007), 110.

2 India Nicole Burton, *Language, Communication, and Power between BIPOC and PWIs in the American Theatre*. September 25, accessed September 27, 2021, https://www.notes.nnpn.org/post/language-communication-and-power-between-bipocs-and-pwis-in-the-american-theater

3 Jeremy O. Harris, "Slave Play Playscript," *American Theatre* (July/August 2019): 42–67. Jeremy O. Harris, "People Say I Wrote Slave Play for White People," *The Guardian*. November 2019, accessed August 29, 2021, https://www.theguardian.com/stage/2019/nov/06/jeremy-o-harris-slave-play-interview, 7

4 Jackie Sibblies Drury, *Fairview: A Play* (New York: Theatre Communications Group, 2019), 5.

5 Patricia Hill Collins, *Another Kind of Public Education: Race, Schools, the Media, and Democratic Possibilities* (Boston: Beacon Press, 2009).

6 Loretta L. C. Brady, "Connected World, Connected Profession: Increased Recognition of Opportunities for Local and Global Engagement by Psychologists in Postcrisis Communities," *Consulting Psychology Journal: Practice and Research* 71, no. 1 (2019): 52.

7 Harris, "Slave Play Playscript," 42–67; Harris, "People Say I Wrote Slave Play for White People."

8 Kirsty Sedgman, *The Reasonable Audience: Theatre Etiquette, Behavior Policing, and the Live Performance Experience* (Switzerland: Palgrave McMillian, 2018).

9 Alice Childress, *Trouble in Mind* (New York: Theatre Communications Group, 2022).

10 Anna Deveare Smith, *We Were the Last of the Nice Negro Girls*. February 9, 2021, accessed February 2021, https://www.theatlantic.com/magazine/archive/2021/03/the-last-of-the-nice-negro-girls/617786/

11 Loretta L. C. Brady, "Performance Review: The White Card," *Texas Theatre Journal* 15 (2018): 88–90.

12 Imani Perry, *Looking for Lorraine: The Radiant and Radical Life of Lorraine Hansberry* (Boston: Beacon Press Books, 2018).

13 Claudia Rankine, "An Excerpt from Help," *The Paris Review* (Winter 2020): 13–41.

14 Marc Lamont Hill, *Nobody: Casualties of America's War on the Vulnerable, from Ferguson to Flint and Beyond* (New York: Atria Paperback, 2016).

15 Ann Elizabeth Armstrong and Joan Lipkin, "The Every 28 Hours Plays and after Orlando Networked, Rapid-Response, Collective Theatre Action – New Forms for a New Age," *Theatre Topics* 28, no. 2 (2018): 159.

16 Armstrong and Lipkin, "Every 28 Hours," 161.

17 Ibid.

18 Aleshea Harris, *What to Send Up When It Goes Down* (New York: Samuel French, 2019).

19 Brandon Jacobs-Jenkins, "What to Send Up When It Goes Down: A Black Gaze," *American Theatre*. April 2019, accessed August 29, 2021, https://www.americantheatre.org/2019/04/05/what-to-send-up-when-it-goes-down-a-black-gaze/

20 Loretta Brady and Suzanne Delle, "Traumaturgy Podcast: Beyond Streaming: Safe Discomfort." *Season 1, Episode 3.*

21 Drury, *Fairview*, 2019.

22 Ibid., 68.

23 Ibid., 98.

24 Brandon Jacobs-Jenkins is a playwright who relies on this theatrical technique to tell his story—most especially in *Appropriate* and *An Octoroon*.

25 Drury, *Fairview*, 102.

26 Rankine, "An Excerpt from Help," 13–41.

In the Trenches: A Conversation with Christina Anderson

Interview Conducted by DeRon S. Williams

Christina Anderson is a Kansas City native, American playwright, and educator who works chiefly on exploring the Black queer woman experience. She received a Tony nomination for Best Book of a Musical for *Paradise Square* and a Harper Lee Award for Playwriting. Christina's plays include *How to Catch Creation*, *Blacktop Sky*, and *Good Goods*, just to name a few. She's a resident playwright at Epic Theatre Ensemble, New Dramatists, and a DNAWORKS Ensemble member. Christina received her BA from Brown University, under the leadership of American playwright, Paula Vogel, and an MFA in playwrighting from the Yale School of Drama.

DeRon S. Williams (DSW) How did you get into playwriting? Were you driven by the need to find community or create solidarity? Or was it in an act of rebellion in of itself, pushing against narratives that you have heard all too often in the world?

Christina Anderson (CA) Well, let's see. I actually got into playwriting when I was a freshman in high school. Before that, I knew that there were playwrights, but I just assumed they were all dead because the ones we were reading in school were [William] Shakespeare and [Eugene] O'Neill. It never really occurred to me that I could write plays. At that time, I knew about Ntozake Shange, but to me, she was a performance poet. I took a drama class freshman year and my teacher had gotten this opportunity to take a handful of students to do a day-long playwriting workshop where they taught the fundamentals of playwriting. Initially, she did not pick me but then someone got sick. A slot opened up and she invited me to attend. It blew my mind. It just opened something in me. Then the Coterie Theatre in Kansas City, Missouri hosted an event called Reaching the Write Minds where they presented playwrighting workshops in middle and high schools. They also had this Young Playwrights Roundtable, and I was selected my freshman year of high school.[1] That was it. It was just a part of my life after that, playwriting. The thing I appreciated about it was I could write what I wanted. There was really no censorship. There was not anything we could not do. I think there was a lot of freedom. It really taught me to just trust my voice and the things I wanted to say and the stories I wanted to tell.

DSW How would you say you found your voice as a playwright?

CA I was fortunate in my early years of high school, and then through undergrad, where I never had anyone steering me away from the things that interested me. I had people who would introduce me to different writers. In undergrad at Brown University, Elmo Terry-Morgan taught this class "Voices Beneath the Veil: African American Plays from 1858 to the Present" that looked at Black queer plays. We studied Sharon Bridgforth, Pomo Afro Homo, and Marlon Riggs' *Brother to Brother*. Seeing that in my sophomore year of college really opened me up to radical Black folks using theatre and performance to express the specificity and also the universality of their existence.

DSW You mentioned radical Black folks, would you consider yourself or your work as a radical?

CA I do not feel like my writing is radical. I write the thing that comes to me. Part of me is channeling these stories. Part of me is figuring out what the stories are that quicken my heartbeat. I never sit down and say, "I am going to write some radical stuff today." However, I can see a difference in the things that I'm doing versus other people, but I do not necessarily think that it is radical. If I were to figure out how radical fits into my work, I would probably say it's the radical approach to play worlds and how Black people exist in those play worlds. I am not particularly a writer who is interested in Black folks' relationship to whiteness. I'm definitely more interested in how systems, like white systems, appear in Black folks' lives. I'm not really interested in writing about Black folks who are invested in engaging with whiteness. If anything, I write about Black folks who figure out how to navigate whiteness to still survive.

DSW Absolutely! Thinking about decentering whiteness, why do you think it is important to divorce your characters from engaging with whiteness? Would you say this is a form of activism, rebellion, or solidarity in the world of playwriting, of theatre, or theatre and art making?

CA I think about those moments when I was younger and see Black folks on stage or see stories that were familiar to me. The work has really been about looking at Black Americans, but also telling a good story, too. It is funny. I cannot tell you how many times after a reading or a production a white person comes up to me, and they will say, "You know, this was really good. These characters don't even have to be Black. They could be anybody." I am always like, well, no. That's a whole other conversation, but I am really committed to having us live and breathe on stage as fully and as complex as we possibly can. I think it is important to see that. I just believe that American culture is Black culture. I think if you don't have Black folks on your stage, you cannot call yourself American.

I also think it is important to note that everyone, even Black playwrights, is all writing different things. There are Black folks who may see a work of mine and be like, yes, and may see another one and say no, or they may see another Black folk's play and be like, yes, and see mine and say no. It is not inherently, oh, there is a Black person who wrote this or the Black person on stage and you automatically fall in love with it. But I would argue there is still, even if it is a thin thread, there's still merit in having those plays exist on stage and why it is important for people to see those plays.

DSW How did *How to Catch Creation* come to be? What is its origin story?

CA It was a commission with the American Conservatory Theatre (ACT) in San Francisco. At the time, I was in residency at the Magic Theatre. It was my first time living on the West Coast. I was out there for a year and was staying at my cousin's [house] in Oakland. It was the first time that I had seen Black folks running in the park and salsa dancing. I grew up in Kansas. I met so many fabulous Black queer women who were living their lives fully and on their own terms. I wanted to capture at least my vision of the type of Black folks that I was meeting. I was meeting this broad spectrum of Black folks. I knew that I wanted to capture that energy or my feeling of that energy in a play. When ACT originally did the commissions, they had just bought their second space, which was kind of at the lip of the Tenderloin [neighborhood]. They initially wanted a handful of playwrights to go through the history of that area, pick a time period, and write a short play about it. They had given us all access to the history of that spot. I am really interested in American cities and how they shift over time. How people get pushed out or brought in. How cities are erected. How they are destroyed. I immediately started thinking about if you had known the Tenderloin as one thing, you would come back and now, all of a sudden, this theatre has bought this building, and there's a hibachi restaurant. I started thinking about what character would have a relationship with an area like that. Also, in multiple plays of mine, I look at the justice system and the prison system in different ways. Then I started looking at men who were falsely accused and exonerated. Almost immediately, I noticed the difference between white men who go through that and Black men who go through that. Then when I knew that the main protagonist was going be this Black man who was falsely imprisoned and released, I started thinking about what someone like that would want. I thought, fatherhood. Then I started doing all this research, and it's actually really difficult for a single man to get a kid. Which I did not know. Then that was really the start of the play. Then I started looking at the community around him, specifically the Black women. Started to build out Tammy. I was with a friend, and we were walking somewhere in San Francisco, and he mentioned Alice Walker used to live in the area. Then I started to think about a Black queer woman writer who came up in the Bay during the '60s. That's where the play kind of got its groove going. I kind of listened to the characters and followed the play. Kind of like it led me.

DSW Your plays shed light and life on Black women in so many different, beautiful ways. What do you hope audiences will understand about Black women through your writing? And how do you believe your work subverts the social narrative of Black women?

CA I mean, I guess the best way to answer, or the way this is coming to me right now is there's a t-shirt that says trust women. Like trust Black women. Yeah. Just trust Black women. Also, Black women existing on stage is enough. I always, when I am writing these Black women, I give them the whole space. My only ask of those Black women characters is to fill it. With a lot of my plays, they always start out with questions. I kind of approach creating these play worlds and working with these characters asking them questions, and then hopefully, having a space that is safe enough for these Black women to answer fully and wholly. I just want Black women to fill the space and see that fullness. I want the audience to see that fullness. Also, there are some things that my characters do where I am like, "that is a huge mistake, girl." I think a lot of them are messy. I think a lot of them make huge mistakes that I would not necessarily do. All the women in my plays, from what I can remember, none of them walk, step shyly into a decision they make. They step boldly into it. Whatever consequences come at them, they face them. Yeah. That is what I would say I want audiences to understand. I just keep hearing this phrase, just trust the story. Also, me as a Black woman writer, trust that I know what I am doing. Trust Black women writers. If something goes against your narrative, acknowledge that, but do not try to put that on my lack of anything.

DSW Absolutely! Let's shift to *Blacktop Sky*. What was the motivation behind creating this particular piece? And how do you feel it's situated in this idea of activism, rebellion, and the creation of solidarity?

CA Yeah. Two things started *Blacktop Sky*. I was living in Harlem, and I was coming out of a barbershop from getting my haircut. There were a bunch of Black folks stock-still, watching the police arrest these two Black men. This was a time period where the instinct to get your cell phone was not so prevalent because we all kind of still had these crappy flip phones. It was something like forty Black folks standing on the street, in the summer, just watching these cops. That's where that opening monologue came from in the play. The larger impetus comes from time studying with Paula Vogel,[2] who created these things or does these things called bakeoffs.[3] It was one of my years in grad school, we had a *Leda and The Swan* bakeoff. I took a lot of the symbolism and metaphors from *Leda and the Swan* and put them into the play. That was kind of how that play came about.

Also, I was interested in how a young Black woman becomes an activist. There was the internet, but Ida learns to protest from the community around her. I do not know if it is irony, but the subtly-ness of it is when she has these encounters, no one says anything. But then when this Black man is assaulted by the police, she learns to go protest. She learns to go down to city hall. But then when she has these encounters, with her boyfriend, with class in the play that make her feel uncomfortable, she is not sure. It looks at how we learn to protest and what we protest. Also, it is kind of that weird time period where you don't know what you want to do. What does it mean to be grown? What does it mean to look grown? I remember at eighteen, I thought I was grown, but now, I'm like, I wasn't grown. So, all those things came together to kind of shape that play.

DSW In your play *Good Goods*, you present these queer characters, but their queerness is never a central part of their existence or the conflict. Why was it important to decenter their queerness and have these characters merely live? And how did you arrive at creating this play?

CA I guess I was more interested in intimacy. Then also this constant need to have a good time. Because when I was younger, I was super obsessed with the Harlem Renaissance and the '70s and *Soul Train*. Black folks looked so good. They were always dancing. It was always this quest to have a good time. But then those moments of being alone with someone were just so uncomfortable. Or not knowing what to do. You always needed somebody else there. I guess in writing the play, it just never really occurred to me to have them being queer to be the action of the play. The action of the play was them deciding to fall into each other and what made that difficult or hard or tricky.

Queerness came into it because between the years of 2003 and 2006, I was going to a lot of queer people of color club party nights in New York. There was just always this partying sense. Always trying to find those connections. I don't know if I thought about putting the queerness in the play. I was just going to queer spaces. I do remember being very purposeful that there was never going be a "Tyler Perry" moment. There is this moment where Truth finds out that Sunny is in love with Patricia. He is never like, "what?!" He just accepts it. Everybody knows about Stacy and Wire, and they just accept it. If Patricia is trying to wedge her way into that, it is not a Tyler Perry thing. It is possession. It is possession and trying to own someone through intimacy. Those are the things I was more interested in.

DSW I want to ask about your use of time because most of your plays span time and do not have a clearly defined location all at the same time. Is this your way of connecting or creating solidarity among generations and regions of Black folks and Blackness? Why is this dramaturgical intervention important to your storytelling?

CA Yeah. I made a decision pretty early on that most of my plays are fictitious cities. That was mostly just me learning history. There is a history of Black folks in America being put places geographically and being pushed out of places. So, I made a strong decision early on that the Black people in my play were going to tell you where they were and invite you into where they were and the location of these Black folks. I try to give Black folks the agency with where they live, how they live, what city they live in, what it looks like, how it functions, and the rules of it. It is unique to every play. Also, in terms of looking at time within the plays, from a personal stance, I think we keep repeating the same things with every generation. The clothes change and the technology changes, but we are still making the same kind of mistakes. I try to show our conversation with time, like Black folks and America's conversation with time. When I'm doing research for my plays, I pull from so many different resources. I have this play called *Pen/man/ship*, set in 1896, but the big conflict in the play came from the Trayvon Martin incident. It is verbatim that encounter he had with George Zimmerman when he murdered him. I just put that in that play. People are never like, that could not happen because I think we are in conversation with the past. We are also in conversation with the future. It is solidarity. It is also a lesson. I feel like the past has given us so many lessons.

Last year, I read this book called *Sister Love*, and in the intro, they talk about how the letters between Pat Parker and Audre Lorde became maps for future queer folks. Queer Black folks. Many of these plays are also in conversation with the future—after I am long gone. That is how time is absolutely a form of solidarity. It is a conversation. Hopefully, it is a lesson. It is history. It is marking time. It is marking existence.

DSW You have this new play you are working on titled *The Ripple, the Wave That Carried Me Home*. What can you tell us about this piece without giving any spoilers?

CA I am currently, slowly writing a series of plays that look at Black folks' relationship to the elements—water, air, fire, and earth. *The Ripple, the Wave That Carried Me Home* is water play. I was doing a bunch of research, trying to figure out a way into the piece. I found this book called *Contested Waters*,[4] which looks at the history of public pools in America. There are a couple of chapters that look at pool segregation. I cannot swim. My mother cannot swim. Very few people in my family can swim. It just never occurred to me that policy and racism would play a part in that. Then I started considering this notion of policing one's recreation. Our way into the play is this Black woman whose parents were, I call them aquatic activists. It's in the city of Beacon, Kansas, which is a fictitious city, but it's a land-locked state, and her parents and her grandparents on her mother's side were committed to teaching Black folks how to swim and giving Black folks access to pools. The play, on one hand, looks at how her parents' activism kind of broke their family in a way. Because I was also really interested in the kids of activists, and the impact that has on them growing up. This Black woman, through direct address, teaches us the history of her parents' activism. You also start to notice how it made her estranged from her parents slightly. The present day of the play is the 1992 Rodney King [brutality] where that video footage is made public. The daughter gets a phone call saying they want to name a public pool after her father, and they want her to come back to Beacon and be a part of the ceremony. That invitation kind of opens up her relationship to water and swimming. I won't give away anything, but there's an encounter that happens that really starts the fracturing of their relationship because it's just the three of them. She's an only child, the daughter.

DSW What I'm noticing about a lot of your plays is most of them center around some activist moment. Is it intentional on your part to center them around these activist moments?

CA Yes and no. Because I do a ton of research for all my plays. It's a mixture of what is surrounding me and what's pulling my attention. It also is a mixture of me having a question and looking for an answer within the research. Because I looked at a bunch of stuff for this water play, and it was really that *Contested Waters* book that helped me with what I can write about. I would say yes. I guess I do gravitate more toward that. A lot of the Black folks in my play are affected and upset by something, either over them being refused access to something or seeing it with someone else, and then them responding. Everyone's activism looks different in all the plays. Some people are out there marching. Some people are doing more intimate, private kind of activism. I don't even know if necessarily the people in the plays would identify themselves as activists, but I don't really sit down, like I'm going to write about these activists or I'm going to write this activist play. Yeah, a lot of times when I'm doing research, those are the things that kind of pull me.

DSW Final Thoughts: Is there anything else you want to offer about your work and the ways in which it serves as a vehicle to create solidarity, rebellion, and activism through contemporary theatre and performance?

CA The only other thing I would say is that I often find when I talk about my plays; people are often surprised by the amount of humor that's in the plays, which I think also has its form of solidarity and rebellion.

Notes

1 Sponsored by the Coterie Theatre in Kansas, Missouri, the Young Playwrights Program is designed to facilitate the growth and development of young playwrights from various school districts throughout Kansas City, Kansas, and Missouri.

2 Paula Vogel is a Pulitzer Prize Award-Winning American playwright and professor. For more information, visit http://paulavogelplaywright.com/about

3 Created by Paula Vogel, bakeoffs are a fast-paced writing exercise where participants have forty-eight hours to write a play based on a specific theme or elements. The activity focuses on reactions to plays and art, continuing the conversation started by the original artist. More information: http://paulavogelplaywright.com/bakeoff

4 *Contested Waters* by Jeff Wiltse is a non-fictional examination of public swimming pools starting from the nineteenth century to today. For more information, visit https://uncpress.org/book/9780807871270/contested-waters/

Part Two

Performance in the Making

4

Re-writing the Declaration: Healing in Theatre from a Black, Queer, Feminist Lens

Quenna L. Barrett

Introduction

"We're not free until we're all free" is a refrain I began to hear often. After Trayvon, after Mike, probably in the midst of Rekia and Sandra, but before Laquan, I followed protests and marches on Twitter until my feet found them in person. I was searching for people who looked like and who were like me, and, in retrospect, looking for a place to lend and become myself as both an artist and organizer. *Re-writing the Declaration* was birthed at the intersection of those selves.

Re-writing the Declaration,[1] a participatory play and arts-based research study, premiered virtually in November 2020. The play was produced by the Program in Educational Theatre at NYU Steinhardt, with support from Free Street Theater in Chicago, and the Speranza Foundation based in Los Angeles. As a doctoral candidate in the Educational Theatre Program at NYU Steinhardt, I proposed to make the play *as* the focus of my dissertation. Since my theatrical investigation already focused on issues that were front and center of the now supercharged sociopolitical sphere, I was invited to direct this play as part of the Steinhardt Ed Theatre Mainstage season.

Barone and Eisner discuss the potential of arts-based research to "raise questions and engender conversation" provide alternatives to pervasive metanarratives, and ultimately make new worlds.[2] This, for me, is what theatre allows us to do—to build new worlds—everyday, and why I see *Re-writing* as an act of rebellion, activism, and solidarity within particular oppressed communities. The play and study are steeped in and informed by the Black, queer, feminist lens, which I first encountered as a member of the Chicago chapter of the Black Youth Project 100.[3] Carruthers illustrates that the Black, queer, feminist lens is beneficial to those who are deemed the "furthest away from normal" ("normal" being white, male, heterosexual, etc.) and that organizing from it can lead to alternatives.[4] Delgado and Stefancic, speaking from a critical race perspective, also argue that we must "look to the bottom" to solve our issues;[5] this is precisely what the Black, queer, feminist lens does. Additionally, critical race, feminist, and queer theories all fall under a framework and philosophy of liberation. As Watkins and Shulman dictate, "[l]iberation arts methodologies are rehearsals for democratic processes that in many cases are still utopian dreams. By breaking down the wall between arts creators and arts spectators, liberation arts begin a process of dialogue and imagination that strengthen individuals and communities to engage their past, present, and future."[6] This was precisely what *Re-writing the Declaration* hoped to engage in.

Ultimately, the ensemble created a journey wherein a high school class of young Black women and non-binary folx of color take a trip to 1776 and realize all of the issues and identities the founding fathers left out. The play was live with a few pre-recorded segments, and videos of folks with marginalized identities we did not have in our cast. Throughout, the audience was invited to participate through the chat, polls, games, padlets, and other tech-based methods.

By recounting certain aspects of building and performing *Re-writing the Declaration*, this chapter seeks to share examples of how one devising process of a participatory play attempted to serve as a site of resistance, and act of rebellion and activism. Grounding in a Black, queer, feminist (BQF) lens, the devising process sought to disrupt the traditional hierarchies of playmaking, incorporate more culturally competent ways of being, and less "standard" ways of working. The play and process sought foremost to center the stories of those most at the margins, and to provide tools for exploring possibilities of liberation with the audience. What we didn't anticipate was how much we, the makers of this play, would be transformed and act-ivated by our own process. Thus, I hope this chapter also demonstrates how transformation, as theatre makers, is necessary for continued acts of activism and solidarity.

We the People—Our Cast

The ensemble who devised *Re-writing the Declaration* was comprised of seven Black women and one genderqueer person of color, with at least half of the total cast identifying as queer. Because the play sought to center the voices and needs of Black women and queer people of color, this is who we asked for in our casting call. Clarke posits, "For a woman to be a lesbian in a male-supremacist, capitalist, misogynist, racist, homophobic, imperialist cultures, such as that of North America, is an act of resistance."[7] By casting in this way and building the show around their experiences, the play centers the stories of oppression experienced by such identities, but just as much centers their stories of rebellion, resistance, and joy, as looking to the healing of marginalized identities tells us as much if not more than the stories of violence against them about how to free them. I, a Black woman, led this process. Discussing the necessity of such frameworks in communities of color, Dillard notes, "Activist praxis on behalf of freedom, and with particular regard for education and research, is not a luxury from an African worldview: It is essential."[8]

From the beginning, we were hyper-aware of our lack of inclusivity despite our stated aims. One ensemble member asked, "how do we more actively include trans gnc in this rewriting?" and after rehearsal I pondered to what extent it was "possible to uphold/work from the BQF lens if those more marginalized identities are not present?"[9] One way we sought to address this was by inviting trans, gnc, and indigenous folks we knew to participate in video interviews that would be incorporated into the show, and to pay them a small stipend for their participation.

Intro Video

You will respect this space by respecting yourself and others.
To understand the difference between equity and equality.
I found God in myself and I loved her. Ntozoke Shange.
You will give people grace and assume best intent.
You will expand your understanding of privilege.
I write for those women who do not speak.
You will be mindful of your language and the impact it may have on others.
If I didn't define myself for myself, I would be crunched into other people's fantasies for me and eaten alive. Audre Lorde.[10]

Notes on Process

We began our devising process with play, intentional community building, and establishing rituals we would return to. We created community agreements to engender a safer and brave space[11]. We answered the prompts "What will make this a brave space for you? What do you need to hold yourself and others accountable?"

Community Agreements:

1. *Give the benefit of the doubt/assume best intentions/give people grace*
2. *Before assuming, ask, "It sounds like you are saying this, is this what you mean?"*
3. *Respect boundaries*
4. *"Ouch" (that hurt) "Oops" (acknowledge pain)*
5. *Make space, take space, Why Am I Talking/Why Aren't I Talking?*
6. *ELMO: Enough, let's move on*
7. *Don't yuck my yum*
8. *Be specific and intentional; don't make assumptions*

9. *Try it on*
10. *Offer alternatives/Solution oriented/Don't consistently be an op*
11. *Let it go! Let it go!*
12. *Lean into the silence*
13. *Accountability:*
    a. *Clear and respectful communication*
    b. *One call out at a time (Name it then)*
    c. *Charge it to the head and not the heart*
    d. *Give second chances*
    e. *Center the person who has been harmed*
    f. *Makes space for learning, growth, and reconciliation*
    g. *Take individual time to process*
    h. *Apologize sincerely*
    i. *Space appropriate discussions; respect power dynamics*

"*Re-writing the Declaration*" Ensemble Community Agreements

In recent years, I have witnessed the growing practice of creating community agreements in rehearsal rooms, and I would urge the theatre community at large to continue instituting such rituals. Our agreements illustrate that from day one the ensemble was permitted to share traits exhibiting their cultural identities (e.g.: "Don't consistently be an op!") as well as their sociocultural sensibilities. This groundwork is essential for challenging norms that have not historically been human centered. In my experience, particularly in theatre spaces, it is also rare that community agreements include *how* we seek to hold each other accountable when someone does break an agreement, or cause harm to another member whether intentionally or not.

Throughout our process, up to moments before opening, we asked copious questions. In fact, one initial ensemble pondering was, "maybe this play is about questions; how do you synthesize or narrow down to get to the right question."[12] This speaks to the level of reflexivity needed for devising and co-creating processes. Landy and Montgomery speak to artistic praxis "as a practice informed by theory (and vice-versa), or, more specifically, a model of action–observation–reflection–re-action, where re-action points to change."[13] *Re-writing* sought to sit in the middle of this loop, "observing" and "reflecting" on the "action" of creating an ensemble-driven play, on the participatory aspects of the production, on making theatre in the new Zoom space, on making theatre in what we hoped to be the middle of a pandemic, on making theatre about and for change—to "re-act" and continue to move forward with change.

Centering BQF throughout Rehearsals: To Queer, or Not to Queer, Should Never be a Question

A core component of our methodology was the ensemble task of looking up and teaching back their own sources on Black, queer, feminist theory. There were two major points of learnings from our BQF teachbacks, one that comes from the research, the other that comes from the act of engaging in this process.

One main idea that came from this research that continually influenced our process was the notion of "queer" as a verb. Andrea, an ensemble member, shared with us, "there's also queer in the way you've been treated in society," relating to Alexis Pauline Gumbs's work.[14] Simone brought in that BQF is different than solely feminism; "they 'queered' it, made it something altogether different because mainstream (read: white) feminism left us out." Simone's summation of some of E. Patrick Johnson's work is that queer, as a verb, means "choosing not to conform." In this view, there is agency in queerness. I could hide and not be who I truly am, as surely many folks have done, or I could choose to be myself, even in a world when that means I am subjected to harm and violence. Being queer itself, we know, is not a choice, but there is agency and power in allowing oneself to be. This notion influenced our process in that it allowed for those of us who didn't identify as queer to understand ourselves as working outside and against the norm.

It also invited us to think about "queering" the act of re-writing itself. We moved from wondering what a literal re-writing of the document might look like, to building ways to engage with the document that were unequivocally queer.

The second learning that arose from the process of this exercise was the realization that yes, the ensemble brought in their own BQF theorists and their own lives as testament of "queer" and "BQF." Not in the "they are research subjects" kind of icky way. Hardly ever was anyone like, "here's my woe-is-me-I'm-queer story," but the mere fact that it was part of who they were. They are "theory" enacted by virtue of living lives as queer-identified folks.

Measures of Rebellion: Cultural Relevance, Spirit Work, and Emergence

Some main elements central to our work, as a company of color, were cultural relevance, spirituality, emergence, and humor as both a tactic of deploying hard conversations, and as a way to resist and continue to center Black joy. I remember feeling during many of our rehearsals how I could be my full self in this space with all folks of color. I didn't have to question if my hair or clothes were appropriate. I could bring in all the kinds of music that I enjoyed. One rehearsal, all the Black women, which is to say seven-eighths of our team, wore bonnets. The entire rehearsal. Again, I think this is a result of us having shared identities, and the fact that we were in our homes, rehearsing (quite literally) from our beds.

One moment I want to highlight as one that might not ever have happened in a different kind of space (read: "traditional," white-led, white-centered) was when twerking was offered, not only as a viable warm-up option, but as a spiritual practice. One ensemble member led us through a "Twerkitation" (yes, a twerking meditation, you're welcome), inviting us to put attention to our sacral chakra. Connecting and freeing ourselves through movement became a regular practice, so much so that a healing movement journey became an on-camera, participatory invitation in the play as one space to find and engage in collective liberation. These were both doubly important when most of our working time was spent seated or lying, having been forced to conduct this process through our computer, iPad, and phone screens.

A related activity from Brownrigg and Johnston's text on devising, "Rants Pants," invited them to just rant.[15] I learned about the necessity of righteous, Black anger from my time organizing with BYP100, and believe in its healing capacity. I noticed that from a previous exercise reading through the declaration "lots of feelings came up," so I invited them to share their feelings in the form of a rant.[16] This activity lived in the space between creating content and feeding ourselves. We, as humans, are still impacted by this document, and as artists working on this piece needed this space to rant and rave and be witnessed in both our real and creative anger. Some of the lines revealed by the rants most certainly made it if not verbatim into the show, surely through the sentiments expressed by characters:

> I just think it's funny how you knew what abolition meant when it applied to separating from Britain but you suddenly could not envision abolition when it applied to slavery. I just think it's funny how you knew the hypocrisy of writing words like 'we' and 'all,' but that didn't stop any of you from signing the document and permanently archiving your hate … I just think it's fucked up how your words get to live on without context and how by writing these words you erase an entire people. Well, you try. We are here, we're writing our own words fuck you thought [sic].
>
> Our ancestors did this shit before. They created societies, agreements, community ways of living that respected and honored the land. So why should we be trying to fit ourselves into a crusty dry toast document that was never made with us in mind.[17]

"Crusty, dusty, old ass white men" is, definitely, a line in the play.

Our warm-up and devising activities were not the only ways in which these tenets showed up in our work, nor were they the only parts of our informal processing that made its way into our play. As our process progressed, our check-ins and -outs became more about witnessing and affirming who we were and how we showed up in the world, less what we'd come to know in "traditional rehearsal spaces," and were increasingly informed by our BQF epistemology. One such check-in, offered by an ensemble member, was what were our go-to hairstyles. I noted, "This is Black Woman AF."[18] In one check-out, we gave "offerings of healing" to one another. We had just workshopped what would become some of the potential healing journeys, and would have a few days off before we would see each other again. What we gave to one another was a blend of both sacred and secular rituals: hydration, deep belly laughs, self-care and kindness, grace to yourself every day, and dancing through frustrations.

During our second week of rehearsals, we began one night by building a collective Spotify playlist. The invitation was to add songs that related to both our process and our play. Unwittingly, this list would serve as a great tool in our relationship building, and in our play. The video that closes the play is set to a choreopoem that the group wrote and choreographed, inspired in part by India.Arie's "I Am Light," which was introduced first in the playlist and brought back up when one of the ensemble led a movement warm-up. This piece, which we call the "I Am" poem, became a turning point and refrain in the play.

Additionally, the journey of "I Am" poem speaks to how we followed the ensemble's instincts and impulses, the relationship of devising activities to what made its way to the script, and to emergence in our process. One of the ensemble members latched onto a refrain of "I Am's" I had written in my previous work, pulled it out as a warm-up activity, and then it became a recurring through line in our story. This was a moment in the devising where we followed (and allowed for) an impulse from the ensemble. Ultimately the "I Am's" served as an affirmation for both ourselves and the characters we created, and hopefully invited the audience to see themselves, too. This segment is one of the few that made it all the way from proposal to devising to the play. What might this process hold for devising? That perhaps a leader in the process must do some groundwork. They must come in with some research and generative material so that the ensemble has something off which to work. And for creating work with folks of color, this anecdote speaks to letting their visions take root and grow. At the intersection of community building and content generation, the "I Am" poem is a great example of all of the very best things about our process merging together: spirit, care, ancestors, play, self, resistance; and in the function of the play was one of our acts of rebellion.

Closing Video

I am choir of women
I am the cackle of tambourines and
the roar of drums

I am Black girl magic
I am my highest self
I am my own best medicine

I am Georgia swamp and peach
Holding so many oceans within me.
I am the soul(s) of the sea.

I am Saturday night sweat
I am sex-positive slut

I am my grandfather's stirring spoon
I am Arkansas aunties with gold teeth
Toni Morrison's spiritual niece (in my head) —
I am a sister, a sistah, a daughter, a granddaughter.

I am from many roots, growing stronger with each attempt to
Chop.
Me.
Down.

I am energy

I am god and goddess and goddexx
I am that I am.
I am creation.

I am learning
to love more ethically every day
I am growing

I'm not a teacher, baby but I can teach you something
I'm not a preacher, but we can pray if you wanna

I am.
I am.
I am.[19]

What these anecdotes also speak to is the necessity of centering care, identity, joy, pleasure, and resilience in both processes with BIPOC folks, and in the work that gets created about them. While as the facilitator of this process I hoped to offer these elements, I could not have anticipated how much we would need them. Perhaps it was the context of the moment (2020 Presidential election + pandemic + racial reckonings). Perhaps it was merely because we were allowed to bring all the weight that our identities held. In a section entitled "Love as Political Resistance," adrienne maree brown reminds us of Audre Lorde's oft-tweeted and memed words that to care for self is "an act of political warfare."[20] brown continues that "we need to learn how to practice love such that care—for ourselves and for others—is understood as political resistance and cultivating resilience." Throughout our rehearsals, the ensemble showed each other much tenderness and grace. We paused when notifications of Ruth Bader-Ginsberg's death rolled in. We brought our ancestors into the space. We encouraged each other to break the rules. We moved and grooved, so much so that one ensemble member exclaimed that she felt like she was at the club often while in rehearsal. We did all this not only because we had to, but because we could.

Shared Healing and Other Tools

Our unintended collective healing served us so that it became particularly intentional in how we invited our audience to heal with us. Our healing progression began with the ancestors arriving in the dream world. They guided the audience in building an altar,[21] sang to them with their own words,[22] and finally invited them on screen to heal through dance. For us, the humor throughout the play and the multiple healing modalities were a tool. As ensemble member Asha noted in rehearsal, "in some ways how we're presenting [the content], it's still a lot of information that can be heavy, and like having a healing meditation session towards the end can help people process ... it might feel angry or you might feel guilt or you might just feel heavy in general. So helping people at least get to the process of processing," became a large part of our goal.[23] We made sure we shared ancestral cultural practices that have been demonized by (white) Christianity, like altars, and invited folks to build with us in case that was a new experience for them. Zanetta brought forward that "everyone has something different to declare in terms of freedom, independence."[24] She posited that our role was to help folks find the tool, to be "inspiring people to find the audacity to declare what they need to declare." This was not the first time the notion of audacity had come up in our process. Early on, we talked about the audacity of the colonizers to do what they did in the first place. We saw that as early-onset white privilege. But for us, Black and colored and queer, something about the mere fact of taking this endeavor on, in showing up to this play/conversation meant that we are taking up space in an audacious way. We hoped to share that with others like us, as well as concrete tools to reflect and analyze and change personal circumstances.

As we deliberated, Deanalis, our one non-binary and non-Black ensemble member, asked, "How do we make like make room and hold space for like all of the possibilities, rather than trying to, like yeah, like reach consensus."[25] This reek of interdependence, perhaps an antithesis to independence, and certainly a foundation for what we I initially hoped to promote through this work. One element of brown's *Emergent Strategy*, a system of actions, interactions, and tools for organizing following principles of the natural world, is interdependence.[26] She lifts interdependence as antithetical, or an antidote, to competition, to capitalism. "[Interdependence] means we have to decentralize our idea of where solutions and decisions happen, where ideas come from."[27] "All possibilities" equal not consensus. Consensus shan't be the goal. All possibilities should be. This challenges the very notion of "democracy," which is rooted in consensus, and in most ways, choosing one side or another. "All possibilities" is a queer sensibility. It demands us to remove the binaries, which, again, do not serve us. And this will be messy,[28] and that's ok. To hold space for all possibilities is seemingly impossible, but so was the abolition of slavery. These are the necessary acts of imagination that move us from one paradigm to another. Re-reading the transcripts, the ensemble was making this proposal of the play and interaction itself.

Repeatedly, audience members shared appreciations for the healing journeys, with particular gratitude for the "gift" of the music journey. On multiple nights, folks engaged at that point in the play who had yet to do so. I say this to acknowledge that this was one of the many moments where I had been wrong in the rehearsal process. I kept trying to cut this music section and the healing journeys overall shorter and shorter, fearing that they were dragging the show out when I thought we should have been moving more swiftly to the resolution. But the ensemble kept pushing back, kept adding in a spaciousness that they themselves needed, and that they knew an audience would need, including reminders to hydrate. This is illustrative of the ways in which directors think they know what's best and can miss beautiful "gifts" when they ignore the impulses of their actors, and how even though I was rooting my process in a Black, queer, feminist lens, habits of white supremacy[29] can still be an interloper. I was falling into the "sense of urgency" in the storytelling itself. This hiccup makes me wonder about the ways in which the habits of white supremacy show up not only in our process and organizational practices, but how they are often even centered in the stories themselves. Should we consider that both our rehearsal processes and the plays that come from them be slower, take up more space, invite in more rituals and other elements of ancestral, indigenous, and non-Western methodologies?

In our final post-show discussion, Andrea remarked that one of the elements she was eager for future iterations was to see the "community chat reiterated in a live space." One of the true gifts of this production as a zoom process was having that chat, as I do not believe we would have been able to achieve as great of an overall sense of community with the audience if we had been in person—theatre spaces are just not set up for that. I coded the chat transcripts primarily looking for what audience members were doing in the chat, and ultimately, they were building community. Content-wise, they pointed out historical wrongs and offered critiques of the Declaration, but often, they were speaking directly to each other. They did this more than even they responded to the prompts that we gave them. They affirmed each other, repeating something that they liked; celebrated each other with emojis and punctuation; and textually complimented each other. They cheered, helped each other answer questions, and asked questions of each other. All to people they didn't know. Particularly with the participatory moments, they provided solutions and problem solved. Through the chat, they were in the play with us. During one show after the unseen administrator rips up the new, inclusive Declaration that the class had built, one audience member responded, "I have a secret copy that I made don't worry," placing themselves in the middle of the action.

The act of inviting an audience to not only chat with each other and play games, but propose real solutions demonstrates care, trust, and belief in their wisdom, especially when that audience is predominantly composed of communities that have been oppressed and marginalized. At this moment, I think theatre can do more of this. When we say, "trust Black women," this is how we demonstrate it. When we say, "the people closest to the problems should have the solutions," perhaps this is one way to make space for them to build them.

Conclusion

As an ensemble working under a Black, queer feminist framework, we knew that our work could not just talk about the issues we faced; it needed to present models for the alternative, for the system, or un-system, we want to see in place. Both Augusto Boal and Paolo Freire believed that when the means of production are in the hands of the oppressed—in *Re-writing*'s case the means of cultural production are in the hands of the queer and of color ensemble and audience members—they become more empowered to change their current situations and future outcomes. I believe that our process holds some seeds for how theatre can serve as a response to both the raging social climate and the internal inequities of how we make theatre. Communities of color, poor communities, queer communities know what they need, and in making art about injustices that affect those communities, it is imperative that the meaning-making and storytelling process not solely center their stories and voices but shift practices to allow those stories to take us somewhere different symbolically and literally.

Transformation was for us, the creators, perhaps more so than for our audience members. This is a notion I tried to share with students I taught this fall, that we shall not expect audiences to be radically moved. But we might start to expect and hope for a shift in ourselves as the play makers. For myself, throughout this process and since, I have only been able to move when spirit has allowed me to. I have learned to submit my whole body and mind to radical rest. When I think about the potential healing and subsequent solidarity in this work and this kind of work—participatory, co-created, made with and for folks of color, rebellious—I'm left really envisioning what is now possible in our rehearsal rooms. After closing night, a few ensemble members shared how they would seek theatre work in spaces with whole or predominant teams of color, of queer folks. That they themselves would look to propagate such spaces. That they would look at care and community with renewed eyes. As facilitators and participants in these processes, what space do we make to pause, to breathe, to witness, to be? How do we welcome in those who came before us? And what new worlds will they allow us to build?

Notes

1 Full video can be viewed at www.bit.ly/RecTheDec
2 Tom Barone and Elliot W. Eisner, *Arts Based Research* (Los Angeles: Sage, 2012), 166.
3 BYP100 (Black Youth Project 100) is a national organization of young, Black activists.
4 Charlene Carruthers, *Unapologetic: A Black, Queer, and Feminist Mandate for Radical Movements* (Boston: Beacon Press, 2018), 8–10.
5 Richaed Delgado and Jean Stelfancic, *Critical Race Theory: An Introduction* (New York: NYU Press, 2017), 27.
6 Mary Watkins and Helene Shulman, *Toward Psychologies of Liberation* (London: Palgrave McMillan, 2008), 264.
7 Cheryl Clarke, "Lesbianism: An Act of Resistance," in *This Bridge Called My Back: Writings by Radical Women of Color*, ed. Cherrie Morega and Gloria Anzaldua (Albany: SUNY Press, 1995), 126.
8 Cynthia Dillard, "When the Ground Is Black, the Ground Is Fertile: Exploring Endarkened Feminist Epistemology and Healing Methodologies in the Spirit," in *Handbook of Ceritical and Indigenous Methodologies* ed. Norman K. Denzin, Yvonna S. Lincoln, and Linda Tuhiwai Smith (Los Angeles: Sage, 2008), 279.
9 Quenna Barrett, rehearsal notes, September 9, 2020.
10 This is the text spoken, shared across the actors, during the opening video of *Re-writing the Declaration*.
11 See Colòn for brave versus safe spaces.
12 Barrett, rehearsal notes, September 9, 2020.
13 Robert Landy and David Montgomery, *Theatre for Change: Education, Social Action, and Therapy* (New York: Palgrave Macmillan, 2012), xvii.
14 Quenna Barrett, zoom transcript, September 12, 2020.

15 Coya Paz Brownrigg and Chloe Johnston, *Ensemble-made Chicago: A Guide to Devised Theater* (Evanston: Northwestern University Press, 2018).

16 Quenna Barrett, rehearsal notes, September 17, 2020.

17 Quenna Barrett, zoom transcript, September 17, 2020.

18 Quenna Barrett, rehearsal notes, September 26, 2020.

19 "I am" poem that closes *Re-writing the Declaration.*

20 adrienne maree brown, *Pleasure Activism* (Chico, CA: AK Press, 2019), 60.

21 Collective altar padlet can be viewed at: www.bit.ly/RWTDaltar

22 The lyric padlet can be viewed at: www.bit.ly/RWTDmusic

23 Quenna Barrett, zoom transcript, September 26, 2020.

24 Quenna Barrett, zoom transcript, September 17, 2020.

25 Ibid.

26 adrienne maree brown, *Emergent Strategy: Shaping Change, Changing Worlds* (Chico, CA: AK Press, 2017).

27 brown, *Emergent Strategy,* 87.

28 I think of the oft-used community agreement, Fail Fast to Learn Fast, which is about embracing failure as an output of growth.

29 "Sense of urgency" is one of the Habits of White Supremacy as identified by Tema Okun and Kenneth Jones.

5

ineffable Dramaturgies: Experiments in Black Queer and Trans Theatre

s. e. callender

In an act of solidarity, three Black performers and peers of mine in Concordia University's Theatre Department—Jahlani Knorren, Maureen Adelson, and Oprah Lemorin—agreed to read aloud my script, *ineffable*, to a playwriting class wherein I was the only Black student. Afterwards, Oprah encouraged me to submit *ineffable* to the March 2019 Revolution They Wrote: Short Works Feminist Theatre and Performance Festival.[1] I applied alongside Oli V, co-founder of Sort Of Productions, our intersectional feminist collective, and we scored a thirty-minute time slot. We spread the word about the project on social media, talked to our classmates, co-workers, and friends, and slid into many local artists' DMs asking them to take a chance on collaborating with us when all we could offer was a first draft, some aspirational values, and a hundred bucks each, which we would scrape together to pay them out of pocket if we had to. Luckily, by the project's end, we were able to fairly compensate everyone as we received university grants and a research residency at the student-run Fine Arts Reading Room, which

A note on naming: In a project involving so many queer and trans collaborators and emerging artists who are in the process of naming and renaming ourselves, the names (and pronouns) my collaborators and I use are often in flux and may not be those that we use in other contexts. This makes us more difficult to enter into the archive, and to find there. For example, at the time of writing this chapter I use they/them pronouns and go by Esi or s. e. callender, employing ambivalent capitalizations and attempting to maintain bridges between past selves and ongoing processes of self-understanding. Meanwhile, a version of my deadname appears in the published script of *ineffable*, alone, without a family name to follow it. And it's a name that I live with as not entirely dead but still breathing in past works, in the demands of bureaucracies, in not-so-distant memories, and in certain relationships.

Figure 5.1 *ineffable*. A play in process. Book cover. Photo courtesy of nafleri.

Figure 5.2 *ineffable*. A play in process. Scan the QR code to access a pdf of the full text online. Photo courtesy of s.e. callender.

also hosted our work-in-progress readings and published *ineffable* alongside notes on its process of creation in April 2019. For many involved, this was their first time working in theatre; many others were undergraduate theatre students like ourselves. As one winter warmed to another spring in Tiohti:áke (Montreal, Canada),[2] we built a community of artists who were able to trust each other, challenge each other, feed each other (sometimes literally), have conflict, fuck up, breathe, and love each other, in the terms through which bell hooks describes "as being about people mutually meeting each other's needs and giving and receiving critical feedback."[3] This chapter briefly summarizes and analyzes *ineffable* as both a play and a process of creation.

ineffable begins with Pharah speaking in the third person about a little girl growing up as the youngest child in a wealthy Catholic family in Port-au-Prince, Haiti. Bright and curious, she asks many wide-eyed questions to her mother, a rigid but loving leader within their community. In the background of her youthful memories, Pharah alludes to the post-Duvalier era political violence that interrupted her teenhood with her family.

Suddenly, Pharah jumps ahead, swinging into the first person to describe the first kiss that she and Mars shared in Tiohti:áke in the early 2000s. Mars joins the storytelling, enacting the moment, and adding their take on that first kiss. From there, the two pass the narration back and forth, playing out moments of significance together, quoting poetry, and sometimes embodying other figures—parents, friends, and other lovers—in each other's memories. Pharah and Mars skip forward and backward through time from their childhoods to middle-age years, recounting the romance they shared, which burned bright over one summer and sent them growing apart by the next.

In her early twenties, we see that Pharah, ever bright and curious, is her mother's daughter, having learned to care deeply about others and what they think of her. She plays within her family's rules, keeping her lesbian identity well hidden, studying political science as its "the closest to liberal arts bullshit that [she] could get away with,"[4] and quietly pursuing her interest in rap. She is close with her parents, frequently calling home for long talks about politics with her father. Pharah looks forward to having a family of her own and has strong friendships. She is critical of the society she comes from and the one she is living in. Through Pharah, Mars sees how much bigger the world is than the North American metropolis where Mars has always lived. Pharah's closeness with her family in Haiti also ignites a curiosity in Mars about their father's life as a government official in Ghana and what futures exist beyond what they have imagined under the insistent white-settler racism that dominates Tiohti:áke. Pharah loves Mars eagerly, showing willingness to commit, so Mars "make[s] U-Haul jokes behind Pharah's back,"[5] but also encourages Pharah's creativity, getting her her first music gig.

Mars is assertive about their sexuality; they are both unashamed of their queer sexual orientation and genderqueer identity, and sexually confident. Mars sees their sexuality as a power they can yield. Raised by a working-class single mother unsupported by their father who returned to his home country shortly after their birth, Mars is ambitious and self-reliant. While they work to put themselves through business school (with a vague and possibly disingenuous goal to "overthrow capitalism"[6]), they're also involved in the local queer, arts and rave scenes and a handful of sexual relationships, some with authority figures. Mars often hurts Pharah with their denial of the depth of the relationship and their insensitivity toward Pharah's needs. Still, Mars' confidence and charm are infectious, and they embolden Pharah to embrace herself and her sexuality.

Disappointed not to be selected for an internship toward the end of their degree, Mars makes the sudden decision to visit their father in Accra, Ghana. During their trip, Mars becomes determined to make a life in their father's homeland, where they feel more powerful. Mars decides that they will conceal their gender and sexuality in order to face less barriers there. Jumping ahead, they describe how they go on to live in Accra, what they achieve, and the "brave friends"[7] that they keep secret.

Bouncing back to when the couple reunites, Pharah can tell that something has changed in Mars, and thinks this must have been the impact of hiding themselves under their dead name during their trip. Wanting to free herself from *her* hiding, Pharah decides to come out to her parents, who then cut her off financially and beg her to take it back. In this moment of vulnerability, Mars pulls away from Pharah without explanation.

We hear how their love story lives on bitter in Pharah's memories of cold-hearted abandonment and sweet in Mars' rose-tinted memories of youthful abandon. The play ends with Pharah describing her life and loves after Mars, her unending fight for acceptance from her family, and how even though her parents beg her to change, they don't give up on her either, still picking up the phone, still sometimes catching her up on their lives, still "leaving the appropriate dead air in the place of a 'mwen renmen'w,'"[8] before hanging up.

Their tragedy is that Pharah and Mars are made to feel that they must choose between their queerness and transness or their African, Caribbean, and Black communities, when the choice is impossible; "I am irreversibly myself,"[9] as Pharah puts it. We *can* choose both. But even confronting this false dichotomy changes us and compels us to feel we must strain to choose all of ourselves. At times, we judge how one another contort under this pressure. This can weigh on Black queer and trans love, on our friendships and communities. It weighed on Pharah and Mars until they broke apart.

This is not the story of any two Black queer and trans people,[10] or of all of us, but of Pharah and Mars specifically, with all their limitations and strengths, their personal histories, and desires, all the ways they were softened, reshaped, and hardened by each other. In terms of representation, this meaningfully mirrors Sarah Ahmed's assertion in an essay first published in *Queer Phenomenology* that our orientations cannot be reduced to our identities (race, gender, sexuality, etc.), though these identities inform whether our society encourages or denies access to that which we are oriented toward, and may thrust unwanted orientations onto us.[11] Interwoven, complex forces, both internal and external, influence the encounter between Pharah and Mars and the paths they take. *ineffable* refers to what they hold back from saying, but also to what is so difficult to articulate about why a particular connection begins or burns out.

Ahmed demonstrates that any object to which we are oriented—for instance, *ineffable* as an art object—cannot be reduced to itself, as it is also constituted by its contact with others, or, in a sense, by its story.[12] *ineffable* must then be understood as the product of a highly collaborative, experimental, and reflective process which shaped its content, form, and meanings. Leading up to and throughout the Revolution They Wrote festival in March 2019 and the readings and publication of *ineffable* by the Fine Arts Reading Room in April 2019, I re-wrote this work in community with many other Black queer and trans people who, as collaborators and as early audiences, shaped the play and its process of creation. They provided feedback based on their lived experiences; they documented, researched, performed, and translated it; they gave it music, poetry, style, and texture; they brought in inspirations, connected to it, and criticized it. Moreover, many Black cishet[13] people and non-Black queer and trans people supported this process with their efforts. So, while I as a playwright am accountable for any criticisms of *ineffable*—and the ideologies it expresses—*ineffable* equally belongs to the community who co-created it.

This communal approach to ownership in artmaking is part of how the process of creating *ineffable* rebelled against the norms of what bell hooks describes as imperialist, white-supremacist, capitalist patriarchy,[14] inherent to much of Canada's theatre scene and culture in general, offering instead a space of solidarity centering Black queer and trans lives. While traditional Western (read white) theatre strives for perfection, our focus was not on the final product. Instead, we were concerned with the process, wherein "people encounter[ed] solidarity by sharing their (un)commonalities."[15] Together, we read the script, discussed the meanings we each got from it, the questions we each had about it, and came to agreements about our budget, process, and shared approach to staging the work. We established a non-realist aesthetic with a strong interplay of music (composed by musician Théo Amo) and silence, few but versatile props and costumes (thrifted, borrowed, and loaned by filmmaker Adam Mbowe), and all performers on stage throughout, sometimes lighting each other with flashlights (eventually documented in video and artful photographs by filmmaker Sara-Claudia Ligondé). Knowing how little we knew, we actively invited in the different forms of knowledge each collaborator held, centering the experiential knowledge of our Black queer and trans collaborators. This opened exciting and difficult discussions, as we circled topics of home, migration, love, "outness," sleeping around, racism, spirituality, political violence, rejection, betrayal, feeling impossible, and feeling free.

Our rehearsals were highly communicative in an attempt to give each participant space to express their creative vision, their feelings, their boundaries, what they struggled with, and what support they needed to grow in their roles, as many were stepping into a new role or into theatre for the first time. Oli and I were also in uncharted waters, as we shared a rehearsal-facilitator role, our subversion of the typical director role. We had no experience directing and took it on because we were unable to find anyone else to. Being rehearsal-facilitators involved animating discussions, bringing in exercises, activities, and workshops facilitators, and providing feedback as the performers brought the play to life themselves. With only five weeks of five-hour weekly rehearsals, we gave each a central theme around which that rehearsal would be focused, based on our understanding of the group's needs, including text analysis, movement/voice, character/acting approach, intimacy, and materiality/culture/space/setting. Through this approach, we built a shared performance vocabulary. For instance, the most experienced performer, Amy Sawyer, shared her knowledge about acting, breathwork, movement, and voice to equip the newer performers, musician Naïka Champaïgne and writer Camille Mankumah, with these foundations; Amy facilitated many deep breathing exercises that eventually translated into the performers attuning to each other's breath and coordinating the timing of certain actions on stage based on responding to one another's breaths. These exercises involved everyone in the rehearsal room, so we were able to learn alongside our performers, noting in our process reflection that we found "Breathing is necessary for everyone, not just the actors."[16] This collaborative approach unsettled the power dynamics in our work; to break the awkwardness of dancing or holding or crawling on the stage barking, we all did all these things together.

We made intentional room for feedback in multiple forms throughout. Sharing food was one way that Oli and I knew to create community and give care, so we fed everyone at each rehearsal, reading, or meeting. Chatting during those shared meals, feedback came up more casually amongst the group. We always began with a check-in and ended with a check-out to voice anything we were carrying in with us or any residual feelings sitting with us as we wrapped up. The group chose if each check-in/out would be out loud or written. If written, collaborators had the option to share aloud what they wrote down, to have Oli and I confidentially collect their written feedback, or to take it home for themselves.

Sometimes, criticism would be easy for us to take. Once, in response to the question "Is there anything you're scared/hesitant to do in the process?" we got written feedback from a performer to the effect of "You're checking on our boundaries *too* much. I'm fine with physical intimacy onstage. We can just kiss or touch or whatever." This feedback opened the door for staging many more acts of Black queer physical affection—dancing konpa, awkwardly hugging hello, cuddling, holding hands, kissing, undressing, clutching to each other, and so on. Each of these moments aching, hopeful, strange, and sweet collided against a dominant culture wherein such images are so hard to find that they often feel taboo and radical when we live them. Chatting with audiences after performances at Revolution They Wrote, we heard repeatedly how good it felt to see this physical intimacy represented, especially alongside exploration of dilemmas that many in the audience said they face but don't often see in arts and popular media. This feedback further emboldened us to add a scene of sexual intimacy to the script.

Other times, receiving criticism took deeper reflection and re-evaluation of the impacts of our behavior. We encouraged collaborators to text, call, or ask for a meeting if they needed to address something we hadn't given space to. Once, a collaborator met with me to ask if the casting of the play had been informed by colorism. They pointed out that the three roles were given to two light-skinned Black queer women and one non-Black genderqueer person of color and noted that the foregrounding of people with their complexions at the expense of the erasure and marginalization of dark-skinned Black women in particular is a dynamic they had observed both in popular media and in our local community. They also contextualized that their question was underpinned by interpersonal conflicts that were exacerbated by their participation in *ineffable*. Regardless of any reasoning behind or circumstances of the casting, making work about Blackness in which dark-skinned Black people are absent or made invisible (as was the case in *ineffable*, wherein many dark-skinned Black people collaborated on the project off-stage but were not represented on-stage) is an expression of our own internalized racism that we had to confront, and work through our disappointment in ourselves. This feedback then became part of a longer process of personal reflection and shared re-evaluation between Oli and I of how we allowed a colorist dynamic to manifest and how we can prevent this from recurring in future projects. We also had to do the uneasy work of rebuilding the trust of the collaborator who spoke up, supporting their feeling of safety in the work, and repairing the damage to the relationships involved, which we were never able to adequately do.

This experience of being asked to do better, of someone sharing their honest feelings with us, also taught us that bringing forward conflict is an act of kindness and solidarity, allowing those responding to the conflict the opportunity to learn, grow, and strengthen the bond that was damaged. We were and continue to be deeply grateful to our collaborator for bringing this forward and helping us to see our ignorance and the harm it caused. While this was the major conflict brought to us by another collaborator, Oli and I also had several conflicts between us. With each, this awareness, and the knowledge that our friendship can withstand moments of tension, disappointment, and discomfort, made us feel safer together.

Oli and I kept process journals and encouraged our collaborators to do so as another form of feedback. We free-wrote (keeping our pens moving for an allotted amount of time, writing without filtering ourselves) after each rehearsal, reading, or meeting, and at the beginning of our one-on-one meetings, either about what was on our minds or in response to a question.[17] These journals brought us perspective within an overwhelming project. I was re-writing *ineffable* and Oli was dramaturging it, while we were also facilitating the rehearsals, and producing—the grants, emails, schedules, and organization of it all. In our attempts to ensure that our collaborators felt cared for, heard, rested, and fed throughout, in our attempts to ensure that they were not being overwhelmed, Oli and I placed too much on our own shoulders. Oli noted in an entry during the weeks leading up to Revolution They Wrote:

> I really wanted to cry but knew that I couldn't or just didn't want to be that vulnerable or accept that something we had created and ensured that it was not stressful for anyone else was actually super stressful and harmful to me and [s e]. Like the process is not protecting us. So like the systems and cultural norms we wanted to break we are still perpetuating in ourselves and then probably indirectly to the group. It's just been more difficult than we thought to uphold our values and ideals. And it's so nice to think or write it down on paper, but honestly so hard to keep in mind.[18]

Crossing our boundaries and sacrificing our own wellbeing to "produce" something is an expression of internalized imperialist, white-supremacist, capitalist patriarchy—the ever-present feeling that we must earn our value in the world through constantly producing. Breaking from these patterns of burnout and self-denial, reproduced many times in our theatre education and low-wage service jobs, remains one of our main challenges. Venting on the pages of our process journals helped us to notice this, to share our feelings, to handle conflicts with each other and work on the issues brought up in conflict, and to stay in conversation with all we were struggling through within ourselves. For instance, some of our journals address our fears of bringing a colonial lens to our research on Haitian and Ghanaian culture and experimental theatre, "continuing this relationship of taking what we want,"[19] and of not being "the right people" to organize this project, as Oli is a white Italian-Canadian queer woman and I am a mixed-race Black Ghanaian-Canadian non-binary person "when the project is so much about and embedded in blackness."[20] We compiled selections from these journals and included them as process notes in the published script.

Alongside staging *ineffable* at Revolution They Wrote, we held work-in-progress readings as part of our research residency at the Fine Arts Reading Room throughout spring 2019. There, we read the script aloud, took questions from the audience, and facilitated discussion amongst them. We broke audiences up into smaller groups that each looked at a different set of prepared questions.[21] In groups, they could write their responses and feedback down to return to us or share it aloud to everyone at the end of the session. Oli and I invited theatre makers, artists, and others who are part of the communities whose realities are addressed by the script to listen, discuss, and offer feedback.

We also invited the other artists participating in Revolution They Wrote after meeting them in a first-look session that the festival hosted. Many of these artists were expanding political, narrative, and aesthetic possibilities beyond the sparse Black queer and trans representations in popular media and established theatre institutions. For example, in *Journey to Free,* Kathleen Charles told "the story of a young black woman rediscovering and affirming her intersectional feminine identity through poetic prose and Haitian folkloric songs."[22] In *2019 boulevard des limites, boundaries,* Christopher Marlot invited audiences into Mademoiselle Marlot's "private life, her sexuality, her wildest dreams."[23] In *Buxton Train* Amanda Benn re-imagined the nineteenth-century women of then-British Guiana who "fed up [with] gender roles and men not getting the job done, [led] the revolution."[24]

As an aside, boundary-pushing works by Black, racialized, queer and trans artists are a recurring strength of Revolution They Wrote. By attending annually since 2016, I have seen an absurdist drama about begging for your mother's love (Mā Ma by Ke Xin Li),[25] a Kurdish pop star's DMs as she heals from intimate-partner abuse and intergenerational trauma (tldr; smh by Burcu Emeç),[26] fragmented pieces of Black girl growing up memories and mourning (Crybaby by Kalale Dalton),[27] peanut butter smeared on the mannequin body of a rapist (Dark Red by Willow Cioppa),[28] and an Afrofuturist Black-supremacist sex-positive musical (The BiG SiSSY Show—The Message by Athena Holmes).[29] The programming of these local artists built a unique audience around the festival, and in the year *ineffable* was staged we further encouraged the participation of Black queer or trans audience members by making free tickets available to them. This is the subaltern counterpublic, "where members of subordinated social groups invent and circulate counter discourses, which in turn permit them to formulate oppositional interpretations of their identities, interests, and needs,"[30] that *ineffable* developed and developed from.

In that first-look session at Revolution They Wrote, we also took notice of Deniz Başar, a Turkish academic and playwright who had just fled from institutional racism at the University of Toronto. She commented that she was concerned about how to present her play, *In the Destructible Flow of a Vast, Monolithic Moment*, which has as its backdrop the cultural taboos and political turmoil in Turkey from the 1990s to the 2013 Gezi Park protests. Deniz feared that Canadian audiences would receive her work with a sense of Western superiority, that they would "sympathize" with her characters while feeling "grateful" for the security and stability of their own country, imagining that this "overseas unrest" has nothing to do with them. Deniz's comment immediately intrigued Oli and I as she put into words something that we had been asking ourselves with *ineffable*, in which Canada, Ghana, and Haiti are all depicted, hopefully without idealizing one or the other, as each geography offers different complicated possibilities and challenges to our Black queer and trans characters.

Deniz also took an interest in *ineffable* (in fact, she has since published its Turkish-language translation).[31] She attended one of our readings and recognized that, though we didn't know it, we were trying to create narrational theatre. A form widely used by Middle Eastern theatre makers, narrational theatre is characterized by performers narrating the story of the play, with the possibility to switch between narration and enactment.[32] Narrational theatre allows for thoroughly researched and often taboo histories and realities, difficult to depict on stage, to be described.[33] It also creates distance between the performer and the character(s) they embody, and allows a single performer to play multiple roles or to perform roles that might otherwise be off limits to them. Deniz used narrational theatre in her latest play *Wine & Halva,* which was produced by Sort of Productions in 2020. In that work, three narrators of differing races and genders take turns in portraying two characters, a white gay man and a Turkish immigrant woman, as they move through different locations, speaking to the relative formation of identity. As Deniz explains in an interview with *The Theatre Times,* "The narrative style allows the performers and audiences to be aware they are engaging in theater; it doesn't pretend to be a 'slice of life' with the audience invited to be voyeurs."[34]

At the reading that Deniz attended, confusion about the multiple voices and narrational form of *ineffable* was voiced by some participants familiar with the conventional (as in Eurocentric) wisdom "show, don't tell" often taught in Canadian theatre schools, which advocates that rather than explaining action, one must show it on stage. Through Deniz's mentorship and friendship, we were able to clarify our narrational theatre approach, and became freer in using it. Originally, two performers playing Pharah and Mars were recollecting and reliving their love story on stage, accompanied by a third performer who embodied the other strong influences in their lives. Through a deeper understanding of narrational theatre, we were able to use Mars and Pharah as unreliable narrators attempting to win the audience over to see the relationship through their eyes—rose-tinted or betrayed. As character-narrators, they can express themselves outside of everyday language, for instance through spoken word poetry, and they can step outside of the narrative to quote poetry and prose that is self-aware of their storytelling. Given that the script covers a large and nonlinear timespan, this form also allows for two performers to portray Pharah and Mars at multiple stages in their lives, and to temporarily give voice to the significant characters in one another's stories—the voices that break through and become internalized. The opening and only stage direction of *ineffable* reads: "Everything on these pages can be said or done by two or more Black performers,"[35] allowing for multiple performers to portray Pharah and Mars intermittently. This was the case in the final reading at the Fine Arts Reading Room in April 2019, wherein five of our collaborators shared the two roles.

Through the readings we also learned from two Haitian artists and dear friends, Maryline Chery and Michael Fanfan, that the portrayal of Pharah's mother felt unrelatable. (In early drafts, after Pharah comes out, her mother leaves her disapproving father to be by Pharah's side, while still begging her to change; Maryline and Michael couldn't buy this unless there were underlying circumstances in the mother's life that would justify this drastic move.) This sparked Oli and I to hire Haitian cultural dramaturges to help us carry out our research related to Haitian politics, music, culture, and conceptions of queerness and transness, in an effort to make Pharah a more grounded and authentic character. This collaboration with Lydie Dubuisson and G3ra burst the process open. It meant questioning many of the assumptions that I'd written into Pharah, which often made her seem like a second-generation immigrant rather than someone who immigrated in her late teens. Better understanding Pharah's cultural background helped to materialize her conflicts with Mars.

> **Pharah** "You don't know that! You don't live with any rules! You don't have parents checking up on you! You don't have to consult anyone about anything you do! You just do whatever the fuck you want and leave everyone else to deal with consequences! You don't live in the real world, Mars!"
>
> **Mars** "Well when you put it like that, I sure wish I did.""[36]

This dramaturgy meant situating Pharah's life within Haitian history and society and flushing out how her family functioned internally. It also meant laughing a couple mornings each week with two Black women a few years older than me, each exploring their queerness, as we shared our research and teased out the world of the play together. It meant bringing the often frustrating and confusing work of trying to *improve* an unconventional play into the light of day, into the playfulness of new friendships.

Building friendships through the process was a goal of ours. We had fun through and around *ineffable*, getting sidetracked in one-on-one meetings, joking around during rehearsal hours, and eating meals together, believing that what happened outside of "the work" can be as important as what happened within it. Friendship also required valuing each collaborator's creativity and voice (rather than prioritizing a single voice like the playwright's or director's, as is often done), valuing our collaborators' wellbeing over the final product, constantly self-questioning, staying open to feedback and intentionally in process.

"When we say show up for black folx we ALSO mean black queer and trans folx—and that means to show up and support us while we're alive and creating, alive and telling y'all to listen to us, that we exist and we matter,"[37] wrote Naïka Champaïgne in an Instagram caption in late June 2020 as we marched to protest racist police violence following the murder of George Floyd by Minneapolis police. In the image above this message, Naïka kneels at Camille Mankumah's feet, looking adoringly at her bare legs. Camille smiles knowingly down at Naïka. Surrounding them, scattered like tiny islands on the dark sea of the Revolution They Wrote stage, are remnants of the performance: a pile of books, a scarf, a suitcase, an armchair, a hibiscus flower, a men's suit, a patch of dirt. This unprompted post seemed to recognize *ineffable* as a site of resistance, one of many needed during another summer of fighting for Black liberation amidst our lifetimes of this fight. If we consider activism as "a wide range of behaviors that are aimed at challenging existing power relations and changing the status quo," then it is not limited to massive, organized protest movements.[38] Instead, "everyday feminist, antiracist, anticapitalist practices" are an equally important form of activism.[39] Within this framework, I believe that *ineffable*—both the play and the process of its creation—is a collection of such everyday transformative practices.[40]

Notes

1 The annual Revolution They Wrote: Short Works Feminist Theatre and Performance Festival was founded in 2014 by Murdoch Schon with the initial support of the Concordia Student Union and later MainLine Theatre in Tiohti:áke. It presents "new and in progress feminist works" that "discuss the intersections of feminism," and incorporates "peer to peer mentorship" through work-in-progress performances prior to the festival at which artists give one another feedback. The festival brings together feminist theatre, performance art, music, and visual arts. "About Us," *Revolution They Wrote*, accessed December 31, 2021, https://revolutiontheywrote.com/about-us/

2 Tiohti:áke is the indigenous Kanien'kéha name for Montreal, popularly used within the city. It translates to "broken in two," referring to how the Saint Lawrence River splits around the island of Montreal. Karonhí:io Delaronde and Jordan Engel, "Montreal in Mohawk," *The Decolonial Atlas*, last modified February 4, 2015, https://decolonialatlas.wordpress.com/2015/02/04/montreal-in-mohawk/

3 bell hooks and Cornel West, *Breaking Bread: Insurgent Black Intellectual Life* (New York: Routledge, 2017), 56.

4 s. e. callender, *ineffable. A Play in Process* (Montreal: Fine Arts Reading Room, 2019), 10.

5 callender, *ineffable*, 11.

6 Ibid., 10.

7 Ibid., 25.

8 "Mwen renmen'w" translates from Haitian Creole to English as "I love you." callender, *ineffable,* 33.

9 callender, *ineffable*, 30.

10 The language used to refer to people who do not exist within the boundaries of heterosexual and/or cisgender identities is varied and evolving. In this chapter, I use the terms queer and trans as umbrella categories to refer to all people with minority sexual orientations and gender identities, respectively, while recognizing that some within these communities will disagree with this use of language for many legitimate personal, spiritual, cultural, and historical reasons. Please note, I include this endnote in multiple pieces of writing to clarify my use of language.

11 Sara Ahmed, "Orientations Matter," in *New Materialisms: Ontology, Agency, and Politics*, ed. Diana Coole and Samantha Frost (Durham: Duke University Press, 2010), 251.

12 Ibid., 240.

13 Cishet is a compound of cisgender and heterosexual.

14 bell hooks and George Yancy, "bell hooks: Buddhism, the Beats and Loving Blackness," *Opinionator*, *The New York Times*, last modified December 10, 2015, https://opinionator.blogs.nytimes.com/author/bell-hooks/

15 Kaciano Barbosa Gadelha, "Friendship, Affect and Capitalism," in *Friendship as Social Justice Activism: Critical Solidarities in a Global Perspective*, ed. Niharika Banerjea, Debanuj DasGupta, Rohit K. Dasgupta, and Jaime M. Grant (London, New York, and Calcutta: Seagull Books, 2018), 13.

16 callender, *ineffable*, 40.

17 Some examples of questions we asked in process journals and in check-ins/outs include:

> What were some obstacles this week? How did you face/overcome them?
>
> What were the dynamics like this week (tension, ran smoothly)? Why were they this way?
>
> How did the roles of dramaturg/playwright coincided with one another/work together this week?
>
> Is there a way that you could improve your work for next week?
>
> Is there anything that you wished you could have communicated, better communicated, or said in general to the group or to your partner?
>
> Is there anything you're scared/hesitant to do in the process?
>
> What's a fun/happy/silly memory from this week?

18 callender, *ineffable*, 46.

19 Ibid., 45.

20 Ibid., 44.

21 Some examples of questions we asked audiences include:

> Who is each character? What are they like? What was each of their journeys?
>
> What do you want to know about the characters? (3 things each)
>
> Who do you identify with? Why?

What were the main themes?

What did you notice? (3 things)

What did you feel? (3 things)

What images stuck out for you? (3 things)

What does time do in this play?

What was the rhythm of the play like? What moments went the slowest? The fastest? Were they effective?

What is the world of the play like?

How was the evolution of the play? What was its shape?

What was the overall effect?

What inconsistencies did you notice?

What did you want to see in this play that was missing?

What are 3 questions that you have about this work?

22 "Journey to Free," *Revolution They Wrote*, accessed December 31, 2021, https://revolutiontheywrote.com/journey-to-free/

23 "2019 boulevard des limites, boundaries," *Revolution They Wrote*, accessed December 31, 2021, https://revolutiontheywrote.com/2019-boulevard-des-limites-boundaries/

24 "Buxton Train," *Revolution They Wrote*, accessed December 31, 2021, https://revolutiontheywrote.com/buxton-train/

25 "Mā Ma," *Revolution They Wrote*, accessed December 31, 2021, https://revolutiontheywrote.com/ma-ma/

26 "tldr; smh," *Revolution They Wrote*, accessed December 31, 2021, https://revolutiontheywrote.com/tldr-smh/

27 "Crybaby," *Revolution They Wrote*, accessed December 31, 2021, https://revolutiontheywrote.com/crybaby/

28 "Dark Red," *Revolution They Wrote*, accessed December 31, 2021, https://revolutiontheywrote.com/dark-red/

29 "The BiG SiSSY Show—The Message," *Revolution They Wrote*, accessed December 31, 2021, https://revolutiontheywrote.com/the-big-sissy-show-the-message/

30 Nancy Fraser, "Rethinking the Public Sphere: A Contribution to the Critique of Existing Democracy," *Social Text*, no. 25/26 (1990): 67.

31 s. e. callender, “söylenemez,” trans. Deniz Başar in *Hevesle Beraberlik Arası Bir Şey—Bir Kritik Kolektif Kitabı/Between Enthusiasm and Cooperation—A Critical Collective Book*, ed. Eylem Ejder and Handan Salta (İstanbul: Mitos Boyut Yayınlar, 2021), 136–58.

32 Marjan Moosavi, “In Conversation with Deniz Başar: ‘Wine & Halva’—A Play That Tests the Limits of Friendship within Canadian Institutional Racism (Part II),” *The Theatre Times*, last modified July 6, 2020, https://thetheatretimes.com/in-conversation-with-deniz-basar-wine-halva-a-play-that-tests-the-limits-of-friendship-within-canadian-institutional-racism-part-ii/

33 Juliet Guzzetta, “Oratory and the Public Sphere: Hearing Italy through Narrative Theater,” *Spaziofilosofico Italia*, no. 2 (2011): 201–8.

34 Marjan Moosavi, “In Conversation with Deniz Başar: ‘Wine & Halva’—A Play That Tests the Limits of Friendship within Canadian Institutional Racism (Part I),” *The Theatre Times*, last modified August 22, 2020, thetheatretimes.com/in-conversation-with-deniz-basar-winehalva-a-play-that-tests-the-limits-of-friendship-within-canadian-institutional-racism-part-i

35 callender, *ineffable*, 2.

36 callender, *ineffable*, 14–15.

37 Naïka Champaïgne, “Y’all Remember the Play I Was Part of ‘Ineffable’?” *Instagram*, last modified June 27, 2020, https://www.instagram.com/p/CB8_vDOHnbe/

38 Catherine A. Faver, “Motivations for Women’s Social Activism,” *Affilia* 16, no. 3 (2001): 320, quoted in Rachel Gouin, “An Antiracist Feminist Analysis for the Study of Learning in Social Struggle,” *Adult Education Quarterly* 59, no. 2 (2009): 158.

39 Chandra Talpade Mohanty, *Feminism without Borders: Decolonizing Theory, Practicing Solidarity* (Durham: Duke University Press, 2003), 4, quoted in Rachel Gouin, “An Antiracist Feminist Analysis for the Study of Learning in Social Struggle,” *Adult Education Quarterly* 59, no. 2 (2009): 158.

40 I want to thank Valérie Bah, Deniz Başar, and Oli V for their assistance with writing this chapter, for keeping me accountable, and for reminding me that my voice is irreverent, curious, and a little flirty, that it’s broken by laughter halfway through sentences and ticks up with a question mark

at the end in a way that I hate but that also forces me to be humble. I also want to thank all the collaborators who co-created *ineffable* but are not already named in the chapter above; thank you to Elsa Orme, Manolis Antoniou, and Max Harry. And to Zoe S. Bailey, thank you for diving in with me; to Quinlan Green, thank you for keeping my heart open and for reading me and letting me read you; to nafleri, thank you for the illustrations that are on the book cover and the ones that are just for us two; to Obakeng Ndebele, thank you for dreaming *ineffable* as a film and always expanding my mind into undefined space.

I hope to create with each of you again someday.

6

Reconsidering and Recasting

John "Ray" Proctor

A *Masterclass* article written in November of 2020 defines *casting* as "a pre-production process that involves choosing actors to fill the roles in a particular television show, movie, commercial, or play."[1] This definition hides the impact and the incalculable social ramifications contained within the reality of what casting is and what it does. What is insidious about of this definition is that it seems so innocuous, simple, and straightforward. All television shows, commercials, movies (films), and plays (live theatre) are hegemonic and ideological mechanisms that have real-world impacts, and consequences, and ramifications. I hope to frame the consideration of the intersection between race and casting practices in America by deferring to Antonio Gramsci's construction of theatre as an ideological social mechanism.[2] Then I hope to narrow the scope of my own argument to consider, specifically, the role *casting* plays within this larger ideological mechanism and, more specifically, how casting decisions with regard to race distort and erase BIPoC subjects from the very narratives that are, theoretically, written and produced to (re)present diverse, equitable, and inclusive theatre. In particular, I would like to consider Lin-Manuel Miranda's reasoning and insistence on the casting of the actors of color in the leading roles of *Hamilton* and what that casting does to the way audiences perceive, or make sense of, the writing of race within the context of that spectacle-text.

Discussing the nature of the relationship between the audience and what they see, or how an audience begins to interpret or make sense of the theatre-event is complicated, complex, difficult, and layered. Philip Zarilli, Richard Shechner, Stuart Hall, and many others wrote extensively about the nature of communication between audiences and performance in the 1970s, 1980s, and 1990s. Critical Race Theorists, such as Derek Bell, Alan Freeman, bell hooks, Kimberlé Crenshaw, Audre Lorde and many many others, have spent their careers examining how societies and communities *read* race. The intersection of research from both of these fields of study generates an interesting lens through which we might begin to understand the cultural phenomenon that was (and continues to be) Lin-Manuel's *Hamilton* and how audiences are confounded by, and make sense of, Miranda's insistence upon racially specific casting of the leading roles in the production.

In 2016, Michael Paulson of the *New York Times* wrote,

> The hit musical *Hamilton* has drawn widespread praise for its use of a diverse cast to explore American history. But a casting call seeking 'nonwhite men and women' to audition for the show drew criticism from the union representing theater actors, prompting *Hamilton* to say Wednesday that it will amend its language to make clear that anyone is welcome to try out for the show.[3]

Quoting *Hamilton* producers, Paulson continued, "[We] regret the confusion that's arisen from the recent posting of an open call casting notice for the show, but it is essential to the storytelling of *Hamilton* that the principal roles, which were written for nonwhite characters (excepting King George), be performed by nonwhite actors." *Hamilton*, however, is not unique in its demand for race-specific casting. *OnStageblog*'s Chris Peterson compares the hypocrisy of outrage regarding racially specific casting, by pointing out the lack of attention that was paid to actors of color who questioned the fairness of the September 2015 casting call for *Brightstar*, which specified, "All characters are Caucasian."[4] It is not uncommon for the author, or the rights holder, to require and demand that their play be cast with individuals who are specific races and specific genders. In 2017 the Albee Estate rescinded the right to a production of *Who's Afraid of Virginia Wolf?* because they had cast a Black actor (Damien Geter) in the supporting role of "Nick."[5] Dramatist Play Service, the rights holders for Robert Harling's *Steel*

Magnolias, may grant exceptions for men to appear in drag, but it is a right expressly held by the playwright and a right that is rarely granted.[6] More than simply their literary script, playwrights have the right to manage and control the spectacle-text, which can include the race or gender of the actors embodying the characters in their plays. Actors/performers of color have known and dealt with this fact for years. The casting controversy of *Hamilton* is interesting and unique because in this instance the demand for casting inclusion is coming from white performers who feel like they are being barred from playing the leading (or featured) roles.

Casting policies in *Hamilton* have garnered antidiscrimination lawsuits against major communication companies. Attorney Paul Clement, representing Charter Communication, argued, "The musical *Hamilton* is notable for its creator's decision to cast exclusively minority actors as the Founding Fathers." Clement continued, "A refusal to contract with a white actor to play George Washington cannot be made an antidiscrimination violation without profoundly undermining First Amendment values."[7] The stakes of *Hamilton* are that, in one way, it *re-presents* a version of the events of Alexander Hamilton's life as documented by Pulitzer Prize-winning author Ron Chernow.[8] Miranda re-envisions Chernow's literary-text into the spectacle-text that is the live production of *Hamilton*. People want biographies and history to be true, but "true" is also complicated and complex. The truth is we weren't in the room when it happened—so we're always getting somebody else's version of the story, colored by their perspective and their biases. The tension of Miranda's *Hamilton*, in performance, is that Miranda's might not ever have intended to tell Alexander Hamilton's truth. It is unlikely that it has ever been Miranda's intention to adhere to, or support, mythologies about America's Founding Fathers. Through his color-conscious casting decisions and demands, Miranda writes race into this spectacle-text which, while it entertains, also ruptures and challenges conceptions of claimants of American identity, writers of American history, as well as calling into question the complicated intersection of race and the complexities of American identity.

Antonio Gramsci's articulation of ideology is a useful place to begin this discussion. According to Gramsci,

> The concept of hegemony refers to the moral, philosophical, and political leadership of a social group, which is not gained by force but by an active consent of other social groups obtained by taking control of culture and ideology. During this process, the leading social group exerts its impact and gains its legitimacy mainly through social mechanisms such as education, religion, family, and the mass media. Based on the definition of hegemony, *media hegemony* means the dominance of certain aspects of life and thought by the penetration of a dominant culture and its values into social life.[9]

Words have meaning and power. Contemporary critical theorists question and challenge the use of phrases like "dominant culture" and now substitute and utilize words, phrases, and concepts such as "global majority" to describe the presence and existence of non-white people. It is important to understand that this global majority exists in the same communities, societies, and share the same worlds as white people. And we understand that *white people* are not monolithic, however the ever-presence and existence of whiteness as a concept might be. Let us recognize that white people and white experience can be, and is, divided into considerations of gender, economies, orientations, and lived experiences. What white people do not experience that non-white people do experience has to do with an awareness of being *other-than* white. W. E. B. DuBois' theory of *double consciousness* describes the experience of recognizing and identifying a *self* that is outside of and other-than the normative subject center of whiteness. Blackness and black identity recognizes that there is a social, structural, pervasive, institution of *whiteness*, and that whiteness also has a sociopolitically vested interest in how blackness is constructed, performed, and broadcast. Theatre is an ideological mechanism that creates, produces, and reproduces a fiction (or narrative) about identity. Often the ideas of what it means to be American get conflated with the idea of whiteness, and that idea of whiteness is also often conflated with the notion that whiteness contains an inherent goodness and "right-ness" of the role white people have played in the building and shaping of America. American stages laud, reflect, and expand upon the humanity and progress of the "dominant culture" by telling stories and producing narratives featuring all-white casts and white heroes.

According to David Altheide, printed in *The Public Quarterly*, "[M]edia hegemony serves as a crucial shaper of culture, values, and ideology of society."[10] That's the trick, the "shuck and jive," that's hidden within the *Masterclass* definition of casting. Television shows, movies, commercials, and plays are fictions. They are composed, designed, constructed, produced, performed, and cast by people and institutions that have vested interests in the very same culture, values, systems, and the institutional structures of the communities and societies in which those productions are performed.

In many plays and spectacles written by white playwrights from the earliest moments of American theatre history Black and non-white characters were tangential, in that they were included at all. Black characters in plays written by white authors were maids, servants, slaves, or comic relief. According to Robert Toll, in the case of minstrelsy, these characters were played by white actors in blackface and later by black performers desperate to earn a wage.[11] By the time theatre producers were at all willing to cast actual Black people in stage plays, Black actors were limited to only playing characters who were maids, servants, slaves, and comic relief. This same casting pattern also followed for film and later television. However, white actors, playing roles written for white characters, got to experience the gamut of human feeling, possibility, and existence. Of course, that stage and cinematic representation of human possibility was divided along the lines of gender and what men could become and accomplish was broader and more expansive than was the representation of women and womanhood. Who and what and how *blackness* could exist in the beginning of American theatre, a medium that was written and produced by white people, for largely white audiences. I acknowledge that this is a broad generalization. The institution and history of American theatre, however, have, at times, simply stricken the non-white experience altogether, through how a play has been cast.

The problem is not simply that Black and non-white people sometimes do not appear at all in white-produced film, television, and plays (like *Friends*), it is particularly odious that when you do see Black and non-white people white-developed content produced by and for white people, the Black and non-white characters are often the thugs, criminals, hypersexualized, or a danger to the nice white leading characters that have to be saved. A hallmark of Black existence in America has been discovering, developing, and demanding modes of resistance to the Black narrative propagated by the dominant culture. An interesting contemporary mode of resistance is the linguistic reframing of the dominant (or white) narrative of Black as *minority* to the recognition that Black people are a part of a collective global majority.[12] Incorporating the use of this idea and phrase, *global majority*, ruptures and interrupts the often unspoken and assumed idea/habit of placing (the concept of) whiteness at the center of bigger ideas, like *America* (or what it means to be *American*). Take, for example, the idea of the American Dream. Sociologist and critical theorist Sarah Churchwell details the sociocultural history and origins of the concept of the American Dream, describing parallels between America's emergence from the Great Depression and upward mobility.[13] This division of access that exists between whiteness and blackness is only one of the privileges (or detriments) that gets hidden when the word America (or American) is used to describe the collective identity of what it means to be American.

Unspoken is the fact that this concept (or idea) is rooted in, and tied to, bigger and much more broad ideological structures and structural systems: patriarchy, white supremacy, and capitalism. That is not meant to be an incendiary statement; rather, it's a fact. The idea of America and the American Dream has to do with perspective and/or identity location. The inherent beneficiary of the American dream has always been the straight white guy, who will deserve and receive reward if he does as he is told, remaining within the confines and boundaries of the structural systems that govern behavior and reward in America. The very concept of what it means to be American occludes the fact that this is a dream specifically for heterosexual white guys. This is not a dream that benefits a collective "we" (as in the "We the People … ")—a *we* that should theoretically/ideologically comprise the center (or identity) of the idea of the American Dream. The very concept of America as a collective noun/identity belies the specifics, lived realities, and particularities of identity. Black and non-white people are certainly not the imagined subjects/centers of the American Dream. Black and non-white people are *other than* the straight white man who is at the ideological center of this idea of American.

In the ideological framing of what it means to be American—if we begin with the premise that this idea of American is straight, white, and male—then we must consider in what roles everyone who is not straight, white, and male is cast. The typical straight, white, male protagonist at the center of this idea of the America includes a house with a white picket fence, two-car garage, a nice car, a beautiful slender wife, two (or 2.5) children, a job, vacations, time off, money for savings, and leisure. Maybe this version of the American Dream seems outdated, but is it? Doesn't this continue to be the imagined fantasy of every romantic comedy and action movie? This is the basic plot structure of all of the *Tarzan* narratives (books and movies included, every iteration of *Planet of the Apes, Pretty Woman, Indiana Jones, Die Hard, Star Wars,* almost all of the movies in the Marvel Cinematic Universe). The hero defeats the threat and wins the girl? Doesn't this continue to be an ideological script, structure, and plot of the way movies continue to be made? And, however, this is a generalization that doesn't make it any less true. So many films and movies end with the white guy saving his family, or the world, and defeating the villainous black or brown threat. And what does it mean that this pattern is broadcast over and over and over?

That is the ideological structure/pattern/process (or the center) of building the idea of who is, and what it means to be, American. These films also, simultaneously, teach and broadcast (or cast) everybody else in relationship to the straight, white, male protagonist. The pretty, slender, white woman is the prize to be won at the end and their man is the hero, protecting them from some threat. Critical Race Theorist, David Childs, says, "From the inception of motion pictures and television, African Americans have often been depicted in unflattering ways; this includes portraying African Americans as being deviant, violent, dim-witted, or as comic relief for the film."[14] White characters are depicted protecting and defending their homes and their way of lives from the threatening *others*. Certainly, there are also movies that feature white people as villains and performing truly heinous acts; *Die Hard* and *Silence of the Lambs* are the first that spring to my mind. The biggest difference is that those villainous representations of whiteness exist within a much broader and much more expansive array of white representation.

Even the notion of "the audience," construed as a singular body, assumes that there is a single reaction that the ideal audience has, or is supposed to have, to the spectacle-text. But this is not the case, because different audience members will be, themselves, associated with the depictions on the screen. A non-white audience member will recognize themselves in the depiction of non-white characters, and the white audience member will do the same with white characters. When a white character is the hero, and the non-white character the villain, these two audience members will be put in different situations. What the film tells you, as an audience member, is to empathize with the hero. For the white audience member, this is no problem—they see themselves in the role of the threatened, triumphant hero. For the non-white audience member, the situation is different. Even though the narrative tells them to empathize with the hero, the process of identifying themselves in the spectacle-text through the reading of visual identifiers (or semiotics) *others* associates themself with the villain. It is implied that their association is wrong; what they should do is empathize with the good, white character. Since the depiction cannot be reacted to similarly by every member of the audience, the idea that there is "an" audience for the depiction is false. There is no "audience."

Thus, it might be more accurate to suggest that "the majority" of the audience is expected to empathize and sympathize with these white protagonists AND audiences are also expected to also recognize, or identify, the Black and non-white representations as threatening to the white protagonists. The protagonists are so often cast with white actors and the antagonists (or the villains) are so so often cast with BIPoC actors that a pattern of representation is both repeated and established, and the idea of whiteness as innocent/hero/justified in their actions; and other than whiteness as villainous and threat and dangerous/threat/to-be-defeated. This trope of *black as threat/white as protector* is so common and pervasive that sometimes it is even repeated in films made by people of color. For example, M. Night Shyamalan's *Unbreakable* falls into this trope; in this instance, however, we end up parsing one minority's proximity to whiteness in relation to another, and complicity with white ideological structure in exchange for fame and celebrity.

In so many of these narratives the important part is to understand that the white characters are being presented as the *victims* of the "savage" and "uncivil" Black and non-whites, and in the end the killing or containment of those Black and non-whites is just. And if we begin to understand that the white characters, particularly the white male characters, *stand in for* the expected idea of "hero (which is the character with which 'the audience' is expected to identify)," what Black and non-white people begin to understand is that they themselves are not the "heroes" of these narratives. The characters through which they (Black and non-white people) identify their own faces and their own families and their relatives, the characters which look like the people who lived in the communities in which they were raised, the faces that look like the people who loved and raised them—these popular cultural narratives are, in fact, (re)presenting them as the threat that the hero/protagonist/imagined ideal American audience, the white folks, are meant to defeat and root out. That is our traditional casting in the

"American" narrative—a fiction, more often than not, constructed and broadcast by white folks.

The idea of Black and non-white people in America being members of a *global majority* ruptures and interrupts this fiction, this pattern, this forced habit of repeating that Black and non-white people are somehow minorities. The fact is that Black and non-white people are not, in fact, villainous in the way that Black and non-white are so often represented in spectacle-texts produced by white authors/producers. The myth that Black and non-white people are inherently devious, dangerous, and violent is as much as lie as is the inherent innocence and goodness of whiteness. Rupturing such narratives forces us, and allows us, to consider a space (or an existence) in which our presence is not something that white people beneficently tolerate; white people are not making room for us at their tables. In *Ways of Seeing* John Berger writes that "[t]he way we see things is affected by what we know or what we believe … We never look at just one thing; we are always looking at the relationship between things and ourselves."[15] Daniel Banks extends this thinking,

> Thus what a person sees—or thinks she sees—is based on how that individual knows the world. The language she uses to represent that worldview both describes her conception of the world while simultaneously codifying it. The reproduction, or performance, of this reproduction is [as Judith Butler writes] the 'ritualized repetition' of certain social norms, which impacts the ways identities are culturally apprehended.[16]

Whiteness, the very idea of whiteness, is always already conflated with and contained within the identity of what it means to be American. Black and non-white people, their experiences, their existence, their presence, can only be marginal to the inherent whiteness always already contained within the idea of that which is American. This implicit whiteness, by identifying itself as the center of American identity, thus only tolerates Black and non-white people's existence and most certainly does not recognize the "other" experience as the American experience. That is the mythology that understanding that Black and non-white people are a part of the global majority ruptures. This embracing of the use and idea of global majority is not only honest and accurate, but it is also a type of linguistic re-casting; and it is imperative to recognize that this re-casting is being done in response to the *traditional* casting of Black and non-white as threat and as other than American.

The casting of Hamilton places the marginal at the center and those who have traditionally occupied the center on the margins. Whiteness is represented in *Hamilton* through the characters King George and Samuel Seabury. The song *The Farmer Refuted* begins with *Seabury* carrying his own soapbox and then getting on top of it, beginning, "Hear ye, hear ye." Seabury would like his audience's silence and attention as he speaks. He would like the authority and respect traditionally given to performers by audiences in a "traditional" theatre-event, which is not, at all, what happens. Seabury brings his own soapbox, stands on it, and is dismissed. Musically Hamilton steals Seabury's melody: he riffs on it, complicates it, adds notes to it—and then they forget about Seabury. Seabury is not dismissed, and he doesn't actually get an exit. The music and the stage swallow him up and he disappears. This wave of people of color forgets about and dismisses the small white man who stood on a soap box.

The Disney staging of this moment initially has Lafayette, Madison, and Hamilton making side-comments to themselves, mocking Seabury—but under their breath, and their staging indicates that they find what he is saying utterly absurd. Burr, on the other hand, adopts a physical posture that might indicate that he is paying attention to Seabury and may be performing respect. The Burr character is aware that they are in public, and that Seabury can see him. He is performing—if not deference, then respect—for Seabury! Or he is performing a show of respect for what Seabury is saying—for Madison, Lafayette, and Hamilton. He is performing (or modeling) behavior to appease whiteness, or to be acceptable to whiteness. In this way the play represents multiple perspectives and ideologies of people of color. Burr, urging Hamilton to be quiet and show Seabury respect, Hamilton unable to conform or acquiesce to Seabury's system (or doctrine),

Lafayette and Madison's mockery, these are stagings of a multiplicity of non-white responses to white assumption (or imposition) of authority.

The second representation of whiteness comes in the character of King George. The chorus—all of the chorus—demands, "Silence! A message from the king! A message from the king!" Every character exits the stage, leaving King George alone in the spotlight. He is draped in markers that signify authority: crown, robe, and scepter. The presence of this white male actor bearing these absurd trappings of authority is an intentional mockery of the idea of white masculinity as the apex of cultural/social power and authority. Through the character King George, Miranda hangs white masculinity in a dramatic effigy. King George—or whiteness—is losing power and the loss of power is driving him mad. Over the course of the play, he is also relegated to sitting off to the side of the stage. He is largely kept distant from the rest of the narrative. The character is meant to be laughed at. He is tangential to the lives of these characters. He is unimportant. This transgression of whiteness is what makes it so important that King George be played by a white actor, and that he is one of only two depictions of whiteness in the play. Whiteness was an interruption to the grace and movement of everything else that was happening on the stage.

Throughout the play Burr vacillates, shifts position, and never takes too firm a stand on anything. He's mercurial until the end of the play when the most defining action he takes is to shoot and kill Hamilton. If it is possible to read these characters as explorations of Black, BIPoC, or "other" existence trying to discover and define itself within the confines and ideological structures of whiteness (this mythologized white history of America, these costumes that hint at, and nod toward, a collective imagining of colonial history), then Burr's killing of Hamilton may be an abstraction of the constant tension people of color (Black people in particular) experience between assimilation and resistance to conform to a set of rules that never intended your success. Miranda's depiction of Hamilton is that he is incapable of conforming to polite structures of this society and that the accoutrement/trappings of this society, his new money, looks absurd, like he doesn't fit, like he's trying too hard.

Hamilton's attempt to keep up with the latest fashion is one of the visual hooks about which Burr mocks him. As Black people we recognize being the object of that exact type of mockery. We "conked" our hair to fit in, some of us have been convinced to use skin lighteners, we spend hours and fortunes on hair extensions and wigs—all of it to adhere to the structures and standards of a whiteness that denigrates and often despises our very presence. And, surprisingly, we (Black people and People of Color)—much like Hamilton—display tenacity in our survival, we define creativity/fashion/style/culture, we exceed and excel in a system that was designed to exclude our presence. The same way that Hamilton thrives in a system that was never intended to include his immigrant presence.

That is what gets lost when you replace people of color in this spectacle-text. Watching a white actor talk about existing in spite of a system that never wanted them is absurd precisely because of the intersection between whiteness (or race), patriarchy, and capitalism; this intersection, by design, makes success much more probable for straight white men. This is not to suggest that there have not been white people who have struggled, nor is it to suggest that there were not poor white people who have struggled. It is, however, a fact that the ideological structures and systems which undergird the America in which we currently exist commingle notions of propriety, civilization, and inherent goodness—with whiteness. Ironically, Burr is trying to negotiate these ideological structures and frameworks—and the black presence of the actor embodying the role (or the presence of any person of color in the role) highlights the reality that people of color are not the beneficiaries of these ideological structures, because race and racism are also a part of the ideological structures that formed, influenced, and impacted the great experiment that is America. The reality is that Leslie Odom's black presence highlights the fact that people of color—Black people in particular—have historically not been at the top of the American food chain. His very presence is a constant reminder to all of the Black people who might be in the audience that Black people existed in the mythology that is American History. His presence reminds white people too that Black people have always been a part of American History, and his presence ruptures the mythology that Black people have always been slaves. It is ironic to watch this disingenuous, inauthentic, manipulative Burr (written on the black body of Odom) follow all of the "rules" that tell him he should win and be rewarded and be successful, fail. It is ironic because, as a Black audience member, as a Black man in America, the spectacle-text itself forces you to question your "place" and your very existence within the system and structure—that is America. The presence of Black actors, and actors of color—whose presence the playwright demands—displaces whiteness in the mythology of American History. That is the subversive transgressive story hidden in the spectacle-text of this production through its casting.

Further, the Hamilton character also cannot "win" in this narrative. He tells his son (Phillip), "If he (George Eacker) is truly a man of honor he'll aim it at the sky," before the duel in which his son is killed. Hamilton also aims his gun at the sky before he is killed by Burr. The idea of adhering to rules and decorum in an event—or during an event—that risks your life and survival, could easily be a metaphor for non-white existence in America. Existence and survival are fraught and tenuous ventures if you are depending on another person's illusion of honor, or if you expect them to adhere to the rules that they wrote. The "rules" of those systems have rarely worked out well for us (Black, BIPoc). History has taught us to never depend upon the kindness of strangers. In so many American stories we are already the villains and bad guys. Defeating us, silencing us, killing us—that is the "traditional" end for people of color in many many American stories.

Too many structures, macrocosms, and institutions are based on an idea of whiteness, a whiteness which needs Blackness and the "other" to be the boogeyman. That is why the staging and casting of *Hamilton* with performers of color is integral to the show itself. *Hamilton: The Musical* was never meant to be an accurate depiction of history, or American history, or even Alexander Hamilton's history. *Hamilton: The Musical* is an act of theft. Lin-Manuel Miranda rooted through the dusty tired mythologies of American history (in the exact same way that William Shakespeare rooted through the *Hecatommithi* and Ovid) and dusted off dry boring stories that everybody had heard of, but no one really remembered in any great detail, then he tore these myths apart and re-imagined his "other" perspective onto the loose framework of these mythologies about Founding Fathers and our glorious past. I don't think he was trying to rewrite history. I don't think *Hamilton* is a play that honors our Founding Fathers. *Hamilton* does not serve as a corrective, simply replacing white people in American history with people of color. What Miranda does, through his insistence on racially specific casting, is both genius and insidious. Like Prometheus, Miranda stole the mythologies of American history—he stole their fire—and in the Spring of 2015 set The Public Theatre, if not the country, ablaze. Displacing, recasting, performers of color in *Hamilton* with white people removes the possibility of this type of critical reading by blanching the spectacle-text itself.

Notes

1 MasterClass, "How to Cast a Film: Understanding the Casting Process—2022," accessed June 15, 2022, https://www.masterclass.com/articles/how-to-cast-a-film

2 Antonio Gramsci, *Selections from the Prison Notebooks*, ed. Quintin Hoare and Geoffrey Nowell Smith (London: International Publishers Co, 1971), 23.

3 Michael Paulson, "A Black Actor in 'Virginia Woolf'? Not Happening, Albee Estate Says," *The New York Times*, accessed May 21, 2017, https://www.nytimes.com/2017/05/21/theater/a-black-actor-in-virginia-woolf-not-happening-albee-estate-says.html

4 Chris Peterson, "The Ridiculousness of the Hamilton Casting Controversy in 5 Images," *OnStage Blog*, accessed June 15, 2022, https://www.onstageblog.com/columns/2016/3/30/the-ridiculousness-of-the-hamilton-casting-controversy-in-5-images

5 Paulson, "A Black Actor in 'Virginia Woolf'?"

6 "Drag Version of 'Steel Magnolias' on Hold after Licensing Issue," accessed June 15, 2022, https://www.wect.com/story/15118202/actors-in-drag-closes-the-curtain-on-wilmington-play/

7 "White Actors Suing 'Hamilton' for Discrimination? Supreme Court Hears Warning—The Hollywood Reporter," accessed June 15, 2022, https://www.hollywoodreporter.com/business/business-news/white-actors-suing-hamilton-discrimination-supreme-court-hears-warning-1195755/

8 Ron Chernow, *Alexander Hamilton* (New York: Penguin Press, 2004).

9 Gramsci, *Selections from the Prison Notebooks*, 25.

10 David L. Altheide, "Media Hegemony: A Failure of Perspective," *Public Opinion Quarterly* 48, no. 2 (1984): 476–90, https://doi.org/10.1086/268844

11 Robert C. Toll, *Blacking up: The Minstrel Show in Nineteenth Century America* (New York: Oxford University Press, 1974), 3–4.

12 Rosemary Campbell-Stephens, "Global Majority: Decolonizing the Language and Reframing the Conversation about Race," 2020, https://www.leedsbeckett.ac.uk/-/media/files/schools/school-of-education/final-leeds-beckett-1102-global-majority.pdf. Campbell-Stephens, "Global Majority: Decolonizing the Language and Reframing the Conversation about Race."

13 Wayne E. Arnold, "Sarah Churchwell, Behold, America: A History of America First and the American Dream," *European Journal of American Studies*, September 23, 2020, https://journals.openedition.org/ejas/16324

14 Crowdcast Inc, "Understanding Critical Race Theory & Education with Dr. David Childs," *Crowdcast*, accessed June 15, 2022, https://www.crowdcast.io/e/understanding-critical

15 John Berger, *Ways of Seeing*. Pelican Book (London: British Broadcasting Corporation, 1972), 84.

16 Daniel Banks, "The Welcome Table: Casting for an Integrated Society," *Theatre Topics* 23, no. 1 (2013): 6, https://doi.org/10.1353/tt.2013.0011

7

Reflecting on "The Work" of *We Are the Canon*: AntiRacist Theatre Pedagogy Workshops

Maya Johnson, Daphnie Sicre, and Karl O'Brian Williams

Introduction: Who We Are & Why We Are Doing This Kind of Work

We Are the Canon: AntiRacist Theatre Pedagogy Workshops are about acknowledging that the work of Black, Indigenous, People of Color (BIPOC) and their multitudes of heritage, experience, and life have always been there and must now be given pride of place and centered. These workshops were created by Daphnie Sicre and Karl O'Brian Williams, after years of discussing how to become antiracist professors. Since 2019, we have conducted over 50+ workshops to high school teachers, college professors, theatre departments, and theatre organizations across the country and the globe.

For this book chapter, we wanted to share our insights through a reflective roundtable conversation with one of our students, Maya Johnson, who served as a research assistant for the workshops. Together, we discuss what we have learned from our practice.

What are the current theatre pedagogical practices that are harmful?

Daphnie Sicre (DS) I can start with erasure. I think it's one of the first types of harms that we are consistently seeing over and over. There's so many types and ways it occurs. For example, I had a young Black man in his early twenties come into the audition room with two pieces from Arthur Miller's work. The plays were *Death of a Salesman* (Willy Loman) and then *All My Sons* (Joe Keller). He did not have anything contemporary that represented him, his story, his music. As a professor, how do you let students spend a whole semester working on pieces that have nothing to do with them or their identity? What is absent becomes forgotten, and eventually erased. Erasure is often perpetuated and fostered by even the best professors, especially when they do not teach material that represents their Black students, their Asian students, their Queer students, etc.

Maya Johnson (MJ) Another erasure, and definitely a harmful strategy, is teaching from a place where whiteness is the default. When this is done, it means every other student who's not white is always playing catch-up. Because if I am not white, how do I relate? Where is the material, you're providing me that's inclusive of my experience as well as other's experiences? There's always going to be a disparity once whiteness is the default.

Karl O'Brian Williams (KOW) I agree, and we see how that disparity is part of a cycle of harm passed down through our teaching practices. It comes in part from the dual action and consequences of silence. Students sitting in classrooms feel like they cannot speak up or say anything about how they are being taught, even when the face teaching them resembles their own. However the silence plaguing teachers of color often looks like disempowerment: fears of making changes to a mandated syllabus, or questioning department policies and practices. To push past that many teachers like myself have had to find ways to insert our own cultures and histories into the syllabus. Before I felt completely empowered to make bold changes I used what I called a comparative approach—and you inspired this Daphnie—I would introduce Caribbean plays based on its positioning in the Western in canon, so Walcott's "Ti-Jean & His Brothers" is a nod to the Greeks Aristophanes' "The Birds," "The Frogs," etc. but it's also a critique on colonialism, but it was a place to start, and it allowed the classroom discussions to move into areas centering more diverse theatre.

MJ Creating and making art, especially collaboratively, is supposed to be a liberating experience, and I come at it from a place of play, and curiosity, and exploration. I feel like BIPOC folks aren't always awarded that, or the ability to do that. There's lots of harm being done, and things being said in classrooms that are very silencing. They make you self-conscious. You're not really afforded the ability to play, to see, explore, and find your way in a manner that other people are allowed to. Although you might feel self-conscious, you have to be extra aware of what's coming out of your mouth and what you're sharing. I feel it's important to be able to create spaces, where folks feel free to explore, play, to have fun, and to have that same liberation with art making like everyone else!

DS Absolutely, I completely agree because when you are the only one in the room, when you are the only student of color, the only Black student in a room, you can't make a mistake. You're not allowed to make mistakes, because if you make a mistake, it's like everyone else is coming after you, and that's why it's important to not just amplify Black voices, but to secure them, make the environment safe and freeing for them to speak and be heard, and affirmed.

KOW The three of us are here, sharing our stories and we know that we're not alone in our love and passion for the arts, or in our acknowledgment that there has been harm done, and that more visibility of our work, and the work of our predecessors is needed. It's the same way, these conversations need repeating, because they give more people insight into the diversity that exists within the myriad of groups of BIPOC. It gives greater perspective, and it makes us know we are not alone. This work benefits everyone, we don't just do it for people who don't look like us, but we do this most importantly, to empower ourselves—to show each other that we exist.

DS It's the only way to break the wheel. Break the way someone has been trained, to get that person to realize what they're doing, because even though they know it's harmful, they're still using these techniques and practices.

KOW It's a go to, it's comfortable and it works for you, but you have to catch yourself, and be accountable. Every time I catch myself centering pronunciation in a way that overshadows everything else a student is doing or pointing out errors in the most deficit-inducing ways, I have to pause and acknowledge where that comes from. Growing up, the British way of speaking English was drummed into me as superior: sounding as close to Received Pronunciation[1] was the target. Let's stop this pronunciation war, and critique, when students don't sound the way, we think they are supposed to when playing certain characters. Juliet can sound 5,000 ways!

DS And we are not just seeing this in acting classes. A costume designer was about to present a PowerPoint where one male character from the play was ethnically ambiguous, but the images presented were all of white models, with the exception of only one Black model. If the character is ethnically ambiguous, why are all the models presented predominately white?

MJ … whiteness becomes the default.

DS Exactly, you're telling these actors, the default is whiteness. I love these inspirations, but I need you to find these inspirations with models of color. And he did after I mentioned it.

KOW I have brought in many plays that were written by writers specific to the ethnicity of my students, with characters that also fit their specific race or ethnicity, and I've watched them take them up and put them right back down, and choose plays they've always heard about, ones turned into films, the ones that have been privileged as part of the canon. It doesn't happen all the time, but it does happen, and I wonder "what's that about?" This is the impact and legacy of centering whiteness in our art. It's like the trauma in Ntozake Shange's *Lady in Red* is too specific and harrowing, but Sophocles' Antigone is somehow more accessible for everyone. And I'm not saying I want to see white women doing "For Colored Girls …, " but I am recognizing how years of centering whiteness in theatre has made it second nature for us to choose it.

DS … and because we're centering that, then we have the white gaze and we're performing for that? Are our stories being created for that? In my theatre classes for social change, I've been assigning "The Characteristics of White Supremacy" by Kenneth Jones and Tema Okun[2] as mandatory reading. The article breaks down how these characteristics of white supremacy show up in culture and how harmful they are. The article gives strategies to help dismantle the following characteristics, paternalism, power hoarding, fear of open conflict, and individualism. For example, perfectionism—you're in an acting program, and English is your second language, you're going to have an *accent*. Perfectionism dictates that we erase the way that people talk and everyone talks the same. We see the same treatment with AAVE. Students feel their voice is not being heard/seen or they don't relate to whatever white character they have been assigned; yet, it's being dictated as the norm, a white norm.

KOW I think of how stories told through ritual, and a non-Eurocentric lens are being featured more in mainstream theatre, and I do hope it's not a moment or a trend. Aleshea Harris' *What to Send Up When It Goes Down*[3] comes to mind and Jackie Sibblies Drury, *Fairview*[4], you know that circle we love so much in theatre, the "circling up" comes straight out of ritual, out of Africa. I'm chasing that as an artist right now: unlocking and freeing myself from Western structures. I'm going back to what I grew up with, the stories I heard as a child from family, from elders.

DS I see you shaking your head, Maya. You got to direct a scene in your directing class, from it. What do you think about that work, in comparison to other plays that you might have read and other classes?

MJ I think about freeing yourself from what you've been taught. I think that *Fairview* did that, for me. It was very shocking to me, but it was very effective in what it was doing and what it was saying. It was a really interesting experience for me to see a Black woman playing with structure and point of view in that way. Before your class, I hadn't read many plays by BIPOC, and so when we're talking about how one group of people is awarded the opportunity to take risks, and do all these things with structure, as opposed to this certain group of people, it was really freeing and inspiring for me to see a woman of color doing that! I was like, can I do this on stage? To have the experience working with that material in a directing class was really inspiring for me as someone who wants to play and experiment.

KOW Yes, I agree. As an audience member, I felt that struggle with strict form and structure, and trying to break from that, the lens which holds our existence hostage. That's why those pieces speak to me, because that's where I am. Every time I sit down with a syllabus, and I'm in front of students, I am literally trying to toss or swap out things I have been taught and trained to do that don't work anymore, or are just harmful. And it's not easy. This past year, I changed things as well. I wanted to explore lesser-known playwrights and theatre practitioners from the African and Caribbean Diaspora who were living and working in New York now and doing the work. I brought in a Jamaican-American, Epiphany Samuels who has her own company Affirmation Theatre. I also brought in Nelson Diaz-Marcano, a Puerto Rican playwright. His play, *World Classic*[5], *is* not published, but he was so excited to talk to the students, and in sharing his experience expressed to the students that what I was doing in the classroom—does not happen, and did not happen when he was in college only learning about white male playwrights. I also had Haitian playwright France-Luce Benson. The students read her interview theatre piece, *Detained*.[6] I had swapped out *The Exonerated* for *Detained* because it's a Commission piece written by a living Black Haitian American female writer, France-Luce Benson. I choose writers who are alive and doing the work because they can come into the class and show the students how the field works. I also had students look at Tarrell Alvin McCraney's *Choirboy*[7] and Jocelyn Bioh's *School Girls or the African Mean Girls Play*.[8] It was frightening to think, "Oh, I'm not gonna to teach known playwrights," but you know what they will come up in the conversation. Living playwrights are out there, doing the work, NOW. I don't want to say, level the playing field, but to fight the hierarchy instilled by white supremacy, we have to. It's been very freeing for me to include more of those voices, and I'm just thinking of ways in which I can just keep doing that.

How do we deconstruct the meaning of "the canon" and include the missing voices, especially Black voices?

DS In teaching our workshop, *We Are the Canon*, we ponder the *questions* and *traditions* being centered. Maybe you're right Karl, maybe these playwrights are going back, looking at different African traditions and bringing them into their work and writing style.

KOW We've got to teach from a more global view. In talking to other Jamaican Diaspora artists, creative writers, and actors like Patrice Johnson, Jeffrey Anderson-Gunter, Jermaine Rowe, and David Heron we always question: do you write in the Creole? Soften it? Erase it altogether? It's a constant debate. I choose to leave it in and let the audience grapple with it. It's about trying to control the art, and you can't take that away from the artist. Allow the artists to be bold, or just be. There's a generation of artists of color, Black writers who were told they had to do it this way; otherwise, you're not getting your plays seen, produced, or published. I think so many people who wanted to experiment were weighted down by limitations. I would've loved to hear first drafts of artists of color from the 70s, 80s, & 90s before they were told they needed to find a Chekhov play and put their culture in it. I think this is what happened to a whole generation of immigrant writers, and Black writers and it's possibly still happening.

DS I was teaching a playwriting workshop, and one of my writers is AfroLatinx. He's writing a historical story in Panama. I can't remember the time period, but he was concerned about standard structures, and who will produce it if it has X-amount of characters, and if the setting or scenic design requires a huge build. Would a theatre produce a play that takes place on a street, with many buildings? It makes me think back to what you were saying about writers of color, who've been brought up to feel as if they have to ask for permission to express themselves, or tell the story how they want, because they felt they needed to fit a white lens or gaze. I told him two things. One: "Take a look at Darrel Alejandro Holnes'[9] work, another AfroLatinx Panamanian US playwright, and see how he's free in his form, yet still following structure." Second: I reminded him of Lin-Manuel Miranda's *In the Heights*[10] and how it takes place on a street. I told him not to fear structures instead write the story he wants to write and place it where he wants to place it. Basically, to not limit himself, and to write. It often begins with what you said Maya, not being allowed to do certain things in the classroom.

What does the antiracist classroom look like?

DS I was in a workshop for educators through the Institute for Teachers of Color Committed to Racial Justice, and this incredible woman Altagracia Montilla[11] was giving a speech about antiracist schools and what an antiracist school should look like. She beautifully broke down how diversity, inclusion, and equity present itself in schools. I sat there, listening to her, and I began to convert what she was saying into the theatre classroom. She said, "Equity is cultural and historical consciousness. Inclusion is empowerment, and Diversity is a representation." As I watched her speak, it all clicked, and I called Karl right away to brainstorm how we could use this model for AntiRacist Theatre Pedagogy.

KOW Equity may have been the most basic thing we wanted, or the part of the puzzle we felt for years was all we needed. The belief is once BIPOC folks are all equal with whites, then the playing field will be level, right? The truth is, it's not enough. We also need justice. What are you doing with these students in front of you? How are you going to create an inclusive antiracist classroom? What does justice in the classroom look like? In order for justice to help build an antiracist space, we've got to understand where we're all coming from, we need historical consciousness and what does that look like? It begins with making space for conversations with students, because you can sit in very beautifully decorated classrooms adorned with great quotes and faces from all the world's ethnicities, but if the students have no real entry point, are not interested, or they feel no ownership, then you just have a classroom that looks great for a brochure.

It's also about accountability, which doesn't happen overnight, and cannot be achieved in one workshop. Our workshop isn't just for a checklist. It doesn't matter how many workshops you do, it's about what you are going to do afterwards … where's the follow-up? Where's the transformative justice? Instructors need to adjust and keep themselves current and accountable.

MJ It's really important to have empowerment, cultural awareness, and representation because it's not really helpful if you're including diverse people and voices in your classrooms without them. These things are amazing so long as the person attempting to implement them is actually doing the work. There has to be accountability and making sure that teachers are actually doing the research and changing things, as well as being flexible. Especially according to the identities of the people who they are teaching because otherwise, when you are the only one in the room, the only one representing a race, or ethnicity, or whatever group you belong to, and the teacher is constantly asking you to teach them and everybody in the room, as well as having to constantly defend your identity, all the time, it is not fair.

DS You are right Maya. Again, trying to break away from white centered classrooms is not easy, especially at PWIs. Both Karl and I use the Liz Lerman critical technique[12] because it's not about sitting and ripping someone's work apart. It's a technique that centers the artist, and allows for the artist to ask questions, then the audience asks you questions, and opinions are last. Not everyone can do it, and some struggle when we first introduce it, but I think it's an important tool to decenter white supremacy culture and build an antiracist space. But Maya, what was it like for you to be in a space, my directing class, where you could hear from other students, where you could give your opinion?

MJ One of the things I really appreciated about your class is that you made our entire syllabus about Black playwrights, which is something that I've never seen or experienced before. It gets away from what we usually see with people who are *trying* to be inclusive, and it's an admirable attempt, but we see a lot of Black exceptionalism on display where you choose the artists who are Pulitzer Prize winners and people like that, and so it's like, here's all of these various white playwrights, but here are the one or two Black playwrights who have done really well and we feel you should know about them. It paints it like the exception to the rule, whereas you really opened our eyes to not just one or two: there's all of these Black playwrights, and these Black plays that we could be reading and learning from and in that way, I think you did decenter whiteness.

As for the Liz Lerman critique, I thought it was really interesting to be able to receive and give feedback to my peers in this way. I've been in film classes where we do the roundtable thing, where you show your film and everyone gives their critique, but I find that space to not be as open or welcoming. In your class, I had a great time hearing what my peers had to say, and it just made it more of a conversation. Even if the feedback wasn't always glowing, it was always constructive, and it was never negative. It was always very helpful and open. In the many weeks we were together, it always felt very comfortable.

DS I am not going to lie, I was scared at what students would say, especially at a predominantly white institution, but I said, I'm gonna do it anyway.

MJ I was scared when you said, "All Black playwrights, all of them!" Ha!

DS From the one-minute plays by Suzan Lori Parks to everyone we staged, I made a point to center Blackness. And it worked. I realized I could do it, and I can't wait to do it again.

For the antiracist classroom you can't stop, once you start. You've got to do this for the rest of your life, otherwise it's no longer an antiracist classroom. Montilla describes antiracist schools as either traditional, progressive, community, or antiracist; thus by adapting her model into the theatre classroom, you can visualize the traditional classroom which has lower representation, lower empowerment, and lower cultural competency, which equates to lower cultural and historical consciousness. This is the kind of classroom where teachers fall back on what they know, or what they've been taught. It's the classroom where they've given a syllabus and they teach that syllabus exactly like they tell them.

In the progressive classroom, you have higher representation, which means more than half of the syllabus may reflect BIPOC playwrights but there's lower empowerment because there may not be enough projects around that. There's also lower cultural, historical consciousness, so the syllabus still centers whiteness and the Western canon. Teachers have added more diversity, but everything else is missing. A lot of educators fall prey to the progressive classroom, they think they have to meet a quota, and be like "Oh, how many playwrights of color do I include?"

The next one is the community classroom—where you see lower representation, higher empowerment, and higher historical consciousness. This is where teachers are exclusive with the type of BIPOC content they include. You only see awarded playwrights. The cultural significance might be there, but still there's a centering around a rewards system, only picking plays with major accolades and Pulitzer acknowledgment, which means it's accepted by white norms, thus centering the Western canon.

Now, the antiracist classroom has higher representation, higher empowerment, higher cultural historical consciousness. It takes a lot of work to achieve this classroom. It's diverse representation and scholarship readings come from diverse authors that are BIPOC scholars. This ultimately leads to a consciousness about the work, where it comes from, its history. Part of the diversity is the inclusion of text and videos and projects that empower the students. Part of that empowerment is getting to know your students, who they are, so that the choices and strategies showcase and empower them.

How do we deconstruct the meaning of the canon and include the missing voices, especially Black voices? Why is it important to amplify Black voices and BIPOC voices and how does the antiracist classroom do this?

MJ The benefit of an antiracist classroom is that it opens your mind up to more possibilities and opportunities. It benefits Black students by showing them what came before the Eurocentric norms or centered whiteness. The canon we've been taught is not the only way to do things. Antiracist classrooms acknowledge what came before and understand how you can go forth, do, and create—knowing what is possible for you instead of being set up with limitations.

KOW I think that's it in a nutshell; it is the actual knowledge of your history not centered in whiteness, and not beginning the exploration through a white lens. The idea that so many people still don't realize our history didn't begin with the ships transporting enslaved Africans needs consistent addressing. The art and theatre that reveal our existence around the world before the fourteenth century just never seems to have space in the curriculum, I think empowerment is very important for Black students, and too often they feel the opposite, they feel invisible … in the very schools they have labeled their "dream schools." It can be a lonely place for them, especially when they attempt to articulate and express their feelings about this. So often these expressions are incorrectly assessed as them having "adjustment issues," as if being one of the few persons of color in a predominantly white institution was somehow their fault and problem to fix, when the history and circumstances have already been baked into the system for them to feel this way.

So, for those who are already doing the work and want to go further, think about what that means: non-stop commitment to the reflective practice of your pedagogy, interrogating its genesis, constantly being accountable for every decision you make in every lesson, do I totally dismantle and throw out, or swap out, or gradually include representation, creating a curriculum that empowers the room? This work if you stay in it is for life!

DS We need to go back to this notion of belief; we need to listen. Listen to Black students, Black voices, listen to the Black experience. We need to listen to the experience of students of color in these spaces. If a student is telling you something is harmful, that you have caused harm—believe them. We've got to start believing our students. Then the follow-up is believing and implementing change.

This is hard and it is not easy, but one has to learn to be ok with feeling uncomfortable. I have spent the last year working on this. I am listening to my students a lot more, and I am advocating for their needs behind closed doors, even if it is the needs of just one student. I have placed myself and my job on the line as not everyone agrees. But someone has to speak up in those rooms. We have to sit in discomfort to learn how to better the way we advocate, teach, and ultimately ourselves.

We have to be ok with making mistakes and failing, failing really badly because we do not know whose life we are affecting or changing. James Baldwin said,

> You write in order to change the world, knowing perfectly well that you probably can't, but also knowing that literature is indispensable to the world. In some way, your aspirations and concern for a single man in fact do begin to change the world. The world changes according to the way people see it, and if you alter, even by a millimeter, the way a person looks or people look at reality, then you can change it.[13]

Thus, we must do this work. Changing cultural norms and starting to implement action may not be easy, but it is necessary. You need that action step, just listening and getting an EDI Certificate without implementing action is not creating an antiracist classroom. Bottom line, many Black students have been harmed, and across this entire country they are standing up and sharing their stories. They are asking for transformative justice, and the antiracist classroom is a step toward a transformative space for them.

MJ Ultimately, I think what I'm really excited to see, moving forward, is how redefining the canon and reassessing the structure of our classrooms will provide BIPOC artists, especially Black artists with a sense of freedom, and how that freedom will manifest in their work. I mean, imagine all of the new stories that we will get to see and tell once we unlearn centuries of conditioning that erases such a rich cultural history in this medium.

Notes

1 Received Pronunciation is a phrase from the late nineteenth-century England, which came to be known as the accent of the social elite and became the standard for British English.

2 Kenneth Jones and Okun Tema, *Dismantling Racism: A Workbook for Social Change Groups* (Portland: Peace Development Fund, 2001).

3 Aleshea Harris, *What to Send Up When It Goes Down* (New York: Samuel French, 2019).
4 Jackie Sibblies Drury, *Fairview: A Play* (New York: Theatre Communications Group, 2019).
5 Nelson Diaz-Marcano, *World Classic* (New York, 2017).
6 France-Luce Benson, *Detained* (Los Angeles, 2020).
7 Tarell Alvin McCraney, *Choir Boy* (New York: Theatre Communications Group, 2016).
8 Jocelyn Bioh, *School Girls; or the African Mean Girls Play* (New York: Dramatists Play Service Incorporated, 2018).
9 Darrel Alejandro Holnes n.d., "Writer, Performer, Educator," accessed 2020, https://www.darrelholnes.com/
10 Lin-Manuel Miranda, *In the Heights* (New York: Theatre Communications Group, 2013).
11 Altagarcia Montilla, *How White Supremacy Lives in Our Schools*, 2020.
12 Liz Lerman, "Critical Response Process," 2022, https://lizlerman.com/critical-response-process/
13 John Romano, "James Baldwin Writing and Talking," *New York Times*, 1979.

In the Trenches: A Conversation with Donja R. Love

Martine Kei Green-Rogers

Donja R. Love is an Afro-Queer filmmaker, poet, and playwright whose creative works center on the lived experiences of Black and Queer folx. He received several awards and honors, including the 2018 Laurent/Hatcher Foundation Award, the 2017 Princess Grace Playwriting Award, and a Eugene O'Neill 2017 National Playwrights Conference finalist. Donja is celebrated for his plays that cover topics that have gone underrepresented in theatre, such as the intersection of Black identity, queer love, and HIV, among other issues. His plays include *The Love* Plays (Sugar in Our Wounds, Fireflies, In the Middle),* and *Soft; Or The Dead N—Poem*. Donja is also celebrated for his web series *Modern Day Black Gay* and the short film *Once a Star.*

Martine Kei Green-Rogers (MKGR) How do you feel you use playwriting as a place of liberation?

Donja R. Love (DRL) Playwriting and the discovery of my HIV status are deeply intertwined. I became a serious writer, or rather, I should say, I took writing seriously, after being diagnosed with HIV. Beforehand, I wrote poems, short stories, and my thoughts and feelings. I was always a writer in that specific way, and I never really thought much of doing anything differently until after being diagnosed with HIV in December of 2008. After being diagnosed, writing was quite literally, as cliché as it may sound, a thing that saved my life. It was the thing that offered me healing. It was a thing that offered me liberation. My writing, on top of having a bomb ass support system that rallied around me during that time, really helped me navigate through my status. And it still helps me navigate through, not just my status, but my queerness, my Blackness. It helps me reimagine what my life and what the world that I live in can look like. And in terms of writing/playwriting being liberatory, I realized during this time of Covid-19, the time of "the Rona," I am trying to tell that Donja who was just diagnosed with HIV, who was sitting alone in a small, cold room, terrified—that he is okay. That he will make it through this moment and the subsequent moments to follow. And letting him know that he will be liberated. Right that he may feel completely unsure, completely unaware, and in the dark right now, but there will be liberating moments to follow.

MKGR That's really powerful. Thank you. My next question gets into the specificity of certain plays that you've written. What spawned *Fireflies*? Also, since this is a book about Black performance, liberation, and activism, how is *Fireflies* those things for you? What was your hope when you put it out into the universe?

DRL *Fireflies* is part of a trilogy, The *Love Plays*, which explores queer love during pivotal times in Black history: the time of enslavement, the time of the Civil Rights movement, and the Black Lives Matter movement. The Black Lives Matter movement inspired *Fireflies* in relation to thinking of the three of Black women who founded it and that two of these Black women are queer. What I found myself so troubled by is, at the time [I wrote the play], the Black Lives Matter movement, felt so heavily saturated. People were galvanizing themselves around cis-Black men, when this movement was founded and organized so deeply by Black women. You see folks going out in the streets—protesting and marching only when an individual who fell victim to state sanctioned violence looked a certain way and presented a certain way. So I was specifically thinking about Black women, thinking of Black queer women and all of the work that Black women have done in terms of organizing, in terms of culture work, in terms of us being us—a collective Black people, us being like the world at large, us being where we are and all of the goodness that we have can oftentimes be traced back to Black women. Just thinking of Black queer women and what was that like specifically during a time where individuals didn't have the amount of agency or authority that individuals have now. So, what was it like to be a Black woman, to be a Black queer woman during that time who is creating pivotal monumental work and speeches and words for a face of a movement? It was such a direct correlation to the Black Lives Matter movement. And it was also very troubling in terms of how it feels like nothing has changed. So much has changed, culturally, but at the same time, little has changed historically. I was really fascinated by that and wanting to be a part of the conversation and ask questions. What was it like to be a Black queer woman during that time? When you talk about hope—what does hope look like for a piece like this? My hope was and still is for the Black women to know and to see how important they are, how much they matter. How there are multiple people who have a deep reverence and love for the work, for the existence, and for the lives of Black women. And I want to be very intentional with saying that this isn't about class as well. This is every Black woman, no matter where you are, no matter what your background is, no matter what your upbringing is—you are worthy, and you deserve! Outside of class, outside of economy, outside of so many things, exactly who you are matters. I want Black women to get their flowers and to feel, be empowered, and to see themselves reflected in the work.

MKGR I find it interesting that, especially in the past couple of election cycles, Black women have been viewed as the people who will save the country, but then no one ever wants to treat us like we're the people who could save the country.

DRL I think it's deeply problematic for us to put so much on Black women. We shouldn't have to expect that if we want change to happen, we shouldn't say, "Oh, let's look to Black women. Black women will, Black women ***have*** to do this thing for us." Y'all don't. If y'all said, "You know what? I'm not doing shit for y'all no more, for the rest of my life?" Absolutely. Because everything that you already did—everything that you already sacrificed is more than enough, and we are no longer worthy. As a whole, the Black community and the world at large, what we need to recognize and what we need to understand, is sometimes, the choices that y'all make, the things that y'all do. It doesn't have to be altruistic at all. It could be coming from a completely selfish place. As much as we're selfish, you all can make choices, saying, "You know what? I wasn't thinking about the community. I wasn't thinking about my babies. I wasn't thinking about this person or that person. I was actually thinking about me. And because of the position that I hold in this world, when I think about me, I'm actually thinking about everybody else as well." With that being said, if Black women said, "You know what? Fuck all y'all, I'm only gonna think about me for the rest of my life," we still need to say thank you because in that thinking, everyone else will still be liberated as well.

MKGR Tell me about the process of writing *Fireflies*. Were there people you were consulting? How did you even just go about cracking into the creation of these characters?

DRL There was a lot of research that took place. With *Fireflies*, there were pivotal moments, specifically thinking about the bombing of the 16th Street Baptist Church in Birmingham, Alabama, where this horrific act that took the lives of four beautiful little girls because of White supremacy, because of anti-Black violence. Thinking about that time and who these four little girls were, their family, and what that meant to exist in the Deep South during that time. I was also thinking about Mrs. Coretta Scott King and her position in the world being married to such a public figure and just by the way of that, being such a public figure, what that meant for her. We often talk about, we often think about, the sacrifices of Dr. Martin Luther King Jr., but we should also look at the sacrifices of Coretta and everything that she had to do. It was hard to be in a marriage where your husband walking out the door could mean that you will be a widow. All of the strength that it took to say okay to something like that. And also, being very clear, Dr. King was a fully realized human being, meaning that there were flaws. Meaning that there was a human nature to him. So also knowing that my husband walking out the door could also mean his adultery. What does that mean? What does that look like? I was really interested, when writing *Fireflies*, about the private life of individuals who live such public lives, and the messiness of those private lives. I found myself really interested and really curious in showing that and painting that picture. I say all that to say—I did a lot of research and readings on not just the 16th Street Baptist Church, but on Dr. King and on Coretta Scott King. And I was privileged enough—I don't like calling them interviews because they weren't at all—to hold space and have conversations with my grandmom and with my great grandmom, who are originally from the South—Amelia, Virginia. Just holding space and hearing what it was like to be a Black woman during that time. And learning—I never knew this about my grandmom—about her picking tobacco when she was like a little kid. And she would do this to get money, to be able to support not just herself but her family. Thinking about the desires and the dreams. I never knew this also about my grandmom—when she was younger, she always dreamt of being a model. And I never, up until that moment, thought about what did my grandmom want to be? What did my grandmom want to do with her life? Outside of being a mom, outside of being a grandmom? She is her own person, and what did she desire in life? What were her hopes? What were her aspirations? So being able to have conversations with my grandmom, or with my great grandmom, and learning of them outside of myself, and how important those conversations were for me and how they helped me shape *Fireflies*, and to be able to, as much as possible, create a full version of a Black woman on stage during that time. I will say though, keeping it all the way "one hundred," my process of writing is that I write the piece first, and then I do all the research later because I don't want it to be a history lesson. However, this time I went against my greater judgment, and I talked to my grandmom and my great grandmom first. Then I started to write. It was one of the hardest pieces for me to write because the entire time as I was writing the piece, I just kept thinking about my mom-mom and my nana. I'm like, "Oh, wait, Donja. mom-mom said this, Nana said that. You gotta make sure you get it in there." It got to a point where I had to say, "Donja, you love mom-mom, you love Nana, you love these two women. Right now, you gotta think about Olivia, and you have to think about what her story is, and then you can come back to the conversation that you had with your grandmom and your great grandmom."

MKGR I'm going to ask you the same question about *Sugar in Our Wounds*. Tell me a little bit about that process and what inspired you to write it? Tell me a little bit about what you feel is its connection to Black activism and liberation, etc.

DRL Absolutely. *Sugar in Our Wounds* is the first play in my trilogy, *The Love Plays*. I remember years ago, I read Tarell Alvin McCraney's *Marcus, or the Secret of Sweet*, and there was a passage where Shaunta, one of the characters in the play, was probing Marcus, her best friend, who's the protagonist in the play, to figure out his sexuality. And one of the things she talked about was when the masters of plantations would find out that their enslaved men were queer, what they would do to them. Essentially, they would pour sugar into their wounds. And I was blown away at this idea of this truth—of queerness during the time of enslavement because I never thought about it before. It was as if, poof, me and my queer self and my queer people just popped onto the scene, when now we know that's actually not the case at all. We actually have long lives and long histories, but how erasure works is that those things were never documented. And so after being blown away, I started to become really upset. One, with myself for not thinking that I existed within history, and then upset at history for erasing me and my people. And I just started to do more readings. I started to do more research. I remember coming across someone's dissertation that they were working on and the piece it explored. It talked about queerness, not only during the time of enslavement, but during the slave Atlantic trade. In that piece, it talked about how during the Middle Passage with individuals being so close to each other that there were moments of intimacy that would happen. I never thought about that before. Just thinking about all of these things, and learning of different cultures in Africa, who saw a great importance in same gender love. I never thought about that before. Just thinking about all of these things, and learning of different cultures in Africa, who saw a great importance in same gender love – it being a part of the cultural make-up, and what that was like and how colonization shifted so many things within our culture. How religious practices shifted so many things within our culture and made what was so normal to cultures and to individuals feel so violent and feel so vile and feel so despicable, and a sin, an abomination, and all of these words love to be thrown. I want to use my gifts of writing to, and being very honest, show myself, myself in the world. Not thinking about community, not thinking about it being something for other people to see themselves reflected. I was actually thinking about myself. How can I see myself reflected? I just started to write *Sugar*. It was so interesting. In my research beforehand and in my imagination work, I knew I had an idea of what the play was before I would sit down to write it. When I started writing it, the first thing that popped into my head was a tree. A tree was the first character to speak. I was like, "Oh, I don't know what the fuck this is. It probably will not make it to subsequent drafts, so I'll just listen to it right now, but I'm sure in rewrites, the tree will no longer be a thing." But the tree became such a pivotal character. Thinking historically, the tree became such a pivotal character as a result of the relationship that Black people in America have with trees. What does that mean? How trees are so embedded into our culture, into our familial structure now. I will say what got me onto this path was I remember rereading Alice Walker's, *The Color Purple*, before starting to write *Sugar In Our Wounds*. I remember in the jacket of the book the author's bio profile. She described herself as a naturist and described herself as being so connected with the universe, with the world, with nature itself. And I was just like, "Ah, I wonder, what does it mean to be so connected with nature? What does it mean to have a relationship with nature, such a deep relationship with nature?" That's how the tree in *Sugar* came to be. What I hoped with the tree and with the piece itself is a showcase of what a beautiful history of queerness looked like. Allowing individuals, not just folks who identify as queer, but folks who are the furthest removed as well can get a sense and can see a history and how there is beauty and there is softness in queer love. Historically, folks don't see that. They don't understand that. So they position themselves and other people in a way where we don't see that beauty. We don't see that softness. We think of shame. We think of violence as it relates to something as beautiful as loving someone.

MKGR It's interesting you mentioned that. I don't understand how people can be so angry about people loving one another. I think as a society, specifically in the United States, we have forgotten what love truly means. It's so weird to me as a dramaturg. I'm always watching people because there is nothing that happened in the human experience that could not end up in a play of someone's. I find that I spend a lot of time absorbing and processing the world around me in order to take what I learn from that and apply that to the text in front of me. I think we lack compassion on a large scale, which, in a lot of ways, is part of what you need in order to love someone else. How can we be so stank?

DRL I know. Being stank and nasty and lacking complete empathy. When I think about *Sugar*, how can people position themselves to despise love? Because that's what they are doing. They are literally saying that this love is an ugly thing. In the rewriting of *Sugar* and the conversations surrounding *Sugar*, I found myself also deeply thinking about capitalism. And I found myself thinking about the time of enslavement within the Antebellum South, that Black people, enslaved people were property. Black people, enslaved people were used to build an economy …

MKGR … And to exploit wealth …

DRL Right. If in any way you did not contribute to building an economy, if you did not contribute yourself to capitalism, then we saw no value in you. If you are a woman who cannot bear children, then we have no value in you, right? If you are an older Black person, we have no value in you. If you are a queer person, we have no value in you. You have no value. So, I literally found myself thinking about, as it relates to queerness, capitalism and how deeply rooted capitalism is into every fiber of our being. Folks can talk about religion, which has caused so much harm and still causes harm to the queer community, but I also believe there's a conversation around capitalism as well and how capitalism also causes harm within the queer community. If you look at it on a very science-based level, are you able to create a child? If yes, there will be more individuals in this world for us to work, for us to exploit, to give us money. If you can't do that, then we see no value in you. Capitalism has positioned itself and made folks positions themselves into having issues with queerness and seeing no love and no beauty and no softness in queerness.

MKGR I taught a class at SUNY New Paltz called Race, Gender, and Performance. One of the things I regret is not renaming that class Race, Gender, Class, and Performance, because you cannot talk about race and gender and not get into conversations about class because where you sit in that spectrum of "the haves and the haves not," makes a huge difference in how you navigate and experience this world. In that class, I'm always railing against capitalism and how much it affects ***everything***. One day, in class, I remember telling them that all of us sitting in that classroom contribute to capitalism. Higher education is set up for people to pay to learn from me, as a professor. That the words coming out of my mouth have a value that they have been told they should pay for. I am there working in order to pay my mortgage; my student loan bills that came from me sitting in a classroom ages ago only to now feed into this system with them as the students. Also, since I do not come from generational wealth, how much did my education actually cost me? Debt is a modern-day form of slavery because as long as I have debt, I will need to work to pay it off. Ok, I am getting off my soapbox now.

DRL Absolutely. Folks knew what they were doing. When you think about specific Black people, within a certain tax bracket, they are talked about as if they had transcended race. I remember people would say that about Oprah Winfrey. They would say things like "I don't see her as this Black woman. I just see her as a woman." Her cultural and economic capital played into that.

MKGR Remember when OJ Simpson was acquitted? People were dancing in the streets. Years later, I remember being in a college classroom and I was the only person of color in that classroom. We were discussing the performative politics of the OJ Simpson case. A white person in the class said they didn't understand why Black people were excited that a murderer got away with murder. And I said, "No, no, no, no, no. You're looking at this all wrong. We weren't dancing in the streets because a murderer got away with murder. People were dancing in the streets because they realized if you have enough money, you might actually be able to buy the white man's justice." But we all learned in the aftermath of all that, that the white man's justice system was not going to let OJ Simpson get away with those shenanigans in the long term. We all know how his story went.

DRL Absolutely. I am thinking about systems and how they work, how they are designed. What it did is exactly what you said. Black people saying, oh, if you have enough money, then this thing can happen. For those of us who didn't, for those of us who don't, we then are still a part of this capitalistic system of "I will work, I will work, I will work, I will work so that I will be able to get to this level, so I can be able to have this happen." It's just all this vicious cycle in the systems that we're trapped in.

MKGR That is truth. Last, but not least, let's talk about *In the Middle*.

DRL *In the Middle*. Yeah, *In the Middle* is the final play in my trilogy, but it was actually the second play that I wrote when I was creating the trilogy. I wrote that play during the summer of 2016, and this was right after, I believe in this order (if I'm not mistaken), Alton Sterling was killed by police. And then the very next day, on Facebook Live, Philando Castile was killed. Because of what happened to these two Black men falling victim to state sanctioned violence, *In the Middle* said you need to work on me. And that piece also holds space for a queerness during the time of the Black Lives Matter movement. What we were talking about earlier was the Black Lives Matter movement starting to shift and change a bit, but not at the speed and to the degree at which it needed to. Individuals protest and march and hold space for individuals who are cis-gendered, who are often male and heterosexual. And I found myself wondering what if a Black queer man fell victim to police violence? What would that conversation be, and what would happen? Specifically, I was really interested in what that would look like for the mom. And thinking of this thing that happens all the time, character assassination, and how we know the cops have to figure out a way to spin a story where it appears that this person deserved what happened to them. So, exploring that question and thinking about a mom who had a troubled past, a mom who battled addiction, and now, your son has died, and the entire world or many folks in the world only can think about your past. Only can think about this thing that you navigated through. They cannot think about where you are right now. As a survivor. As a victor. They cannot think of you as a mother of an individual who was just killed. They're just thinking about what you did in the past. I was really interested in what this intersection looked like, of queerness, of character assassination, and also of healing because another element to *In the Middle* is the Babemba tribe, which is a tribe in South Africa. And what they do, which is so revolutionary, is really practice transformative justice in a way that, before I even had the language of what transformative justice was, the Babemba tribe showed me what that meant. Essentially, what happens is if someone in their tribe, if someone in their village "falls short," and "falls short" can mean a multitude of things. "Falls short" can mean stealing, it could be lying. It could be whatever. Everyone in the tribe stops everything, they take the person who has fallen short and place them in the middle, and everyone says one positive thing about this person, to remind them of who they are. Not the act that they did, but who they are. And this can take hours. It can take days. It can take weeks. But everyone says a positive thing about this person to build them back up again. So, I found myself thinking about that with *In the Middle*, and what would it be like for a mother who is going through this? And the people in her life seeing what she's going through, seeing her past being brought up again. Seeing her being triggered by her past on top of already being traumatized by what's happening to her son. These people and I were also, again, thinking of Black women, of what does it look like for this play to be predominantly Black women. We have this mom who lost her son. We have her mom who is the grandmom. We have her sister who is the auntie. We have her daughter, who is the sister of this individual who fell short, who was killed. What if all these Black women are trying to build up this mom. Place her in the middle and build her up again. *In the Middle,* really, it holds space for a multitude of things—queerness during the time of the Black Lives Matter Movement, character assassination, and transformative justice as well. What do all these things look like in this moment, in this time?

MKGR I love that you are attempting to answer this question. It is deliciously complex.

DRL It made me think about transformative justice in a way that I never thought about it before. Oftentimes, when we think about holding folks accountable, it's done with so much softness. It's done with so much grace, it's done with so much love, but what I heard, which blew my mind, is it doesn't always have to look that way. It can be hard. It can be dangerous. It can cost. Specifically, I find myself thinking about how he killed his abusers. That was transformative justice. I found myself thinking about Harriet Tubman and her having her shotgun ready to blow a motherfucker's head off. That's also transformative justice. And so, us being very clear when we talk about transformative justice—What does it look like? It doesn't look this one way. It is individual. What transformative justice looks like to me can be completely different to what transformative justice looks like to you. I found myself thinking about the violence that can be with transformative justice because Nat Turner showed us that. It also holds space for transformative justice to look a multitude of ways. It can be messy. It can be uncomfortable. It can be confrontational, if need be.

MKGR Understood! Thank you for sharing yourself so fully today. I really appreciate it.

Part Three

Performance and/as Protest

8

(W)Right of Way: Black Geographies and American Interstates

Jenny Henderson

On July 26, 2020, in Selma, Alabama, a whole geography expands in a moment of silence on the Edmund Pettus Bridge. Representative John Lewis had passed away about a week earlier, his belief in "good trouble" looming over a summer hot with grief.[1] His hearse journeyed along Freedom Summer's former routes. It wove in concert with the ghosts of marchers and riders past and the still-haunted landscapes that stirred their movements: geographies of racial capitalism and its carceral containments; sites of voter suppression and the seats of the Confederacy which made them so; and Southern trees, "blood on the leaves and blood at the root."[2]

While Lewis' course spatially remembered the South's terrors and activist legacies, it also situated the region's significance within Black American culture and history: as one example, his service was held at the Ebenezer Baptist Church, where Atlanta's Black community has gathered and organized for over 134 years.[3] His final highway voyage celebrated the grassroots politics of groups such as the Student Non-Violent Coordinating Committee (SNCC), which Lewis once chaired, by moving through sites of local community leadership.[4] While mainstream media portrayals of the highway uphold a lone, typically white and male, driver as the aspirational emblem of America—a pattern viewers can see across mediums, from Jack Kerouac's *On the Road* to contemporary car commercials—Lewis' pathway and its emphasis on community suggest a different relationship to the interstate. Public discourses about the highway put into tension the figure of the white lone driver and the carcerality of Black Americans. Though automobiles afforded Black communities unprecedented autonomy and access in the twentieth century, interstates remain profound places of anti-Black violence: from the state-authorized surveillance which criminalizes "driving while Black," to urban planners' deliberate construction that routed highways through Black neighborhoods.[5] Lewis' procession, however, and other performances, such as Black Lives Matter protests that take place on interstates and New Orleans jazz funerals orchestrated under overpasses, move through cities in ways that revise the narrative of Black life and mobility on the highway. These performances might be thought of as counter-maps, a term originated by Nancy Lee Peluso to describe Indigenous activists' use of sketch maps to reclaim forest areas in Kalimantan.[6] Humanities and geography scholars have widely used "counter-map" to think about community resistance to State possession of space; I argue that the highway performance I explore throughout this chapter are acts of activism that occur through the process of counter-mapping. I explore roads and their counter-maps to emphasize how the latter, rooted in Black geographies and performance traditions, imagines another way of being on the road, while still remembering its past.

In this chapter, I locate the highway as a site of repertoire, working from Diana Taylor's famous "rift" between "the archive of supposedly enduring materials … and the so-called ephemeral repertoire of embodied practice."[7] In doing so, I trace how Black activists, artists, and community members have performed acts of activism on highways over time and history and how those performances are tailored to their material realities and geographical contexts. Put differently, these performances "both keep and transform choreographies of meaning" within the highway's "repertoire."[8] Deviating from reductive narratives that relegate Black history into a novel series of "firsts," I instead take a longer approach to consider how highway repertoires are sustained through performance rituals across generations. These performances make visible the State's anti-Blackness, while also offering alternate maps, which transmit cultural memory and form networks of solidarity and caregiving. Such counter-maps recruit performance to rehearse, map, safekeep, and tend to local Black communities' reckonings and remembrances of space. To illustrate these acts of activism, I will study Lewis' funeral procession and the Bridge Crossing Jubilee, in which mourners and commemorators both walked across the Edmund Pettus Bridge. The Bridge is the site of Civil Rights Foot Soldiers' traumatic 1965 encounter with State troopers, an event commonly referred to as Bloody Sunday. Each year, Selma hosts the Jubilee to honor the anniversary of Bloody Sunday with a ritual march over the Edmund Pettus Bridge and through sharing local music, arts, and history. I conclude with Black Lives Matter protestors highway blockade tactic following the murders of Michael Brown and Eric Garner. I suggest that BLM's blockades exist within the repertoire of Black highway performance and informed activists' movements during the 2020 uprisings. While many news outlets framed 2020's activism as spontaneous and sudden, I highlight Black counter-maps of freeways as continued, place-making practices. Ultimately, I argue that the interstate is an urgent site where Americans repeatedly rehearse their identities through their own maneuverings of the road and popular media. It is where settler capitalism's spatial logics manifest through State troopers' criminalization of Black people and city planners' bulldozing and displacement of historic Black, Brown, working-class, and immigrant neighborhoods. And, yet, it is also a powerful location of community organizing, liberatory politics, and cultural memory.[9] Black communities' reroutings of interstates that I explore here stage an intervention into dominant scripts of the highway and might be thought of as recuperative acts of resistance.

By analyzing these highway performances, I am building on Katherine McKittrick's readings of Black geographies. In discussing the creative work of Black women writers, such as Dionne Brand and Octavia Butler, McKittrick helps reterritorialize sites of colonization and domination and makes possible the "envisioning [of] an interpretive alterable world."[10] Following McKittrick's offering of locations such as slave plantations, I consider the interstate as a site of racist terror where Black communities have employed performance and kinship to map safety networks and alternate geographies.

The acts of activism I discuss here follow in the tradition of what Harry Elam Jr. has called "(w)righting" in his study of August Wilson's Century Cycle—an atlas itself. Elam plays on the many possible meanings of "(w)right" to situate Wilson's dramaturgical interventions as "righting" history through invoking Black American "rites that connect the spiritual, the cultural, the social, and the political, not simply to correct the past but to interpret it in ways that powerfully impact the present."[11] I extend Elam's reading of Wilson to consider how "performative rites" on interstates bring the past into the present in order to "(w)right" place. John Lewis' procession, for example, mapped out genealogies of Black Southern history onto roadways named after Confederate generals. Accordingly, these "rites" set the record straight on highways' white supremacy and present a more just account of such routes. Using counter-maps as my analytic, I meditate on how Black communities' performances rupture highways' anti-Black spatial logic by saying its violent histories and insisting against forgetting; I foreground how counter-mappers (w)right new landscapes within that remembering.

Counter-mapped geographical performances, like John Lewis' procession or Black Lives Matter protests, emerge through rituals, poetry, stories, sayings, dances, aesthetics, chants, and marches, rehearsed on and off the road. Every day, Black organizers, activists, artists, intellectuals, and communities regularly and rigorously theorize alternate geographies; the freeway is a critical location where this thinking and place-making is felt and shared. Here, in the transitory spaces of radical potential and mobility, communities draw counter-maps daily—whole atlases of loss, culture, memory, refusal, dreaming, and demand. By emphasizing the continued geographical performances of Black Americans who navigate, resist, and refuse the interstate system, I hope to move toward a vision of the road in which Black lives truly matter.[12]

US Highway-80: Selma, Alabama

John Lewis' procession traveled the length of the Selma to Montgomery march, culminating on the road a twenty-five-year-old Lewis marched on 1965's Bloody Sunday. His casket was carried across that bridge in Selma, where red rose petals lined Highway-80, once stained by the Alabama state troopers' attacks on the protestors who walked there fifty-five years ago. Lewis' immediate family followed the horse-drawn hearse as the carriage's Black driver brought his hat to his heart and horses to a halt, recalling the "free and enslaved Black hack drivers of yesteryear."[13] In this moment, an ancestral atlas opened wide, holding Representative John Lewis' memory close, revealing how his life, his visions of freedom and democracy, and the trauma inflicted on him here, too, transform this place. Although his casket was draped in an American flag, the service offered a reminder that the state remains anti-Black at its foundations. For example, the Edmund Pettus Bridge is named after a former US senator, Confederate general, and Ku Klux Klan leader.

Lewis' memorial route illustrates distinctly Black American "oppositional geographic practices" which work from a place of Black life, not Black death.[14] More specifically, Highway-80,[15] including the Edmund Pettus Bridge, provides a useful site for critiquing how white and state spatial logics of domination manifest. The procession began in Lewis' birthplace of Troy, Alabama, along the Highway-80 route of the Selma to Montgomery March, through Atlanta, and up to DC, retracing Lewis' life and the steps of Freedom Riders' protests and Black Southerners' moves throughout the early twentieth century. Along the path, Lewis' loved ones and mourners testified to his person and politics through signs and songs, mapping their memories onto the Southern roadways.

Lewis' procession along Highway-80 fits within a longer tradition of refuting white supremacist claims to the interstate. One of the ways in which white supremacists' marking of highways is readily apparent is through naming practices. That is, white Southern organizations have named parts of Highway-80 as the Dixie Overland Highway, Lee Highway, Jefferson Davis Highway, and Edmund Pettus Bridge. These named roads perform, thus signaling who is welcome where and shaping these sites' dominant discourse and map. Katherine McKittrick calls this "transparent space," which "works to hierarchically position individuals, communities, regions, and nations."[16] If maps are "an instrument of power," as geographer Yves Lacoste has proposed, white Southerners' naming of highways after well-known Confederates are also attempts to assert an anti-Black social order geographically.[17] Even more, they stage nostalgia for the antebellum era of enslavement onto the road, linking a false, beautified image of the South's past with present mobility. This ethos is encapsulated in the official slogan that the Daughters of the Confederacy, who commissioned Jefferson Davis Highway and its name, chose for the interstate: "Lest We Forget."[18] When the Daughters conceived of the highway, they wrote that it would "stretch a broad white ribbon across our continent."[19] Their use of "our" and aims of expansion echo the imperialism Dwight Eisenhower embedded within the founding of the interstate. Eisenhower's 1956 Highway Federal Aid Act was based on the German autobahn's totalitarian model and grew from his goals of increased military productivity and commercial access.[20] These stories underpin the highway and trouble the US Department of Transportation's designation of the Selma to Montgomery byway as an officially recognized "All-American Road" for its historic qualities: this award joins Highway-80 with 184 other "significant" and "scenic" American roads and belies interstates' repeated association with patriotism, even as their realities often represent a far more white supremacist nationalism.

While enduring endorsements of white terrorism are represented in the Jefferson Davis Highway and Edmund Pettus Bridge's namesakes, John Lewis and local Selma-based Civil Rights veteran, Lynda Lowry, have opposed the Bridge's renaming, instead pointing toward alternate maps upheld by Selma residents, including the ritual of marching across the Bridge every year at the Jubilee. In a 2015 editorial, John Lewis and Alabama Congresswoman Teri Sewell wrote, "The Edmund

Pettus name represents the truth of the American story … [and] as Americans we need to learn the unvarnished truth about what happened in Selma."[21] Lowry, who marched in Selma on Bloody Sunday at age fourteen, advocates against renaming the Bridge after Lewis, as some have suggested, calling the act a "whitewashing" of history.[22] She implores those who "really want to do something" to "find out what Selma is [and] what it needs" and that "to honor John Lewis would be … to restore the Voting Rights Act," instead of retitling the bridge in his name.[23] Lowry's strategy suggests a political and mapping praxis in which people and their lived experiences illustrate cities more acutely than the state's deployments of liberal optics do. In an interview with *WBUR*, Lowry avowed "our blood and tears is embedded in the cement of that bridge."[24] Marchers renew that relationship every spring at the Selma Jubilee's Bridge Crossing event, inviting new witnesses and walkers. Lowry's sister says, "Pettus is rolling in his grave every time we walk across the bridge."[25] This is in and of itself is an act of rebellion, epitomizing how (w)righting place—as a spiritual, social, and spatial practice—reclaims highways while actively revising their histories.

Selma's Jubilee, which honors the 1965 march through a variety of programming, tenders a counter-map to Highway-80's background of white supremacy. It also opposes some historians' and white spectators' tendency to locate Bloody Sunday as the dramatic pinnacle of the Civil Rights movement, rather than center Black Southern voters' and organizers' continued fights for justice.[26] Founded by Hank Sanders and Faya Ora Rose Touré, two Civil Rights activists and a former Black Alabaman State senator and judge, respectively, the Jubilee is attended by both local community members and a range of notable politicians, activists, and artists across age and race.[27] There are highly broadcasted elements of the festival, such as the fiftieth anniversary ceremonial bridge crossing, in which then-President Barack Obama walked arm in arm with veteran Selma marchers and Former President George Bush. Visually they presented a tableau of unity and progress that Obama's own speech that day challenged as a yet-to-be realized aspiration.[28] While I am mindful of the ways in which the Jubilee is vulnerable to and perhaps already co-opted by politics which do very little to mobilize material change, my focus here is the Selma locals and Black Southerners who make the pilgrimage to Selma each year and how that rite shapes the place's memory.

As such, organizers and participants of the Jubilee foreground Black joy, while stressing the incomplete struggle for Black liberation. Step shows, marching bands, and a Jubilee Street Festival overtake Highway-80 each year, creating a cadence on the interstate that celebrates Black Southern culture. In 2020, for instance, street festival performers included Selma-based blues singer L. Honey Brown and Houston gospel artist Kathy Taylor, who would minister George Floyd's homegoing service later that summer. By transforming Highway-80's haunted space into a repository for sharing Black Southern performance traditions, Jubilee goers fill the road with cultural and communal memory. Performance transforms the highway and illuminates its counter-maps, while leaving sites open to improvisation.

Perhaps the most profound piece of this counter-map is the Jubilee's centerpiece—the annual Edmund Pettus Bridge crossing. Every March, Selma residents and Jubilee visitors crowd the highway, remembering and honoring the footsteps of those before them. One regular Jubilee attendee and activist, Kenneth Glasgow, annually marches "backwards," with other pastors and formerly incarcerated persons. Glasgow says: "We march backwards .... to remind us of everyone who's been left behind. We've got to go back and get them, and get things right, so we can move forward."[29] The Backwards March geographically maps abolition and solidarity onto a crucial site for racial justice history. In this way, Jubilee marchers like Glasgow accentuate the structural transformation that is still needed as they traverse the Bridge and ruminate on its place among their ancestors. Jubilee marchers' celebration and remembrance reroute the highway within Black geographies. Lewis' oft-quoted axiom, "get in the way," is chanted at the Bridge each year, thus marking a spatial and historiographical intervention, as walkers "get in the way" of the whitewashing of Highway-80 and its past.[30]

From the 1965 march in Montgomery to the annual Selma Jubilees to the streets of Atlanta during Lewis' funeral, Black marchers and mourners have resuscitated the Civil Rights anthem "We Shall Overcome," weaving through time and space to repeatedly insert the song's memory and message onto the road.[31] The song itself lives and moves deep in Black American cultural memory as enslaved Africans remixed the tune into similar songs "I'll Be Alright" and "No More Auction Block for Me," and in 1945 Black women first used "We Shall Overcome" in protest during a labor strike against American Tobacco in Charleston, South Carolina.[32] The women's version also transformed the original's "I" into a "we," gifting it the spirit of united protest it carries on to this day. When the 1965 marchers sang "We Shall Overcome" at the conclusion of their famous highway journey, they stood at the Alabama statehouse face to face with state troopers and a statue of Jefferson Davis.[33] The marchers, who were mostly Black Alabamans, chose to resound their protest anthem in front of Davis at the end of highway named for him is an insurgent instance of performance and memory (w)righting the road.

Nearly six decades later, some of the same Civil Rights foot soldiers and many younger Black freedom-fighters gathered further down the same route in Atlanta, rallying as their forebears once did. They marched on the freeway throughout Black Lives Matter protests and then, following John Lewis' death, they stood outside the Ebenezer Baptist Church, in the elbow of Atlanta's knot of interstates, no more than two blocks from I-86 and I-10. "His footprint is in this city," one local attendee said of Lewis to *11Alive Atlanta News*. The attendee further stated that "his life is part of this city. So it is fitting that he would be honored here among people who love him."[34] That "footprint" spreads across the South, just as Lewis' procession remapped it. Outside the church, the sound of "We Shall Overcome" swept across the surrounding highways, crossing over the interstate yet again, as its singers wrote onto a counter-map of song and memory that their ancestors began drawing many generations ago.

Interstate 35-W: Minneapolis, Minnesota

To close my meditation on the US interstate and Black geographies, I turn to one more act of activism: Black Lives Matter protestors' highway blockades. During the summer of 2020, waves of protestors rerouted American freeways demanding justice in the wake of Breonna Taylor, George Floyd, and Ahmaud Arbery's murders. Interstates usually streaming with motor and metal now teemed with marchers and movement and in communion with one another, in the spaces between oft-masked breaths, Black community organizers led masses in chants and pathways across their cities. While their walking created new roads, their refrains of "I can't breathe" and resuscitations of the names of Black men and women murdered by police officers "defended the dead," as Christina Sharpe might suggest, and held space on the freeway for their memory.[35] In these moments, where Black activists remapped city geographies, breathing and spoken ritual acted as practices which rupture highway logic through the centering of Black life and living.

The highway blockades protestors employed in 2020 are an intentional and choreographed tactic particularly developed within Black Lives Matter's repertoire. They also recall John Lewis' own activist practices and his earlier cited words: "You must be bold, brave, and courageous and find a way .... to get in the way."[36] In an effort to counter narratives of activists' social choreography and their activism in 2020's novelty, I turn to the history of BLM highway activism in Minneapolis-St. Paul prior to its central role in 2020's uprisings and read a 2014 protest on 35-W, which followed the murders of Michael Brown and Eric Garner.

Dressed in neon orange and lime green vests, Mica Grimm, Lesley Anne Crosby, and other local organizers gathered demonstrators on December 4, 2014, near the freeway at the intersection of 34th Street and Nicollett Avenue. Grimm began by reading the names of Black men and women killed by law enforcement officers; the saying of names, which is repeated across BLM protests, brings those lives lost into the present. The city air holds their names like prayers. At one point, Grimm said, "I literally can't finish this list ... we don't have time to finish this list."[37] Anti-Black violence in America is exhaustive and disturbs linear time in its relentlessness, overwhelms it with its magnitude. Grimm's unfinished list marks names unsaid and names unknown. The protestors' subsequent die-in is a method for staying in that mourning and demonstrating how it continues into the present.

Moving to the freeway, marchers overtook 35-W, halting traffic for over an hour as they moved toward the skyline. They slowed mobility and called attention to its use as a streamlined divider. Since urban planners and policymakers constructed highways for capitalist efficiency, the activist-led interruptions agitated that function and forced drivers to see the breadth of city space that interstates splice apart. Blockades are also an inventive tactic. Precisely, travelers leaving the highway are derailed by the protest, thus leaving them less sure of alternative routes. After passing under the Franklin Bridge, many protestors laid down in the middle of the freeway, a choreography that cites historic die-ins and the slain bodies of Black men and women killed on American roadways.[38] Though the protestors' positions expressed vulnerability and collectivity, organizers' bright vests and the groups' linked arms suggest care and safety. Laying on the asphalt, their coats curled into one another, and their cardboard signs tangled up into outstretched arms. This reminded me of the energy at many of 2020's protests, including those I attended and watched online, in which aid supplies—such as hand sanitizer packets, snack bags, water, and extra masks—were passed out freely as protestors sought to protect and nourish one another, even amidst pandemic concerns and National Guard officers' threatening postures. Demonstrators reveal the precarity of Black lives in America, while also practicing support and solidarity. Thinking again with Sharpe, Black protestors "inhabit" the road while "rupture[ing]" it;[39] their acts illuminate enslavement's afterlives, its terrors and geographies, and also create spaces to remember and breathe together.

Black Lives Matter groups have returned to the highway blockade tactic repeatedly and the movement's nonhierarchical structure allows each protest to respond to its region's specific histories. Just as the

Minneapolis chapter rerouted 35-W and I-94, BLM chapters across America have staged road interventions and wrote Black geographies on their own equivalent freeways. Many chapters stage their protests on roads with legacies of State violence. In Minneapolis, 35-W cuts through a historically Black neighborhood (in this case, Old Southside Minneapolis). BLM highway protests, through denying mostly white drivers' unfettered freedom of the roadways, surface the inequities that have always existed there. In proudly "liberal" and "nice" Midwestern cities like Minneapolis, this embodied truth-telling disrupts literal passage of roads and fictions of openness and neutrality.

Minnesota's complicity in American systemic racism has been consistently illuminated by local activists, researchers, and residents in studies such as MPD150's "Enough is Enough" report, the Mapping Prejudice Project, and the Public History of I-35W.[40] These projects, along with locals' lived experiences, reveal that Minnesota's racism stretches across generations and cities. The 35-W project compiles oral histories and archives to illustrate the loss of homes and community green spaces' effects on life quality. Like at Selma's annual Jubilee, performance might be thought of as a way residents rehearse and keep the residues of place, while also critiquing the state's anti-Black actions and how harm directs geography—in other words, they (w)right their roads' histories. BLM protestors' selection of 35-W stages a reckoning with state and white violence at large and on the local level. Activists render this point through their collective choreography, repetition, and thoughtful routing. Led by community organizers like Mica Grimm, one of the founders of BLM Minneapolis, marchers traveled from 35-W to City Hall, to demand answers for state injustice. Grimm's map links white violence on the road to bureaucratic offices and offers an example of critical Black geography.

As Black Lives Matter protestors rested their bodies against 35-W's cold pavement in 2014, they repeated Eric Garner's last words, "I can't breathe," into the blue winter sky. Garner spoke out "I can't breathe" eleven times before his death and George Floyd repeated the phrase some six years later. For Black demonstrators, this phrase calls out to ancestors, grieves them, and keeps them nearby. It captures the difficulty of breathing while being Black in America. It moves through the plantation, the hold of the ship, the "weaponized"[41] sidewalk, the freeway, the hospital room. What would the interstate look like if it became a space where Black Americans could breathe easily? Is this even possible with its histories? Black geographers of the highway dare to bring love, breath, and revolution onto roads, in marches and song, in measures of memory, that cartography, its justice, blooms wide with dimension and demands more from this American landscape.

Notes

1 By "good trouble," I am referring to John Lewis' call to activists, made from the Edmund Pettus Bridge at the March 1, 2020, Bloody Sunday commemoration: "Get in good trouble, necessary trouble, and redeem the soul of America." That these words were spoken on the same bridge that would feature in his procession, I argue, is part of its ancestral geography. John Lewis quoted in Associated Press, "From Rep. John Lewis, quoted in a Long Life of Activism," *The Washington Post*, July 18, 2020, https://www.washingtonpost.com/national/from-rep-john-lewis-quotes-in-a-long-life-of-activism/2020/07/18/7ee684d8-c8b0-11ea-a825-8722004e4150_story.html

2 Billie Holiday, "Strange Fruit," recorded April 20, 1939, Commodore.

3 Martin Luther King Jr.'s funeral was also held at Ebenezer Baptist Church, thus propelling its significance.

4 For more background on John Lewis' vital role in the Student Non-Violent Coordinating Committee (SNCC), see: "John Lewis," *Digital SNCC Gateway*, https://snccdigital.org/people/john-lewis/

5 For further meditation on "Driving while Black," see Gretchen Sorin's text and film of the same name: *Driving While Black: African American Travel and the Road to Civil Rights* (New York, NY: Liveright Publishing Corporation, 2020). Additionally, some examples of city planners' anti-Black highway construction can be found here (though these are only starting points in interrogating this pattern): See: Richard Rothstein, *The*

Color of Law: A Forgotten History of How Our Government Segregated America (New York, NY: Liveright: 2017); John Oliphant, "The Roots of Columbus' Ongoing Color Divide," *Columbus Alive*, accessed June 27, 2018, https://www.columbusalive.com/news/20180627/cover-roots-of-columbus-ongoing-color-divide; the 1619 Project's article by Kevin Kruse, "What Does a Traffic Jam in Atlanta Have to Do Withsegregation? Quite a Lot," *The New York Times Magazine*, accessed August 24, 2019, https://www.nytimes.com/interactive/2019/08/14/magazine/traffic-atlanta-segregation.html; Matthew Fleischer, "Opinion: Want to Tear Down Insidious Monuments to Racism and Segregation? Bulldoze L.A. Freeways," *Los Angeles Times*, accessed June 24, 2020, https://www.latimes.com/opinion/story/2020-06-24/bulldoze-la-freeways-racism-monument; and Charisse Gibson, "Tremé: How 'Urban Renewal' Destroyed the Cultural Heart of New Orleans," *WWLTV*, accessed November 26, 2019, https://www.youtube.com/watch?v=1AIG7HwM7y0

6 Nancy Lee Peluso, "Whose Woods Are These? Counter-mapping Forest Territories in Kalimantan, Indonesia," *Antipode* 27, no. 4 (October 1995): 383–406.

7 Diana Taylor, "Acts of Transfer," *The Archive and the Repertoire: Performing Cultural Memory in the Americas* (2003): 1–52.

8 Ibid., 20.

9 Other communities across the United States and Canada have transformed and rerouted the highway through coalition, art-making, and protest, such as the Missing and Murdered Indigenous Women's highway marches and Boston-based artist Lily Xie's recent project, *Washing 洗作*, which collaborated with Chinatown residents to tell the story of Boston's interstate construction through the neighborhood. My focus here, however, is on Black geographies of the freeway. To read more about these projects, see: Carey Dunne, "No More Stolen Sisters': 12,000-mile Ride to Highlight Missing Indigenous Women," *The Guardian*, accessed June 7, 2019, https://www.theguardian.com/us-news/2019/jun/07/indigenous-women-missing-murdered-activists-ride-north-america and "Washing," washingchinatown.com

10 Katherine McKittrick, *Demonic Grounds: Black Women and the Cartographies of Struggle* (Minneapolis: University of Minnesota, 2006), xiii.

11 Harry Elam Jr., "Introduction: (W)righting History: A Meditation in Four Beats," in *The Past as Present in the Drama of August Wilson* (Ann Arbor: University of Michigan Press, 2006), 4.

12 Throughout this chapter, I aim to emphasize the extremity of the State's anti-Blackness on the road, while not falling into a repetition of trauma; or rather, I have tried to center "desire" instead of "damage" in my writing. Christina Sharpe, in her recent text *In the Wake: On Blackness and Being*, offers a crucial model for this, when she invites scholars to understand this reckoning with histories in a way that creates space for connection and care, while moving through the depths of trauma. See Christina Sharpe, *In the Wake: On Blackness and Being* (Durham: Duke University Press, 2016).

13 Crystal DeGregory, "Congressman John Lewis Remembered in Selma, Alabama with Carriage Ride across Edmund Pettus Bridge," *The Atlanta Voice*, accessed July 26, 2020, https://www.theatlantavoice.com/articles/congressman-john-lewis-remembered-in-selma-alabama-with-carriage-ride-across-edmund-pettus-bridge/

14 McKittrick, *Demonic Grounds*, xxvii.

15 It is important to note that "Highway 80," or US Route 80, refers to a different roadway than "I-80," or Interstate-80; while the former was originally conceived of as an "Atlantic to Pacific" interstate, terminating in San Diego, it now begins in Savannah and splinters into several other Interstate and state highways in Dallas, running through much of the Deep South. I-80, on the other hand, journeys from the New York City Metro Area to San Francisco. My discussion pertains to the first freeway.

16 McKittrick, *Demonic Grounds*, 6.

17 Yves Lacoste, "An Illustration of Geographical Warfare (trans. A Buttimer)," *Antipode* 5, no. 2 (1973): 1–13.

18 It is well-worth noting that many Confederate monuments and namesakes were commissioned and funded by *white women's* groups. See John T. Winberry, "'Lest We Forget': The Confederate Monument and the Southern Townscape," *Southeastern Geographer* 23, no. 2 (1983): 107–21.

19 See: Robert F. Weingroff, "U.S. Route 80: The Dixie Overland Highway," *U.S. Department of Transportation – Federal Highway Administration*, https://www.fhwa.dot.gov/infrastructure/us80.cfm

20 Note that the Autobahn was not invented by the Third Reich, but was fervently embraced by Hitler, who oversaw its advancement and completion. Dwight D. Eisenhower, *At Ease: Stories I Tell to Friends* (New York: Doubleday, 1967) and Dwight Eisenhower, "Message to the Congress Regarding Highways, February 22, 1955," Dwight D. Eisenhower Presidential Library, White House Office, Office of the Press Secretary to the President, Box 4, Press Releases February 8–March 14, 1955; NAID #16857605.

21 Terri Sewell and John Lewis, "Editorial: John Lewis, Terri Sewell Defend Keeping Selma Bridge Named after Edmund Pettus," *Sewell.house.gov*, accessed June 17 2015, https://sewell.house.gov/media-center/in-the-news/alcom-john-lewis-terri-sewell-defend-keeping-selma-bridge-named-after

22 Lynda Lowry quoted in "Civil Rights Veteran on Why She Opposes Renaming the Edmund Pettus Bridge," *WBUR.org*, accessed August 13, 2020, https://www.wbur.org/hereandnow/2020/08/13/edmund-pettus-bridge-renaming

23 Lowry in "Civil Rights Veteran."

24 Ibid.

25 Ibid.

26 In her book *Equal Time*, Aniko Bodroghkozy cites Linda Williams' analysis of American melodrama to argue that white spectators of the Selma broadcast would have placed the television's images of "the suffering black body" within melodrama's moralizing, theatrical tradition; I argue that a white savior's eye centered the white Christian middle class in the wake of the police brutality in Selma. Similarly, in the summer of 2020 many white people took to social media to express their newfound awareness of racial injustice. See: Aniko Bodroghkozy, *Equal Time: Television and the Civil Rights Movement* (Urbana and Chicago: University of Illinois Press, 2013).

27 Some more background on the Selma Bridge Crossing Jubilee, including a list of its past attendees, can be found on the event's website and its archives: "About Us," https://www.selmajubilee.com/about

28 In Barack Obama's fiftieth anniversary Selma speech, he explicitly called out America's de jure segregation and correlated the events at Selma with the racial injustice in Ferguson at the time.

29 Kenneth Glasgow, "Marching Backwards for Freedom," *Common Dreams*, accessed March 12, 2018, https://www.commondreams.org/views/2018/03/12/marching-backwards-freedom

30 "John Lewis: Get in the Way," directed by Kathleen Dowdey, *PBS* (2020).

31 Weingroff, "U.S. Route 80."

32 "We Shall Overcome: The Story behind the Song," *The Kennedy Center*, https://www.kennedy-center.org/education/resources-for-educators/classroom-resources/media-and-interactives/media/music/story-behind-the-song/the-story-behind-the-song/we-shall-overcome/

33 Davis' inauguration, a celebration of the Confederacy recently commemorated in 2011 by its con supporters, was also held on the same avenue as the statehouse. See: Campbell Robertson, "Marking Davis's Confederate Inauguration," *The New York Times*, accessed February 20, 2011, https://www.nytimes.com/2011/02/21/us/21davis.html

34 11Alive, "Large Crowds Gathered outside Ebenezer Baptist for John Lewis' Funeral," *YouTube*, accessed July 30, 2020, https://www.youtube.com/watch?v=s8xxz6sLmFM&ab_channel=11Alive

35 Sharpe, *In the Wake.*

36 Associated Press, "From Rep. John Lewis."

37 Mica Grimm quoted in Brandt Williams, "Protests Shut Down Part of I-35-W for over an Hour," *MPR News*, accessed December 4, 2014, https://www.mprnews.org/story/2014/12/04/protesters-close-i35w

38 Theresa Incampo, *"But What if Instead We Imagine Black Life": Femininity, Performance, and the Black Lives Matter Movement* (Proquest Dissertations and Theses, 2018), 50

39 Sharpe, *In the Wake*, 17.

40 MPD150's "Enough Is Enough" report is a ground-breaking examination, or "150-year performance review," of the Minneapolis Police Department. It "is meant to be a toolkit for people, both here in Minneapolis and beyond, to keep pushing." The Mapping Prejudice Project exposes structural racism in Minneapolis by mapping its redlining and predatory lending histories. The Public History of I-35W documents the history of the neighborhood prior to and throughout highway construction and pollution. I highly encourage reviewing each of these important projects.

41 Sharpe writes this in response to Trayvon Martin's murder. Sharpe, *In the Wake*, 15.

9

Honk for Justice Chicago

Jocelyn Prince and Harvey Young

In the aftermath of the murder of George Floyd on May 25, 2020, artist-activist Jocelyn Prince attended protests and marches on the South Side of Chicago. She witnessed the overwhelming show of force by the Chicago Police Department (CPD). Their intimidating presence seemed out of proportion to the peaceful demonstration which itself was a response to the killing of an unarmed Black man by a police officer. Several Chicago protestors would be beaten by members of the CPD on that day. Others at subsequent protests. Prince remembers,

> I began to get frustrated that while people on the South Side of Chicago were being beaten in the streets protesting murder by police, white people on the North Side were going about their daily business, chatting about their kids' summer camp programs or how long the line is at Whole Foods. When Madison reached out to me to ask me if I knew of any protests happening [elsewhere] in the city, I said we should make our own.[1]

Madison Kamp and Prince both are part of the Bradley University Speech Team alumni group and had mutual friends. Prince and Kamp started their own protest, Honk for Justice Chicago, which would become the longest sustained demonstration related to George Floyd's murder in the city. Prince researched city ordinances concerning street demonstrations. Together, they devised a concept for a visibility protest which could take place on sidewalks and, therefore, would not require permits. Although simple in design, they understood that the impact of these initial events would increase if they could attract people to join and participate in the protest over successive days. They leveraged social media, creating "Facebook events" initially for the first two protests and circulating information via other outlets such as Instagram and Twitter. Comments and interactions on the Honk for Justice Facebook page varied. For some, the page was a way to find out when and where the next protest would be and to express their support. People posted comments like "Appreciate you all" and "Nice." Some volunteers and potential volunteers tagged their friends and families on events, which helped spread the word and get more people involved. Facebook also served as a way to connect with other organizations and organizers. One person wrote, "I saw your group for the first time about 15 minutes ago [...]. Good work. You might be interested in my Anti-Racists Club." What began with fewer than a dozen volunteers on the first day quickly expanded.

The next day's protest in Rogers Park on the North Side of the city, one of Chicago's most diverse neighborhoods with approximately forty different languages spoken, began with a couple dozen participants. At the start, Prince gathered the small group in a circle on the grass near a fieldhouse. She used the "people's microphone," when a crowd repeats everything that a speaker says for amplification, to point out a comfort station with water, first aid and other supplies. Prince led the group to repeat the words of Assata Shakur, "It is our duty to fight for our freedom. It is our duty to win. We must love each other and support each other. We have nothing to lose but our chains."[2] Within a few hours, the crowd swelled to several hundred people who gathered for blocks along Sheridan Road, a major four-lane street, in the city. Protestors held up signs with slogans reading "Honk for Justice" and "White Silence is Violence." Some were passersby who found themselves compelled to join in. Most were people who learned about it less than twenty-four hours earlier via Facebook. People of all ages and races attended the protest. Some banged pots and pans. Another person played a trombone. Police officers in riot gear arrived. They came with empty buses for mass arrests.

Figure 9.1 Honk for Justice Chicago protestors. Photo courtesy of Madison Kamp.

A History of Activism

Although other places such as Selma, Montgomery, Greensboro, and Los Angeles are remembered for specific marches, boycotts, sit-ins, and uprisings, Chicago stands apart for the frequency with which its residents have taken to the streets. “If world history is often told as a history of wars,” journalist Don Rose writes, “Much of Chicago history can be told as a history of protest—labor, civil rights, anti-war and other campaigns against injustice.”[3] This culture of civic engagement as well as civil disagreement is endemic to the Windy City and has defined social life in the region for centuries.

Among the more memorable neighborhood-based demonstrations are the series of activist events in Marquette Park, a formerly all-white, redlined neighborhood in Chicago whose residents were opposed to integration. It was the destination point of Martin Luther King, Jr.’s best-remembered marches in the Windy City. Over a series of weeks in August 1966, King led protestors calling for civil rights, as part of the Chicago Freedom Movement, through the streets and was confronted by mobs, comprised of thousands of angry white men, determined to maintain the status quo. Epithets, rocks, and bottles were thrown at the peaceful marchers. The racist hatred that the civil rights leader experienced was sufficiently great that he declared, "I've been in many demonstrations all across the south. But I can say that I have never seen, even in Mississippi and Alabama, mobs as hostile and as hate-filled as I've seen in Chicago."[4] Over subsequent years, decennial marches would be held in Marquette Park to continue the push to end residential segregation and later to celebrate the gradual diversifying of a community. To mark the fiftieth anniversary of King's march, a memorial, designed by Sonja Henderson and John Pittman Weber, was erected in Marquette Park in 2016.

The protests surrounding the 1968 Democratic National Convention (DNC) also linger in public memory. Whereas presidential nominating contests often attract protestors, the DNC activism is notable for its size, scale, and intensity. More than ten thousand protestors, a mixture of Chicagoans and those who traveled to the Windy City, participated in the multiday campaign which ended violently with beatings by police officers and numerous arrests. As John Schultz writes in his study on the convention riot, "The main stimulus for their coming, at source, was that they felt the war in Vietnam to be naturally self-destructive, in every sense."[5] Democratic voters had lost confidence in President Lyndon Baines Johnson. Although LBJ had previously announced that he would not seek nomination and indeed was not a candidate under consideration for the presidential nomination, activists shouted (in reference to the Vietnam War) "Hey, Hey, LBJ, how many kids did you kill today." Vice President Hubert Humphrey who would receive the nomination was similarly rejected by protestors. They chanted, "Dump the Hump."[6]

In addition to these acts of activism within Chicago's histories, there are thousands more protests of all sizes, from the Haymarket Affair to Honk for Justice Chicago. Indeed, there is not a year in Chicago's past in which people failed to gather, take to the streets (or the sidewalks), and collectively voice alarm and demand change. Beach wade-ins and school boycotts occurred against racial segregation (and the effects of segregationist policies) in the city. Workers went on strike to protest labor conditions. Chicagoans occupied buildings as well as public spaces to call attention to destructive gentrification efforts as well as corporate greed. Unfortunately, "most of the city's best-remembered protests turned violent only after the police attacked protestors," writes Don Rose.[7] Within a culture of activism and nonviolent assembly, it is the rare event in which violence ensues. However, those are the ones that garner headlines.

Honk for Justice

Despite the presence of the police and their buses, the second Honk for Justice protest in Rogers Park ended peacefully. There were no acts of physical violence. None of the hundreds of protestors were arrested. Nevertheless, the presence of law enforcement officers dressed in preparation for violence reminded participants why Honk for Justice Chicago was necessary.

On May 25, 2020, George Floyd, a Black man who was accused of using a fake twenty-dollar bill at a convenience store, was murdered by a white police officer in Minneapolis. Handcuffed, with hands behind his back, he was forced facedown on the street with multiple officers kneeling on him, including one who kneeled on his neck. George Floyd pleaded for breath repeatedly saying "I can't breathe." He repeated these words more than twenty times. A crowd gathered, calling for the officers to stop and to allow the man to breathe. For nearly nine minutes—eight minutes and forty-six seconds to be exact—the lead officer continued to kneel on George Floyd's neck until life drained from his body. The murder, recorded on cellular phones and police body cameras, was replayed on the news and shared across social media. Nationally, people took to the streets in protest of this particular death as well as the dozens of recent murders of Black people by the police that had inspired the Black Lives Matter movement. Among them was Honk for Justice Chicago.

The first Honk for Justice Chicago protest in West Town, a neighborhood on the West Side of the city that includes Ukranian Village composed of a large immigrant population, occurred eight days after the murder of George Floyd. It was a death that resonated because of both its alignment with other death by police scenarios and its unavoidable spectacularity. Prince remembers,

> I will never be the same after watching that video. It was like watching a televised lynching. I cried for days. I had nightmares. I dreamt that my brother or other black men I loved were under that officer's knee. I was most horrified by what I saw in the following days, white people going about their business as if nothing had happened. I found that sort of desensitization to violence against black bodies disturbing.

What was needed was an intervention to help folks, especially those who lived on Chicago's North Side, to understand that had George Floyd's skin complexion been different—had he been white—he likely would still be alive. To raise awareness, Honk for Justice Chicago needed to be a durational event, perhaps a marathon protest, that occurred not just on one day in one part of the city but rather everyday throughout Chicago. It would run for sixty consecutive days, between June 2, 2020, and August 1, 2020.

In the style of a field organizer on a political campaign, Jocelyn Prince hosted volunteer trainings. Each began with her telling her story—who she was; why and how she got here. Prince was born and raised on the South Side of Chicago. Her father was a lawyer active in local politics, who ran in three judicial races. Although he lost each election, he was later appointed a judge by Illinois' Secretary of State Jesse White. Prince knocked on her first doors when she was twelve years old, getting petition signatures to get her father's name on the ballot. She would become a staff organizer on the 2008 Obama for America and 2016 Hillary for America presidential campaigns. In the year preceding Honk for Justice Chicago, Prince worked in Iowa for the Kamala Harris for the People presidential campaign. With a parallel career in theatre, she organized and facilitated town halls designed to foster a dialogue among activists, academics, and artists and to encourage grassroots organizing among community members, as Connectivity Director at Woolly Mammoth Theatre Company in Washington, DC. Partnering with Prince was Madison Kamp, a strong advocate for diversity and inclusion. Originally from Peoria, IL, a southwest suburb of Chicago, she relocated to the West Side of Chicago after graduating from Bradley University with a BS in Family Consumer Science. Kamp and Madison met through a Bradley University debate team alumni group.

Joining Prince and Kamp were a core group of volunteers, the "yellow jackets." The yellow jackets were engaged artists who, like the cofounders, felt compelled to act and speak out. They were Thom Cox, Sunny Serres, David O'Donnell, Dana Buccheri, and Stacy Bergland. Cox, a professional theatre actor and a founding member of the Tony Award-winning regional theatre Lookingglass Theatre Company, recalls feeling "angry" at the murder of George Floyd and possessing a desire to "take action in the face of power that knew it wasn't accountable."[8] Sunny Serres, a professor at Harold Washington College, remembers deliberately avoiding the video of George Floyd's murder for a week and, upon watching it, "believed it to be the first lynching that I've ever seen."[9] The "yellow jackets" became a cast and crew of sorts. They set up a staging area for other volunteers and participants, which included bottled water, snacks, poster board and markers, signs and other supplies.

Daily, "pop up" protests continued with the location announced on Facebook the night before. The logistics of this proved cumbersome which led Prince and Kamp alongside the "yellow jackets" to choose seven locations on the North Side of the city, one for each day of the week: Uptown, West Town, Logan Square, Lincoln Square, Lincoln Park, Rogers Park, and West Ridge. This cycle was repeated every week for nearly two months. To further promote Honk for Justice Chicago, a website was created: www.honkforjusticechicago.com. Offering a succinct overview of Honk for Justice Chicago, the website included a schedule of events, photos, and published pieces about the protest.

> Every day, we protest at a different intersection on the North Side of Chicago from 4–6 pm, occupying the sidewalks, waving signs, chanting, making noise, and getting drivers to honk their car horns in support. This event is family friendly. Kids are more than welcome!
>
> Bring signs and anything that makes noise (pots and pans, whistles, musical instruments). We have a limited stock of premade signs, as well as poster board and markers. We have water, snacks, masks, and basic first aid supplies on hand. Helium black balloons are also a great thing to bring for children (and even adults!). Sign suggestions include—"Black Lives Matter," "Silence is Violence," "Black is Beautiful," and "Justice for George Floyd."
>
> When you arrive at the intersection, please look for volunteers in yellow jackets. You can show up at Honk for Justice anytime between 4 and 6 pm, but we encourage you to attend our 10 minute training, which begins promptly at 4 pm.
>
> We protest RAIN OR SHINE. We encourage all participants to wear a mask and practice social distancing.
>
> Although we are not directly affiliated with the Black Lives Matter organization, we ask that you support the great work that they do to organize us all around racial justice. Donate at blacklivesmatter.com.[10]

Face coverings were requested not for the purpose of anonymity but rather in accordance with city and state guidelines requiring masking in an effort to curtail the Covid-19 public health crisis that was occurring concurrent with Honk for Justice Chicago. The "yellow jackets" wore neon yellow vests with thin orange stripes similar to those worn by crossing guards or construction workers. The vests served multiple functions. They helped volunteers and first-time protestors to identify key organizers for that particular protest. They further marked Honk for Justice Chicago as a formally organized event rather than an accidental gathering. In addition, they helped to provide visual consistency from event to event. As the days passed, the "yellow jackets" replaced Jocelyn Prince as the person, with megaphone in hand, training volunteers.

Kamp remembers those moments of "leading the team" to be the most challenging even for a person like herself who "like[s] speaking in front of people."[11] She remembers, thinking about service to and for community each time she addressed volunteers, "This is not about you Madison. It's about the movement and the support of the black community." Madison's experience as a white organizer leading a street action supporting the Black Lives Matter movement presented a challenging dynamic for some of the white volunteers. They wrestled with their access to white privilege and the power dynamics at play while working with Black protesters during the events. Knowing when to "step up" and "step back" was an ongoing negotiation for the white "yellow jackets."

Honk for Justice Chicago worked with two volunteer publicists, Seth Zurer and Rachael Perrotta, who coordinated press releases, handled outreach, and provided media training to Prince, Kamp, and the "yellow jackets." Protests were covered by the gamut of local, regional, and national press. WTTW, Chicago's PBS news station, featured Honk for Justice as part of a neighborhood profile series on Lincoln Square. Nick Blumberg reports, "And as with many Chicago neighborhoods, demonstrations for racial justice have been making noise—in this case, literally. The demonstration 'Honk for Justice' has been coming to Lincoln Square every Thursday."[12] In the televised segment, Prince appears saying, "We want to keep the volume up so that people here on the North Side understand what Black people are going through not just here in Chicago but around the country." In a video essay on Chicago protests created and published by the *Washington Post*, Honk for Justice Chicago appears prominently with Prince interviewed.[13]

As enthusiasm for the daily protests began to wane, Prince, who became the sole lead organizer after other obligations limited Kamp's involvement in late July, found herself having to do more and more organizing work to get people to attend. She reflected on her own efforts and, by extension, the labor of Black women which often drives social justice movements. Prince considered the inability of Black women to rest which, in turn, inspired a performance which would last for the remainder of the Honk for Justice Chicago protest series. She thought what would it feel like if instead of standing and wearing a bright yellow jacket, she wore a pretty summer dress, brought a beach chair and just sat down.

The theatricality of the daily protests increased. In addition to the summer dress and beach chair, Prince added a variety of new costume and set pieces including a large straw beach hat, a beach towel, a white tub for soaking her feet, magazines, a parasol, and a hand fan. Throughout the protest, she refused to speak with passersby. If someone approached her, a "yellow jacket" would intervene and let the person know that Jocelyn is resting and cannot be disturbed. This improvisational schtick became a ritual that symbolized how Black women consistently are asked for unpaid labor and the ways white allies might interrupt that dynamic. In its coverage of Honk for Justice Chicago, the *Chicago Reader*, a regional free newspaper, spotlighted this "performance art twist": "When Prince is there, she sits in a lawn chair reading. White volunteers serve as mediators between her and anyone who wants to interact with her, telling them, as Prince says, 'No,

Figure 9.2 "Far past time for Black people to rest." Photo courtesy of Seth Zurer.

she's resting. She needs to rest. You can talk to me.'"[14] In the *Washington Post* coverage, Prince offers, "Black women have been doing a lot of organizing work for progressive politics for centuries. It's time for white people to do that work. It is far past time for black people to rest."[15]

With her performance art, Prince drew inspiration from performance artists damali ayo and Tricia Hersey-Patrick. damali ayo created her interactive street performance, *Living Flag: Panhandling for Reparations*, to raise awareness about the issue of reparations for the descendants of Black Americans enslaved by white people in the United States. During the performance, damali occupied public spaces like street corners, library steps, and parks. She collected money from white passersby and immediately paid those funds to Black pedestrians. Tricia Patrick Hersey founded The Nap Ministry in 2016 to provide spaces for rest with immersive workshops and performance art. Hersey's performance art positions rest as a form of liberation. The Nap Ministry creates striking images, some of which provide commentary on the history of Black women and labor.

Rain or Shine

Honk for Justice Chicago aligns with the history of social activism and protest within Chicago. Its emergence, beginning with an exchange between Madison Kamp and Jocelyn Price, has its roots in the sympathy strikes of the past in which Chicagoans felt compelled to stand up and step out in support of an outrage occurring elsewhere. Indeed, it was the lack of attention and awareness of residents on Chicago's North Side (despite the activism on Chicago's South Side as well as elsewhere within the city) that spurred a protest which would last for two months and capture the attention of the city as well as the regional and national press.

Although successful, there were numerous challenges encountered by Prince and Kamp and their team of "yellow jackets." Among the more significant were the efforts required to sustain Honk for Justice

Figure 9.3 Rain or Shine. Photo courtesy of David O'Donnell.

Chicago over sixty days. Every day, volunteers were needed to occupy sidewalks and publicly call for justice. These individuals had to be recruited. New participants required training. Whereas recruitment on sunny and warm weekends was not difficult, rainy weekdays proved more complicated. Participation could range from hundreds of people to just two people depending on the day. Cox remembers, "To continue showing up knowing that there may be very few people coming. Rainstorm. Or days and times where there are only two, three people showing up. It takes an extra heft." Part of the required "extra heft" was the realization that, at times, an entire movement can rest on the shoulders of one or two people. It is literally a pair of people standing up (and almost seeming to stand against a city) for justice. Serres recalls her most challenging times as "those moments when I was by myself and it was just [Jocelyn] and me. I was really in a vulnerable spot. I noticed that I would get yelled at and picked on when it was just me, but it was also some of the most rewarding too." In part, the reward was the self-acknowledgment of the importance of individual activism.

Prince, Kamp, Honk for Justice Chicago yellow jackets as well as the many volunteers also were impacted by the reactions of passersby. History sometimes records activism as a series of dynamic snapshots: a person holding a sign or standing up to (and directly) facing the police. However, protests have a soundtrack. Honk for Justice Chicago was no exception. There were the voices of people repeating—essentially chanting—the words of Assata Shakur in that first gathering. There were the amplified words of Prince, Kamp, or the "yellow jackets" by the megaphones for the daily trainings. There were the improvisatory statements of participants, the banging of pots and pans, and, yes, even the sound of a trombone. Serres fondly remembers, the large number of "bus drivers, post office workers, Fed Ex drivers, Amazon [delivery] drivers who would honk and wave and yell." She adds, "I remember just being on the North Side and having people hanging out of their cars with excitement that there was a protest happening in their neighborhood." Serres also notes the positive impact of supportive passersby on low attendance days: "You're alone? We respect you."

There were also detractors. With the protest occurring in summer 2020, in the months leading up to a presidential contest between incumbent Donald Trump, who increasingly supported violent white nationalism and seemed unwilling to empathize with Black and Brown communities targeted by police violence, and former Vice President Joseph Biden, who served in the administration of former Chicagoan Barack Obama, Honk for Justice Chicago attracted the ire of people who viewed the protest as activism against Trump. Serres notes, "The amount of rage people had is surprising. How can you feel rage about someone standing up for themselves? That level of rage was mind blowing." Cox remembers people approaching him in an intimidating manner and launching into "aggressive debate."

Referring to the sense of being "physically threatened," he reflected, "That has always been the case with any protest against racial oppression. That is the nature of the conversation and it already has been. I had to return myself to feeling that [I] had to be willing to be unsafe. I was putting myself at risk in a way that I wasn't accustomed to." Participation in these daily protests, especially the rainy weekday gatherings, prompted self-examination—a "return to self"—that helped the volunteer to see themselves as part of a larger community and, equally importantly, to understand how their activism can make a difference and effect change.

The visibility and extended duration of the protest not only raised awareness to the justifiable outrage at George Floyd's murder but also captured the attention of a city on the power of activist performance. The impact of Honk for Justice Chicago extended beyond the individual responses of participants. It also affected passersby who found themselves in the midst of a protest as it rotated daily among seven distinct neighborhoods. They became participant-observers in a manner reminiscent of theatrical in-the-round or runway spectators. As performance scholar Jordan Schildcrout writes,

> Even if an audience member is focused on the performers, they inevitably see their fellow audience members on the other side of the stage—and are reciprocally seen. This mutual visibility could produce a variety of effects—curiousity, anxiety, desire—but it necessarily makes one more aware of one's own visibility in relation to others sharing this same space.[16]

Some people felt antagonized. Serres notes that when she participated in a Honk for Justice Chicago protests "someone would yell Trump 2020 everytime." Thom Cox remembers a man who was "being territorial" at the last protest in West Ridge. The man declared, "Why are you doing this in a residential neighborhood? You're in my neighborhood. This is why people come to hate Black Lives Matter." The man walked away only to return with a megaphone. Cox remembers, "He pointed it at my ear and turned on the siren. 'How did you like it? That's what it sounds like.' Then he walked away. What if that had been a gun? He lifted it and pointed it at my head in the way you would a gun."[17] Other passersby found inspiration and hope. An especially poignant moment for Serres was when "a bus driver got off the bus to thank me." These experiences evidenced theatre scholar Harry Elam's assertion, "In these turbulent times social activists [become] protagonists in their own real-life drama."[18]

"American society is rife with loud, moral protest," writes James Jasper.[19] Honk for Justice Chicago represents the spirit of activism within the Windy City. For weeks and across seven distinct neighborhoods, Chicagoans gathered to protest injustice afar (specifically George Floyd's murder in Minneapolis) and also closer to home. Consisting of sixty individual events, Honk for Justice Chicago evidences the depth of activist spirit in Chicago. It also served as a reminder that activism can incite resistance to change. There were honks for justice. There were passersby who sought to silence the protest. In making the challenges to justice and process visible, Prince and Kamp's campaign spotlighted not only the labor but also the real obstacles to creating lasting change. The effort to bring about change needs to be ongoing and must be of an extended duration. As Sheila Radford Hill has observed, "Deep within the soul of grassroots organizing are a thirst for freedom that cannot be quenched, a hunger for justice that cannot be satiated, a will to succeed that cannot be denied, and a desire to build a legacy of change that will pass on to new generations."[20] This thirst, hunger, will, and desire inspired Honk for Justice Chicago.

Notes

1 Jocelyn Prince, HJC Interview (February 6, 2021), unpublished.

2 Assata Shakur, "To My People" (letter, July 4, 1973); www.assatashakur.org/mypeople.htm

3 Don Rose, "A Brief History of Protest in Chicago," *chicagostories.org*

4 Martin Luther King, Jr. quoted in, Ron Grossman, "50 Years Ago: MLK's March in Marquette Park Turned Violent, Exposed Hate," *Chicago Tribune*, July 28, 2016.

5 John Schultz, *No One Was Killed: The National Democratic Convention, August 1968* (Chicago: University of Chicago Press, 2009), 2.
6 Joel Achenbach, "A Party That Had Lost Its Mind," *Washington Post*, August 24, 2018.
7 Rose, "A Brief History of Protest in Chicago," *chicagostories.org*
8 Thom Cox, HJC Interview (February 6, 2021), unpublished.
9 Sunny Serres, HJC Interview (February 6, 2021), unpublished.
10 "Participation Details," Honk for Justice website, https://honkforjusticechicago.com/
11 Madison Kamp, HJC Interview (February 6, 2021), unpublished.
12 Nick Blumberg, "'Chicago Tonight' in Your Neighborhood: Lincoln Square," July 9, 2020, https://news.wttw.com/2020/07/09/chicago-tonight-your-neighborhood-lincoln-square
13 "With More Protests, More Gun Violence and More Coronavirus Cases, Chicago Is a City on Edge," *Washington Post*, July 26, 2020, https://www.washingtonpost.com/video/national/with-more-protests-more-gun-violence-and-more-coronavirus-cases-chicago-is-a-city-on-edge/2020/07/26/615e904f-29ab-4c98-818f-0e46c265b0de_video.html
14 Kerry Reid, "A Manifesto, a Performance Art Protest, and the Return of (some) Live Theater," *Chicago Reader*, July 16, 2020.
15 Quoted in "With More Protests."
16 Jordan Schildcrout, "Envisioning Queer Liberation in Doric Wilson's *Street Theater*," *Modern Drama* 61, no. 1 (2018): 95.
17 Cox, interview.
18 Harry J. Elam, Jr., *Taking It to the Streets* (Ann Arbor: University of Michigan Press, 1997), 25.
19 James Jasper, *The Art of Moral Protest* (Chicago: University of Chicago Press, 1998), 2.
20 Shiela Radford Hill, "Foreword," in *The Dignity of Resistance*, ed. Roberta M. Feldman and Susan Stall (Cambridge: Cambridge University Press, 2014), xiv.

10

Grunt Work: Serena Williams' Black Sound Acts As Resistance

Leticia Ridley

It is the quarterfinal match at 2015 Wimbledon and Serena is in the second set in the quarterfinal match against Belarusian Victoria Azarenka. Deadlocked in a 30-30 score for the game, an intense rally ensues between Azarenka and Serena. As they clash for the advantage in the game, so too do their grunts—constantly battling for sonic dominance. Serena begins this game with a noticeable aural difference from the game prior; rather than staying silent during her serve as she did in the previous match, she shoots out a husky and gruff grunt from her mouth. As if aurally transferring herself into a different place or time, Serena's grunt begins to dance with her tennis racket hitting the ball. Breaking open space on the tennis court through her grunt, Serena, akin to Fred Moten's assertions, situates Black sound as simultaneously theory and praxis, a way to theorize and perform "an ongoing performance of encounter: rupture, collision, and passionate response."[1] Serena's aural responses serve as a refusal of whiteness' goal to police and discipline her body into submission. In this way, Serena can be placed into a genealogy of black sonic ruptures in the face of objectification and subjugation.

Like a musical score, Serena's grunt establishes a guttural rhythm, and as a Black feminist listener, I can almost anticipate the frequency in which she expels the grunt. The sheer force in which she hits the ball is evidenced by the sharp intensity of her grunt as she fights Azarenka's competing soundscape and shots. But I also notice something else—

perhaps Serena is fighting another opponent that hopes to stay invisible to the white spectator: the compounded racism and sexism.

As the precision of her racket and the intense ferocity of her grunt coalesce to flood and exceed the aural field, Serena's serenade vocalizes a desire to defeat the anti-blackness and patriarchy that she faces on the court—the game within the game. When Serena grunts, she growls back to these forces, utilizing her voice as a reminder of the oft-cited first line of Moten's classic book *In the Break: The Aesthetics of the Black Radical Tradition*: "The history of blackness is testament to the fact that objects can and do resist."[2] Serena's grunt embodies Moten's argument as a sonic eruption and space of possibility that reverberates through the history of Black performance, one by which Black people (considered objects at one point in time) can speak back to and resist-dominant structures. Serena's grunt builds upon Moten's keen observation and theorization that "passionate utterances and responses" such as Aunt Hester's screams (Fredrick Douglass' aunt whose beating by Captain Anthony he detailed visually and aurally in his popular slave narrative, *Narrative of the Life of Frederick Douglass, An American Slave*) are acts of sonic disruptions that Black performance can theorize and resist through.[3]

Separated by time and space, I am not proposing that Serena's grunting is symmetrical with that of Aunt Hester's screams—due to the complete subjugation of Aunt Hester's status as an enslaved person versus Serena's position as a wealthy athlete—but rather to listen closely as Moten suggests to how the "commodity's aurality" is less about what the commodity says, but rather the fact that the commodity decides to sound at all.[4] Moten, drawing on Karl Marx's conceptualization of commodity speech, contends that the aural interruptions, which I apply to Serena, do not overdetermine *what* is said when she sounds, but to consider the *act* of sounding itself as a moment of interruption. Thus, I follow Moten and listen to Serena's grunts. To be sure, Serena sounds back to those who attempt to discipline her body: while she has sometimes employed profanity or her grunt has been characterized as bothersome noise, her commitment to her vocality solidifies its function as a sonic response to the critical nexus of white supremacy, patriarchy, and anti-blackness.

Returning to the game at hand, as I watch, and listen, I begin to think Serena will be victorious against Azarenka (and, subsequently, defeat the white tennis powers that be)—but then Serena falters. The rhythm and precision of the grunt is lost as Serena's body is caught out of position, unaware of Azarenka's placement of the tennis ball. She just barely recovers, and her grunt begins to tremble. The grunt recklessly pleas on behalf of Serena for the security and comfort of the rhythmic growl of a few moments ago. Her grunt sounds desperate, as she seemingly worries that this is the moment that she will break, the point where Azarenka will win. I theorize Serena's grunt not as something that can be easily understood, but as an aural performative signature that attempts to name the un-nameable event or the violent structures that tennis sits upon. In the moment of this potential break, Serena's grunt compels and challenges us to take note of not only the repetitive emotional and psychological violence enacted on her body, but more importantly, the labor that it requires for Serena to gain the (hyper)visibility that allows her to refuse the white hegemonic space of the tennis court. This profound attention to Serena's labor, signaled by her strenuous and trembling grunt, creates an alternative way to imagine Black women's athletic bodies through sound. For Serena, the grunt strongholds the sports world in which she occupies to make space for her even as it constantly refuses not to. Serena's insistence on sounding despite the attacks that soon follow is a process of imagining, inventing, and living for a future where Black sound is not policed and punished.

As I continue to watch the match unfold, relief meets my mounting concern. Serena does not get defeated. As soon as the trembling grunt comes, it quickly escapes and Serena, back in position, finds the precise and rhythmic sound that she had momentarily lost. It is now Azarenka who seems unsure of herself, as Serena's grunt roars louder and louder, building into a crescendo of elation as the tennis ball slips past Azarenka. The grunt reverberates louder as Serena erupts into an elongated and sustained yell; she pumps her fist in victory at defeating Azarenka in the tennis match. In her act of sonic reverberation, Serena asserts not only her dominance within tennis, but calls for the viewers to listen to how Black women sound themselves into being.

I follow suit of many scholars of Black women's popular music—among them, Farah Griffin, Angela Davis, Daphne Brooks, and Emily Lordi—who examine how Black women musicians wield their sound to their own sociopolitical ends. The "intellectual revolution in Black feminist sound" that these thinkers contribute to is invested in understanding how Black women use sound to rip through the white noise, as Daphne Brooks might say.[5] Serena's Black feminist sonic practice insists that we listen deeply to the cultural work that Black women do in the popular domain.

These "Black feminist speech acts" are articulated by Brooks as serving a larger Black feminist project of "the ways in which said [sonic] practices forecast and execute the viability and potentiality of Black life."[6] Taking inspiration from the litany of aforementioned Black feminist sound scholars, it is through the framework of Black feminist sound in which I orient my analysis of Serena, reading the ways that sound becomes a Black feminist strategy by which Serena (re)claims her own body and voice on the tennis court. For Serena, the grunt becomes one way for her to invest in her own epistemologies—epistemologies that, in turn, do not require the acceptance nor recognition of whiteness. The energy behind Serena's grunt is unique, even though she is not the only tennis player that grunts in the game.

The History of the Grunt

The history of the grunt in tennis is imprecise, with multiple stakeholders situating the phenomenon's entrance into the game roughly around the 1960s. A 1962 *Sports Illustrated* article, "Rod Rockets into Orbit," supports this claim when the journalist referred to tennis newcomer

Vicki Palmer by the name "The Grunter."[7] This nickname continued to follow Palmer, and when asked about her grunt in an interview with *Slate* journalist Josh Levin in 2011, Palmer said that her grunt was a breathing technique for when she hit the ball.[8] Despite the frequency of Palmer's grunt it didn't evoke the controversy it has today; in fact, her fellow competitor—hall of famer Nancy Richey—echoes Palmer's early statement about her grunt, stating that it seemed to "help with [Palmer's] timing," and was not as loud as contemporary players' grunts.[9] It was not until the 1990s that grunting became an increasing staple of tennis players with white Yugoslavian tennis player Monica Seles being the most highly regulated and stigmatized for her grunt. Seles' grunt famously led the International Tennis Federation to place a machine that measured the decibel levels of her grunt when she played. Notably, the backlash that Seles' faced for her grunt illuminated how the regulation of grunting is gendered, as male tennis players such as Jimmy Conners rarely faced criticism for his grunting during matches. Even former female tennis player Chris Evert has sided with keeping grunting out of women's tennis arguing that grunting is a "distraction" that "throws off guard the [opposing] players."[10] By contrast, Serena Williams credits Seles for her own grunt, noting that Seles "was a role model."[11]

Despite the conscious connection that Serena makes with Seles and her grunt, her aurality is separated by one notable fact—the body in which the grunt is expelled from. As sound studies scholar Nina Sun Eidsheim reminds us, "vocal choices are based on the vocalizer's position within the collective rather than arising solely as individual expression."[12] Eidsheim's astute observation that sound is impacted by the perspectives and socialization of the communities in which one sits makes visible the way that race and its intersections with gender comes to matter in *how* one hears. Although sound can and does operate as a control mechanism, and one must always be aware of these dimensions, I want to focus on how the grunt becomes a space where Black women, and specifically how Serena rebels from dominant prescriptions of what Black women's bodies sounds like.

Serena's grunt is what performance scholar Alexandra T. Vasquez would call a "vocal detail," a detail that she also locates in the grunt of Cuban musician Perez Prado.[13] In Vasquez's examination of Prado's grunt, she argues that the property and power of the grunt lies in its unknowability and inability to be contained.[14] Thus, Vasquez deftly illustrates how the grunt itself ruptures the American soundscape and requires that scholars approach it in ways that do not stifle its fluidity; the grunt refuses to be held or to stay around long enough for others to grasp it. I contend that these characteristics render the grunt a space of profound theorization for Black performance. Keeping this in mind, I follow Vasquez's pathway for thinking through the grunt with a critical difference: I trace it not through music, but through the athletic body. I examine Serena's grunt through its appearance in her cultural production, specifically her endorsement commercials.

Sounding Black Life

In August 2018, Serena Williams posted a new Nike commercial on her personal Instagram profile: a one-minute video blending archival footage of her being trained by her father as a child and footage of her playing matches at multiple US Opens.[15] This commercial, a part of the Nike campaign "Voice of Belief," was billed as a homage to her return to the US Open after giving birth to her daughter Olympia in 2017. The commercial builds upon Serena's frequently revisited origin story of growing up in Compton, California, where her father Richard Williams trained her and her sister, Venus, to become tennis champions.[16] The short film begins in the past, with grainy footage of a young Serena practicing her serve. In between her father's instructions, he tells her to imagine that she is "at the U.S. Open." Acknowledging this imagination work as necessary, a young Serena nods along with her father and throws the tennis ball up to serve. Just as the serve is about to be completed by a young Serena, the commercial cuts to an older Serena hitting the ball as she lets out a ferocious grunt. Among her father's consistent instructions, the commercial travels through various US Open matches as viewers watch Serena serve and her subsequent celebration of her scoring points, while also briefly returning to the archival footage of a young Serena practicing. As her father's words of encouragement and coaching pick up pace, footage of Serena hitting the ball with her racket is shown in rapid succession while she repeatedly grunts. The commercial culminates back at the Compton practice court with a young Serena and her father replaying the footage from the beginning of the commercial. This time, a young Serena completes the serve with a grunt as the screen goes black with the following words: "It's only crazy until you do it. Just do it."

Serena's representation in this commercial, both the archival footage of her practicing and the ideal outcome of playing at the US Open, challenges the oft-assumed belief that Black athletes are naturally athletic and do not need to train as hard as their counterparts. More specifically, Nike, alongside Serena, dispels the idea that the labor required to capture the athletic success that Serena has gained is innate, underscored by the persistent coaching that is illustrated through her father's voiceover throughout the duration of the commercial alongside her practicing. The persistent and deliberate usage of footage where Serena can be heard grunting compels the viewer to listen to the strength, power, and effort that Serena places behind her racket. The voiceover of Richard Williams coaching Serena—interspersed throughout the commercial—earns a privileged position within it. Ultimately, it is *his* imagination and *his* words that inspire a young Serena to believe and work toward her goal of playing at the US Open. Even the naming of the commercial spot "Voice of Belief" solidifies the importance of not only the action of doing, but also centralizes the voice to enact futures that may not be able to be seen.

Notably, while Serena is visually represented in both childhood and adulthood, any replies or words spoken by her are absent; rather, it is her first coach and father that must envision this possibility for her through his words of encouragement and coaching. While his aurality serves a temporary escape from the scopic regimes of white supremacy at the root of tennis—perhaps even activating her own enactment of futurity—Nike posits her father as the driving force behind her success, even as the commercial is visually inundated with her laboring body both at practice and during her matches at the US Open.[17] Though the primacy of his voice is central to the commercial and can lead to easy disavowal of Serena's own sonic participation, I want to offer that we listen closely to how Serena's grunt is reframed and strategically used to signal to the energy that it takes to pursue and enact visions of the future.

The subtext of the grunt within the commercial, I argue, goes beyond merely illustrating the external work of the body, but also signals to the internal work of breathing. Specifically, the grunt serves as the lifeblood of the commercial; it is Serena's grunting that punctures the footage, moving us in and out of her athletic life similar to the breath. This repetition of the grunt requires the breath to be expelled and centers what the performer is doing, what Black dance theorist Thomas DeFrantz might call "action born of breath."[18] In other words, the grunt emerges through living bodies in and across time and space. Breathing has a particular resonance with Black people's experiences with anti-blackness, from enslavement to environmental racism to Eric Garner and George Floyd's pleas of "I can't breathe."[19] These soundscapes are not new; they resonate across geographies and temporalities, circulating through the soundwaves of our present. To these points, our contemporary listening patterns are never situated only in the present, but are entangled with the auditory imaginations of the past.[20]

Nonetheless, these sonic perceptions of sounds and Black breath do not go unchallenged, as Ashon T. Crawley argues in *Blackpentecostal Breath: An Aesthetics of Possibility.* Breath has been a vital tool of resistance for those in the African diaspora. Crawley situates the breath as critique, as a "disruption with [and of] normative conceptions."[21] Linking the physicality of breathing to what he calls "otherwise possibilities" that can name and depict "things existing other than what is given, what is known,"[22] Crawley situates breathing as disrupting the normative ways of listening. Crawley's work is instructive, not only for his attention to breathing as a sonic practice, but for situating breathing itself as a performative that refuses the disposability of Black life.[23] Thus, Serena's grunting, both when she is competing and in the commercial, insists on Black aliveness.

Breathing also has personal resonance for Serena. In 2017, when undergoing an emergency cesarean section (C-Section) after her heart rate dropped too low during contractions, Serena complained of feeling short of breath. Previously, having suffered from blood clots in the past and knowing that any operation increased her risk of developing blood clots, Serena told her doctors (who at first dismissed her after an ultrasound cleared her) that they needed to order a CT scan of her lungs. Obliging with Serena's request, her medical team discovered a pulmonary embolism in her lung. Serena's literal inability to breathe, a life-threatening situation that stemmed from both unanticipated medical complications as well as the anti-blackness and gender discrimination that Black mothers face when giving birth, violently collided to expose the persistent push for Black people to be able to breathe. Ushering in new breath through her daughter Olympia while trying to maintain her own ability to breathe, Serena illuminates the conundrum of her own hypervisibility. On one end, her celebrity garners her a lot of attention and the resources necessary to stay alive, while simultaneously—despite being a world-class tennis champion—she was ignored. In this case, her celebrity did not aid her; to a certain extent, she was invisible and unheard. Quite literally, her impetus to sound off and insist on action—moments of disrupting the status quo—was wielded at this moment as she demanded that she be heard, and it saved her life. I offer this aside to exemplify the real stakes of the (Black) breath, and the ways that Serena's grunting and vocal outbursts produce distinct sonic vocabularies of Black life that persist even within the structure of anti-Black violence. But as Serena's grunt illuminates, it is not only what structures attempt to limit the boundaries of Black life, but how Black people respond through sound. Black aurality can both be seen and heard outside of racist epistemologies that claim that Black sound is merely noise that needs to be silenced.[24]

In tracing alternative soundscapes, I situate the professional athlete as a performer to animate how Black celebrity athletes adopt and incorporate the practices of performance as a means to disrupt and challenge the varying discourses that surround their corporeal presence in the public sphere. As Nicole Fleetwood contends, sports "focuse[s] our attention on the performance of the body"; therefore, an emphasis on the connections between sports and performance prompts one to consider how both cultural terrains produce ideas around Black embodiment.[25] Serena's illustrious career shows that sports are a highly contested and complex field that sustain and mobilize certain narratives about Black women's bodies. When read through the lens of performance, Black women athletes' enactments (both visually and sonically) are understood as a critical source of self-making.

Serena's vocality magnifies how resistance registers on a sonic level. In other words, Serena's commitment to (and persistence of) sonically responding to her detractors is an investment in her own desire and right to be fully acknowledged and established within the public sphere of her choosing. Through her sonic responses, Serena challenges, questions, and rejects the racist, sexist, and classist ideologies within the sports world at-large, and the world of tennis in particular. Accordingly, I contend that the (hyper)visibility that Serena has in tennis and beyond is directly correlated to her athletic skill and stands in direct opposition to what the cultural gatekeepers of tennis desire, which is her *in*visibility. The issue that Serena's presence poses to tennis is not simply that she is competing at a professional level, but the fact that she was never "supposed to" dominate tennis in the way she does, to win as much as she does, to be the face of tennis for over a decade, and to vocalize anything besides gratitude for even being *allowed* to compete. I recognize the power that is waged against Serena by her detractors so that her presence within tennis is seen as out of place. Nonetheless, I contend that while Serena is shaped by her surrounding soundscapes, she strategically intervenes in them through her sonic praxis.

Serena Williams uses the sound of her voice and/or grunt to remake the boundaries of her present, insisting that tennis and sports at large readjust their frames to future "that hasn't yet happened but must."[26] In her Black feminist sonic performances, she refuses to be withheld within dominant discursive production and devises her worlds based in her own self-definition. It is noteworthy that Serena has never shied away from the way that race nor gender influences her treatment on and off the tennis courts; she has been vocal about it at every stage of her career. Serena Williams asks us to consider the presumably deviant sonic performances as a site of possibility, even if these moments are fleeting.

Notes

1 Nina Sun Eidsheim, *The Race of Sound: Listening, Timbre, and Vocality in African American Music* (Durham: Duke University Press Books, 2019), 2.
2 Fred Moten, *In The Break: The Aesthetics of the Black Radical Tradition* (Minneapolis: University of Minnesota Press, 2003), 1.
3 Ibid., 14.
4 Ibid., 9.
5 Daphne A. Brooks, *Liner Notes for the Revolution: The Intellectual Life of Black Feminist Sound* (Cambridge, MA: Belknap Press: An Imprint of Harvard University Press, 2021), 9.
6 Ibid., 3.
7 "Rod Rockets into Orbit," *Sports Illustrated*, August 27, 1962, 51.
8 Josh Levin, "Tennis: An Aural History," *Slate*, accessed September 14, 2011, http://www.slate.com/articles/sports/sports_nut/2011/09/tennis_an_aural_history.html
9 Ibid.
10 "Chris Evert: Women's 'grunting' Getting out of Hand," *ESPN.Com*, accessed December 11, 2020, https://www.espn.com/sports/tennis/news/story?id=4293867
11 Darren Rovell, "Top Tennis Stars Have to Do the Grunt Work," *ESPN.Com*, accessed August 30, 2005, https://www.espn.com/sports/tennis/usopen05/columns/story?columnist=rovell_darren&id=2147218

12 Eidsheim, *The Race of Sound*, 11.

13 Vasquez focuses is less on theorizing the grunt, and more to how the grunt has a performative afterlife in other mediums such as literary lexicons.

14 Alexandra T. Vazquez, *Listening in Detail: Performances of Cuban Music*, Illustrated edition (Durham: Duke University Press Books, 2013), 165.

15 "Voice of Belief Feat. Serena Williams—Nike News," accessed December 11, 2020, https://news.nike.com/featured_video/voice-of-belief-serena-williams-just-do-it-film

16 Tim Adams, "Venus and Serena: How the 'ghetto Cinderellas' Swept All before Them | Tim Adams," *The Guardian*, accessed June 15, 2013, sec. Sport, https://www.theguardian.com/sport/blog/2013/jun/15/venus-serena-williams-film

17 This can also be argued of the recent film, *King Richard*, executive produced by Venus and Serena Williams. Recently, the choice to focus the film on Richard Williams has led to a debate on social media sites such as *Twitter* for the film's focus on Richard. For me, the film gives a nuanced portrayal of Richard's vision and pitfalls in assisting his daughter's tennis success, while also highlighting their mother's own labor in their tennis success. Nonetheless, I do think the respect of women athletes is often dictated by the approval or connection with a male coach or male professional athlete that is asked to cosign their athletic greatness.

18 Thomas F. DeFrantz and Anita Gonzalez, eds., *Black Performance Theory*, Illustrated edition (Durham and London: Duke University Press Books, 2014), 6.

19 Maanvi Singh, "George Floyd Told Officers 'I Can't Breathe' More Than 20 Times, Transcripts Show," *The Guardian*, accessed July 9, 2020, sec. US news, https://www.theguardian.com/us-news/2020/jul/08/george-floyd-police-killing-transcript-i-cant-breathe

20 Ibid., 1.

21 Ashon T. Crawley, *Blackpentecostal Breath: The Aesthetics of Possibility* (New York: American Literatures Initiative, 2016), 41.

22 Ibid., 24.

23 Ibid., 1.

24 Of critical importance to my own project is how Stoever privileges Black thinkers and artists in listening and the productions of sound,

particularly attentive to the ways they mobilize sound "as a critical modality through which subjects (re)produce, apprehend, and resists imposed racial identities and structures of racist violence." (4) In so doing, Stoever makes clear that white listening has created misunderstanding of blackness and that Black people have a long history of employing sound as a medium and process to intervene in this racialization.

25 Nicole R. Fleetwood, *On Racial Icons: Blackness and the Public Imagination* (New Brunswick, NJ: Rutgers University Press, 2015), 110.

26 Tina M. Campt, *Listening to Images* (Durham: Duke University Press Books, 2017), 34.

11

Black Squares, White Faces: Cancel Culture and Protest in the Age of Digital Blackface

Aviva Helena Neff

Over the past decade, the function of social media platforms has developed from photo sharing and diary-like status updates into a site for resistance and community organization. In 2013, the Black Lives Matter movement grew into an international call for change on Twitter and over the summer of 2020, Facebook and Instagram transformed into spaces for rapid communication and cultural discourse, while TikTok was co-opted by youth movements to expose racists and homophobes. Despite this political progressivism, beneath the countless memes, songs, and dances lurks the dark underside of viral internet transmission: videos and images of police brutality and anti-Black racism. Galvanized by a tumultuous year, in 2020, a groundswell of social justice accounts, digital protest movements, and live conversations about race in America have crossed billions of screens, inspiring likes, shares, retweets, and duets that complicate and personalize the struggle for equity, both in America and globally.

Conversely, social media have revealed uncomfortable fractures within movements for solidarity, such as the oft-criticized "Blackout Instagram" effort and the troubling memeification of Breonna Taylor's unlawful slaying by police officers.[1] Black-identified content creators across Facebook, Twitter, Instagram, and TikTok have founded movements for solidarity, expressing disdain with alleged "shadowbanning" and other silencing techniques, yet many protests have been met with unsatisfactory promises of change from social media platforms. As the intersections of Covid-19, a contentious election cycle, and calls for racial justice complicate the form and function of social media protests, a question emerges: can pro-Black movements succeed in spaces that are anti-Black by design?

This essay explores the ways in which acts of solidarity, such as content creation strikes, are complicated by systemic racism on social media platforms like Facebook, Twitter, TikTok, and Instagram. Relevant to this conversation are perceptions of celebrity culture's relationship with race and capital, as demonstrated by the popularity of "digital blackface," a form of linguistic and cultural appropriation that appears frequently across social media platforms. Coupled with the recent outing of "blackfishes," or non-Black people who appropriate Black language, aesthetics, and most disturbingly, assume Black identities, these contemporary forms of race-play have provoked conversations about professional inequality and representation, such as the 2019 cases of "activist" blackfishes Rachel Dolezal and Jessica Krug. Viewed holistically, social media have enhanced and troubled contemporary conversations regarding race and identity, furnishing forth a complex topography of accountability culture and virtual expressions of solidarity.

Black Squares, White Faces: Creating and Consuming

The rampant appropriation of Black culture on social media is underscored by the emergence of one of the first digital protests: the Black Lives Matter movement. Founded by Alicia Garza, Opal Tometi, and Patrisse Cullors on Twitter in 2013 after Trayvon Martin's murder, Black Lives Matter experienced a mainstream renaissance in the midst of the Covid-19 pandemic and the regime of former President Donald Trump. On May 25, 2020, while many Americans were hosting socially distant cook-outs, Christian Cooper, a Black birdwatcher, recorded his own racially charged harassment by a white stranger in Central Park.[2] The same day, George Floyd, an unarmed Black man, was deliberately suffocated in Minneapolis by a police officer.[3] In what will be remembered as an historic turning point, the consecutive slayings of unarmed Black Americans nudged previously unengaged institutions into action, with many corporations releasing statements, promising workplace reforms, and occasionally ousting old leadership. Unfortunately, these gestures of solidarity failed to take root without persistent pressure from grassroots organizations, much of which took place on social media. Nonetheless, many users of social media across social demographics felt that platforms such as Instagram and its parent company, Facebook, failed to take action against misinformation and white supremacist violence across the nation.[4]

On March 27, 2019, Facebook announced a new algorithm designed to target hate speech and harmful content after "conversations with members of civil society and academics who are experts in race relations [...]" identified that the social media giant had a hate-speech problem.[5] In 2020, amidst several months of tense hearings and criticisms of Zuckerberg's app, NBC News reported that "users on the Facebook-owned Instagram in the United States, whose activity on the app suggested they were Black, were about 50 percent more likely under the new rules to have their accounts automatically disabled by the moderation system than those whose activity indicated they were white[...]."[6] The algorithms designed to hold white-supremacists accountable ironically targeted those they were intended to protect, forcing employees and users to take matters into their own hands. In a rare public protest, for example, Facebook employees in Oakland staged a digital "walkout," circulating petitions, writing public blogposts about company culture, and condemned Facebook's tacit support of anti-Black language and imagery. One employee wrote that "Along with Black employees in the company, and all persons with a moral conscience, I am calling Mark to immediately take down the President's post advocating violence, murder, and imminent threat against Black people."[7]

Unfortunately, much like the now proverbial #BlackoutTuesday "black square" posts of 2020—in which social media users were encouraged to post black squares in lieu of photographs—Facebook's brief flirtation with equitable restructuring has yet to produce actionable change, calling into question the efficacy of pro-Black protest movements on structurally anti-Black platforms. White supremacists have openly organized across several social media platforms—namely Twitter, YouTube, and Facebook, but it wasn't until 2017's deadly "Unite the Right" rally that news outlets began to echo public cries for accountability across these internet giants.[8] Facebook's failure to take action against white supremacist groups while censoring Black activists demonstrates the possible limits of solidarity when using inherently racist platforms. Author and activist Ijeoma Olua, who had an anti-racism post removed by Facebook, reflects, "I write and speak about race in America because I already see this hate every day. It's the complicity of [Facebook,] one of the few platforms that people of color have to speak out about this hate that gets me."[9] The frequency with which Facebook (and many other platforms) censors Black content begs the question, can we protest systemic racism in a space that traffics in white supremacy?

Social media has steadily transformed our communication, consumer markets, and political spheres into performative spaces that quantify and financially reward popularity. Through "likes" and "shares," users are encouraged to grow their follower count, with many platforms offering users the ability to monitor the "engagement" of their posts, which include a spectrum of users across age, location, and gender. A blue check-mark next to a social media handle previously signaled that the user belonged to an elite echelon of "verified" users, those who were experts in their field, or a celebrity whose account was "real." On Twitter and Instagram, verification can be earned in a roundabout way—those who generate more clicks, leading to more engagements with advertisements, are eligible for the coveted "blue check" status based on their perceived popularity by the app.[10] TikTok allows users who demonstrate significant follower growth (+500–2000 a day) to apply for verification, regardless of a creator's offline celebrity status.[11] By amassing a small army of "influencers" who are paid to create content and advertise products, TikTok has become a titan in setting fashion, lifestyle, and political trends, which are fed to both users and laypeople alike. In other words, creating more social media celebrities, or influencers, is profitable both for the influencer and the app.

This process has not proven to be work equitably for non-white users. In a 2020 *Wired* article, TikTok rapper Brianna Blackmon reflected on her experience as a Black artist generating content on the cusp of civil unrest:

> Isn't this funny—TikTok doesn't silence Black creators?" she says in a mocking tone. "Then why did they take my sound down from my video, from my pro-Black rap that went viral yesterday? I wonder." It was almost too absurd. Blackmon made a video protesting censorship—and was censored. Is this what it meant to be Black and unapologetic on TikTok?[12]

Blackmon, who creates free-style raps for her 500,000 followers, engaged in one of TikTok's early Black creator-driven protest movements by doing what she loves—rapping. Blackmon's lyrics stated: "Black creators on this app have had enough, so we switched our pictures put our fists up." Soon after her video gained traction, Blackmon's newest viral protest hit was deemed "unfit for community standards" by TikTok, further exacerbating tensions between Black influencers and the applications that benefit from their labor and ingenuity.[13] Blackmon's video was an expression of solidarity, synthesizing a protest movement founded by actress and Influencer Lex Scott in May 2020 in order to call out TikTok algorithms for allegedly favoring white creators.[14] Users changed profile pictures, posted videos expressing evidence of "shadowbanning," a silent punishment that TikTok has fervently denied, and cited TikTok's troubling history of suppressing queer, disabled, and fat content creators.[15]

On June 2, 2020, TikTok released a statement acknowledging the May protest and promising action items designed to "create a supportive environment for the Black community and everyone across the world."[16] Despite pledging to create a more equitable community for Black creators, applications such as TikTok have yet to discover an effective mitigation effort where user bias is concerned.

According to a "social strategy" report from tech company Hootsuite, "The TikTok algorithm is a recommendation system that determines which videos will appear on your For You page. No two users will see the same videos on their For You page, and the videos you see might change over time based on your viewing preferences and even your current state of mind."[17] Per TikTok's algorithm, users who tend to engage more with white creators are less likely to see Black accounts populated into their home page, even when white creators are re-presenting, or "dueting" (a side-by-side response video to an original work) with Black creators. TikTok rewards users who consume videos with a finely tuned algorithm, ensuring that with each video that is viewed, several more that correspond with a topic or specific creator are shuffled into a user's queue.

In *Renegades: Digital Dance Cultures from Dubsmash to TikTok*, author Trevor Buffone describes the emergence of Dubsmash (TikTok's New York-based predecessor) and the racial undertones that divide the two apps. According to Buffone, Dubsmash was the original stomping ground for many Black created viral dance hits that were copied by white TikTok users.[18] Dance challenges such as "Renegade," and "Savage," created by Black teenage dancers Jalaiah Harmon and Keara Wilson, offer an exchange of embodiment designed to go viral, but the virality of Dubsmash and TikTok allows the embodied act of dance to exist independently of the body that created it. Buffone writes,

> But as Renegade helped propel the careers of [white influencers] K-Camp and [Charlie] D'Amelio and drive up TikTok's popularity with Gen Z, little changed for Harmon. She had created the iconic viral dance; the world had "discovered" her, yet no one knew that she was the original Renegade [...] The more popular the dance, the further it gets away from its creator, and, thus, the more difficult it is to track.[19]

Virality on TikTok fosters a system of seemingly deracialized simulacra, as it is desirable for an account to go viral, spawning endless copies of the original, however, increasing popularity beckons an inverse reaction, a decay in "authenticity" and the removal of Black creators from choreography, as the impersonation takes on a life of its own, existing as a set of rote movements performed by anyone with a phone, rather than the original embodied gestures of cultural signifiers. Thus, the videos of dance challenges with the highest viewer count often come from popular influencers, who are more likely to be white, due to algorithmic bias. Social media platforms crave and commodify Black content, yet Black creators are often sidelined in favor of white bodies "performing" Blackness. Similar to the continuing debate over whether non-Black people mimicking Black dance, hairstyles, and speech idioms are a demonstrating appropriation or appreciation, viral videos and memes beg a similar question: when and how do these acts shift from the virtual realm of "digital blackface," to literal acts of "blackfishing?"

A School of Blackfish: Dolezal and Krug

Published the same year that Twitter was founded, Joshua Lumpkin Green's *Digital Blackface: The Repackaging of the Black Masculine Image* (2006) introduced the term "digital blackface" to describe both the use of Black avatars in video games such as "Grand Theft Auto: San Andreas," and their impact on perceptions of Black masculinity.[20] Fifteen years later, "digital blackface" now encompasses the act of performing Blackness through the appropriation of colloquial AAVE, the use of Black emojis, and reaction gifs, for the purpose of social media "clout." On social media, those who engage in digital blackface have enjoyed financial success rather than negative consequences, signaling that social media audiences approve of Black culture when it is re-inscribed on white bodies. In recent years, digital blackface has made the uncomfortable jump from virtual spheres to social and professional culture, conjuring memories of blackface minstrelsy, through what is often deemed “blackfishing.”

In 2014, Rachel Dolezal won an election for president of the National Association for the Advancement of Colored People (NAACP) in Spokane, Washington. She had plans to revitalize the chapter, aided by her experience lecturing at Eastern Washington University, where she taught classes in the Africana Education program.[21] Dolezal claimed to have overcome her fair share of adversity, from her humble upbringing to several well-documented experiences with discrimination—a noose placed on her porch, a hate mail package delivered to her NAACP post office box, and a Swastika inscribed on the door of her previous place of employment.[22] Dolezal’s “street cred” as a Black woman went beyond her teaching and activism, for she prided herself on her ability to braid hair, a skill she claims to have honed over the course of 20 years.[23] Dolezal felt poised to bring her experience as a “Black” artist, activist, and scholar into conversations about race in the Pacific Northwest. The problem? Rachel Dolezal is a white woman.

According to her brother, Dolezal began using Black hair products, tanning lotion, and modifying her biography to claim a Black identity as early as 2009.[24] Warning her brother not to “blow her cover,” Dolezal successfully utilized an invented history of racist trauma, poverty, and ability to perform Black cultural gestures such as hair braiding to claim an invented Black identity.[25] Social media users were swift to pass judgement; “Black Twitter” reacted with disgust, mirth, and disbelief at photographs of Dolezal’s bronzer-laden cheeks and tight box-braids, which were designed to curate a “racially ambiguous” appearance. Dolezal lost her teaching job, her NAACP presidency, and her personal reputation, due to so-called social media “cancel culture,” which occurs when users turn en-masse against an individual to register their disapproval of the person. Ironically, the permanence of Dolezal’s “cancellation” is disputed by her media legacy: a Netflix documentary, countless interviews in print and electronic media, and an online channel where she posts her braiding tutorials. Despite the internet solidarity that brought attention to her story, Dolezal was rescued by capitalist interveners such as Netflix and *The Today Show*. Although she may never teach or lead a social justice organization again, Dolezal has neither renounced nor apologized for her claims of Blackness, nor has she performed any sort of reparations or given any public accountability for her actions, demonstrating that "cancel culture" and accountability are conflicting premises.

As the tumultuous summer of 2020 drew to a close, Jessica "La Bombalera" Krug, a Fulbright scholar and Associate Professor at George Washington University, washed the burnt cork off her face and revealed herself to be a white woman posing as an Afro-Latina. Having made a career identifying as a Bronx-raised Afro-Boricua scholar and dancer, Krug admitted to having "eschewed [her] lived experience as a white Jewish child in suburban Kansas City under various assumed identities within a Blackness that [she] had no right to claim[...]."[26] What was lost in the midst of Krug's dramatic "reveal" was her true motivation for dropping her disguise—several BIPOC junior scholars allegedly discovered her secret and were preparing to report her to the university.

Claiming to be of Algerian origin, Krug told a colleague that she was "the product of rape between her mother and father."[27] This demonstrates an uncomfortable alignment of Black male identity with sexual assault, and Black female identify with sexual victimhood, suggesting that an "authentic" Black experience is one of sexual trauma. Both Krug and Dolezal's constructed histories are rooted in intimate partner violence and experiences with racism.

In *Embodying Black Experience* (2010), Harvey Young examines the modality in which Black life is affected by "racializing projections," which often take the form of physical and emotional trauma. Young contends that these projections, though far from homogenous, are common throughout the Black American experience: " ... a repetition with a difference, exists among embodied black experiences."[28] Dolezal and Krug's race play extends beyond the realm of social media, taking shape as a fake, embodied form of racial projection. Through hair braiding, street activism, dance, and renaming, Krug and Dolezal offer an astonishing commitment to a lie, an observation that prompted the creation of the term "blackfishing," a reframing of the term "catfishing," coined by journalist Wanna Thompson in 2018.[29] Unlike those using digital blackface, "blackfishes" consciously move their appropriation beyond the constraints of the digital sphere through physically darkening one's skin, undergoing plastic surgery, or donning other socially constructed aesthetic impersonations of Blackness. Dolezal represents one of the first publicly revealed instances of blackfishing, a title that has since been bestowed on celebrity and layman Black impersonators alike.

Bodies Online: Celebrity, Race, and the Instagram Face

In *White Negroes: When Cornrows were in Vogue.. and Other Thoughts on Cultural Appropriation* (2019), Lauren Michele Jackson writes, "Leading discussions about appropriation have been limited to debates about freedom and choice, when everyone should be talking about power."[30] Many celebrities have been accused of applying a virtual form of "burnt cork" to their identities for cultural clout, intentionally muddying the waters of their authentic racial identity in order to increase their desirability through self-exoticism. Social media platforms are rife with blackfishes and digital blackface; some are popular influencers, while others are non-Black users appropriating queer Black language in their comments (i.e., "go awf, sis!" or "that's the tea!"), mocking malapropisms designed to trigger race-sensitive algorithms and increase views and "likes." In "Linguistic Profiling" (2006), John Baugh suggests that both the racial identity and socio-economic class of anonymous speakers are determined by their dialects and accents, producing some of the same "devastating consequences" as racial profiling.[31] The impact of "sounding Black" can be measured in inequitable fiscal, legal, and housing treatment, as noted by a 2015 National Fair Housing Alliance investigation.[32] Linguistic discrimination falls into a liminal space when applied to social media interactions, for white users "performing" Blackness often abandon their appropriation of African American

Vernacular English (AAVE) when they are not operating in the realm of Twitter, Instagram, or TikTok. An additional form of digital blackface occurs when white users write in supposed Black dialect.

The tangible consequences Black Americans face through linguistic discrimination make threats of "cancel culture" inconsequential, considering the ways in which white influencers and celebrities are rewarded for fostering a culturally and racially ambiguous identity. While overt digital blackface is illustrated by the aesthetic appropriation of Blackness, as evidenced by Dolezal, it operates more covertly in the case of celebrities such as the Kardashian-Jenner clan, who despite having been widely accused of cultural appropriation, have yet to experience "cancel culture" consequences. Kim Kardashian West's commercial success reflects an aesthetics of "absence" seen in American literature and entertainment since the advent of the trans-Atlantic slave trade. By removing Black people from Black culture and aesthetics, socially respected white bodies ironically performing Blackness become the dominant vessels promoting Black popular culture and reaping the financial benefits and colonizing cultural gestures not intended for non-Black consumption.

The pervasiveness of colorism within American society is partly to blame for Dolezal, Krug, Sharp, and other blackfishes' ability to "pass" for almost Black. In an article for *The New Yorker,* Lauren Michele Jackson writes: "But then there is another story that helps account for how someone who looks like Krug can blend in, so to speak: the story of how the lightest among us have a way of perpetuating their lightness over generations, prizing it as it is prized by the institutions they move within."[33] Jackson is primarily referring to academic institutions in her article, yet Krug and Dolezal demonstrate how easily colorism can be weaponized in order to infiltrate Black spaces and separate Black gestures from Black people. Singers such as Ariana Grande and Rita Ora are ethnically white and European, yet they often sport tanned skin, traditionally Black American hairstyles, and have appropriated AAVE both in their music and casual language. Much like the Kardashian-Jenners, both Grande and Ora have engaged in cosmetic surgery, while "earning" their Blackness by association with hip-hop and R&B artists such as Big Sean and Jay-Z. The problem with this celebrity race-play is the way in which surgical and aesthetic ambiguity empowers their desirability.

Here, we encounter another dimension of Harvey Young's "racialized projections," embodied by the perceived sexual availability of Black women. It is not the *whiteness* of Grande, Ora, and the Kardashian-Jenners that make them desirable, but the fetishization of their transgression of racial boundaries. Kardashian-West has deftly capitalized on her relationships with Black culture—from a salacious sex-tape with singer Ray-J in 2007, her current union with rapper Kanye West, and her trendsetting "reinvention" of French and box braids as "boxer braids" and "festival braids," Kardashian West (and the rest of her sisters) are experts at selling Blackness—sans Black women.

Searching for Solidarity: #BlackTikTokStrike

In March 2021, Jimmy Fallon brought white TikTok influencer Addison Rae on his talk show to perform eight TikTok dances, none of which were created by Rae.[34] Rae, who has since been given a production deal with Netflix, was quickly called out for her "cringey" and plagiaristic segment on Fallon, claiming it was "kind of hard to credit during the show."[35] Dissatisfied with the consistent exclusion of Black creators from viral content, and now, television and film, #BlackTikTokStrike was launched in tandem with the release of Megan Thee Stallion's 2021 hit single "Thot Shit." Users expecting the next viral choreography were met with videos such as Erick Louis', a Black TikTok creator who refused to dance, instead stating: "This app would be nothing without [Black] people."[36] The strike, which protests what Louis deemed "digital colonizing," seeks to expose the labor of Black creators, which algorithms and the public's adoration of white influencers made invisible.[37] While the strike has no definite end or structured demands, it forced non-Black users to attempt their own choreography, which was met with glee by Black Twitter, creating a new kind of solidarity—laughing at paltry, poorly executed choreography which lacked cultural gestures of Black identity.[38]

It is difficult to draw definitive lines around technological transmission, considering the ephemerality of social media, yet it is critical to wrestle with the shifting power dynamics of the virtual sphere. When our timelines and news feeds are flooded with hash-tagged names and blacked-out profile pictures, we drown ourselves in racial projections of pain and death. Mindlessly scrolling on apps such as Twitter and TikTok offers a breath of air, yet we are quickly submerged in a sea full of blackfishes, continually mouthing along to Black humor, creativity, and lyrics—emitting from white faces. While social media protests such as #BlackTikTokStrike may lack the efficacy of more centralized and structured protest movements, these acts of solidarity work to emphasize inequality among content creators. The true "renegades" of social media, Black youth, continue to push for change, one "like," comment, or retweet at a time.

Notes

1 Aja Romano, "Arrest the cops who killed Breonna Taylor": The Power and the Peril of a Catchphrase," *Vox*, 8/10/20, https://www.vox.com/21327268/breonna-taylor-say-her-name-meme-hashtag

2 David Betancourt, "Christian Cooper Hopes America Can Change. Because He's Not Going to," *The Washington Post*, 7/23/20, https://www.washingtonpost.com/arts-entertainment/2020/06/23/christian-cooper-central-park-birder-comics/

3 Justin Sondel, Knowles, Hannah, "George Floyd Died after Officers Didn't Step in. These Police Say They Did — and Paid a Price," *The Washington Post*, 6/13/2020, https://www.washingtonpost.com/nation/2020/06/10/police-culture-duty-to-intervene/

4 Olivia Solon, "Facebook Ignored Racial Bias Research, Employees Say," *NBC News*, 7/23/2020, https://www.nbcnews.com/tech/tech-news/facebook-management-ignored-internal-research-showing-racial-bias-current-former-n1234746

5 Ibid.

6 Ibid.

7 Sheera Frenkel, Mike Isaac, Cecilia Kang, and Gabriel J.X. Dance. "Facebook Employees Stage Virtual Walkout to Protest Trump Posts," *The New York Times*, 6/1/20. Web, accessed 12/15/20, https://www.nytimes.com/2020/06/01/technology/facebook-employee-protest-trump.html

8 Julia Carrie Wong, "White Nationalists Are Openly Operating on Facebook. The Company Won't Act," *The Guardian*, 11/ 21/2019, https://www.theguardian.com/technology/2019/nov/21/facebook-white-nationalists-ban-vdare-red-ice

9 Jessica Guynn, "Facebook Apologizes to Black Activist Who Was Censored for Calling Out Racism," *USA Today*, 8/3/2017, https://www.usatoday.com/story/tech/2017/08/03/facebook-ijeoma-oluo-hate-speech/537682001/

10 Twitter, "About Verified accounts:" "Activists, Organizers, and Other Influential Individuals: Outside the Professional Categories Defined above, People Who Are Using Twitter Effectively to Bring Awareness, Share Information, and Galvanize Community Members around a Cause, to Bring about Socioeconomic, Political, or Cultural Change, or to Otherwise Foster Community, May Be Verified," https://help.twitter.com/en/managing-your-account/about-twitter-verified-accounts

11 Rosalyn Boder, "How to Get Verified on TikTok," *SpinUp*, 4/12/21, https://spinnup.com/blog/how-to-get-verified-on-tiktok/

12 Jason Parham, "TikTok and the Evolution of Digital Blackface," *Wired Magazine*, 8/4/2020, https://www.wired.com/story/tiktok-evolution-digital-blackface/

13 Ibid.

14 Ibid.

15 Elena Botella, "TikTok Admits It Suppressed Videos by Disabled, Queer, and Fat Creators," *Slate*, 12/4/19, https://slate.com/technology/2019/12/tiktok-disabled-users-videos-suppressed.html

16 Vanessa Pappas, Kudzi Chikumbo, "A Message to Our Black Community," 9/2/20, https://newsroom.tiktok.com/en-us/a-message-to-our-black-community

17 Christina Newberry, "How the TikTok Algorithm Works in 2021 (and How to Work With It)," 8/23/21, https://blog.hootsuite.com/tiktok-algorithm/

18 Trevor Buffone, *Renegades: Digital Dance Cultures from Dubsmash to TikTok* (Oxford: Oxford University Press, 2021), 4.

19 Ibid.

20 Joshua Green, "Digital Blackface: The Repackaging of the Black Masculine Image," Electronic thesis, Miami University, 2006, https://etd.ohiolink.edu/

21 Allison Samuels, "Rachel Dolezal's True Lies," *Vanity Fair*, 7/19/15, https://www.vanityfair.com/news/2015/07/rachel-dolezal-new-interview-pictures-exclusive

22 Jeff Humphrey, "Questions Raised about NAACP Hate Mail Report," *KXLY*, and "Human Rights Advocate Finds Noose On Porch," *KXLY*, 6/10/2015.

23 Ashley Weatherford, "The Rachel Dolezal Documentary Gave Us the Hair Tutorial We Didn't Ask For," 4/27/18, https://www.thecut.com/2018/04/the-rachel-divide-netflix-rachel-dolezal-hair.html

24 Tasneem Nashrulla, "Rachel Dolezal's Brother Says She Warned: 'Don't Blow My Cover,'" *Buzzfeed News*, 6/12/2015, https://www.buzzfeednews.com/article/tasneemnashrulla/rachel-dolezals-brother-says-she-warned-dont-blow-my-cover#.ogrRQaZYy

25 Ibid.

26 Jessica A. Krug, "The Truth, and the Anti-Black Violence of My Lies," *Medium*, 10/3/20, https://medium.com/@jessakrug/the-truth-and-the-anti-black-violence-of-my-lies-9a9621401f85

27 Lauren Michele Jackson, "The Layered Deceptions of Jessica Krug, the Black-Studies Professor Who Hid That She Is White," *The New Yorker*, 9/12/20, https://www.newyorker.com/culture/cultural-comment/the-layered-deceptions-of-jessica-krug-the-black-studies-professor-who-hid-that-she-is-white

28 Harvey Young, *Embodying Black Experience: Stillness, Critical Memory, and the Black Body* (Ann Arbor: University of Michigan Press, 2010), 5.

29 Wanna Thompson, Twitter, 11/28/20, https://twitter.com/WannasWorld/status/1059989652487069696

30 Lauren Michele Jackson, *When Cornrows Were in Vogue and Other Thoughts on Cultural Appropriation* (Boston: Beacon Press, 2019), 4.

31 John Baugh, "Linguistic Profiling," in *Black Linguistics: Language Society, and Politics in Africa and the Americas* (Oxford: Routledge 2006), 35.

32 National Fair Housing Alliance, *Fair Housing: The Case for Fair Housing*, 2017 Fair Housing Trends Report, 2017, 35.

33 White Negros: When Cornrows Were in Vogue … And Other Thoughts on Cultural Appropriation.

34 Cache McClay, "Why Black TikTok Creators Have Gone on Strike," *BBC News*, 7/15/21, https://www.bbc.com/news/world-us-canada-57841055

35 Hannah Yasharoff, "Jimmy Fallon Addresses His TikTok Dance Segment with Addison Rae. Here's Why It Sparked Backlash," *USA Today*, 3/30/21, https://www.usatoday.com/story/entertainment/tv/2021/03/30/tiktok-dances-why-addison-rae-jimmy-fallon-clip-sparked-backlash/7058920002/

36 Sharon Pruitt-Young, "Black TikTok Creators Are on Strike to Protest a Lack of Credit for Their Work," *NPR*, 7/1/21, https://www.npr.org/2021/07/01/1011899328/black-tiktok-creators-are-on-strike-to-protest-a-lack-of-credit-for-their-work

37 Ibid.

38 Ibid.

In the Trenches: A Conversation with Willa J. Taylor

Khalid Y. Long

A prominent staple in the Chicago theatre community, Willa Taylor has developed educational programming for many theatrical institutions, including Arena Stage (Washington, DC), Lincoln Center for the Performing Arts (New York), and New Victory Theatre (New York). Currently, Taylor serves as the Walter Director of Education and Engagement at Goodman Theatre in Chicago, where she oversees all school-based education programs, including visiting musicals in elementary schools, school matinee series for high schools, and all professional development for educators and teachers. In her role, Taylor is directly responsible for collaborating with educators, school administrations, and community-based partners across the Chicagoland area to implement innovative learning experiences through arts-based programming. In addition to her role at the Goodman Theatre, Taylor is an adjunct professor at DePaul University.

Khalid Y. Long (KYL) The Goodman Theatre has a lengthy history of producing Black theatre.

Willa Taylor (WT) And not just in February.

KYL To be more specific, the Goodman Theatre hires Black directors as well as commission Black playwrights. What makes the Goodman Theatre different?

WT I think the first thing that makes us different is that Bob Falls, who's the artistic director, decided when he came that he did not want to be the lone voice of building a season, and so created an artistic collective. The majority of people in the artistic collective are directors and playwrights, including Harry Lennox, Regina Taylor, Chuck Smith, and Henry Godinez, to name some of the people, and certainly some of the voices of color in that collective. When any of those directors or playwrights have a project that they want to put up, it sort of comes into the season automatically. Chuck says, for example, "I want to direct August Wilson's *Gem of the Ocean*," it automatically goes into the season. I also think that we had an incredible director of new play development and literary manager, Tanya Palmer, who really understood the necessity for diverse forces on a stage and fought vociferously to have those voices get on our stage, for example, Suzan-Lori Parks' *Father Comes Home from the War*, that's a project that she really championed. I think the third thing is we've had relationships. The Goodman is almost 100 years old. We've had long-term relationships with people like August Wilson that have allowed the powers that be, and the institution connections and ways into seeing what theatre can be in a community like Chicago. We were the first theatre in the country to do all of August Wilson's work because August wanted the work at the Goodman. We pride ourselves on being able to try whenever we do a play to do the best production of that play that can be done. I think that commitment permeates the whole staff, especially when it's a new play or a writer or director who has not worked at the theatre before. In particular, when it's a BIPOC voice, we rally in a way to give as much support so it can be as successful as it possibly can. That reputation then attracts different voices and different directors to the theatre.

KYL I want to go back to something you said earlier about the folks in the collective and how they're able to champion certain plays to be produced. What it sounds like is that there is a level of trust among the collective and the leadership.

WT The collective, as a body, is unique. Membership into that club is not easy to get. There must be a level of trust developed, not about just the quality of the work that you can do, but your commitment to the vision and the values of the institution about what kind of work you want to do and what the message of that work is. That builds a level of trust between the institution and the members of the collective in a way that's different from just being an artistic associate.

KYL That is an example of solidarity.

WT It is also the collective's commitment to the institution. Not just to make it their artistic home, but to help make it a fully fleshed member of the community, not just the artistic community, but the community in which we live. Almost everybody teaches. Everybody who lives in Chicago does other work around the city. But there are no members of that collective that haven't contributed, for example, to the education programs or to an engagement piece, or to a fundraiser. They are part and parcel of the family. It's not just an artist who comes in to do some work, but they are fabric of the institution.

KYL Who do you think at the Goodman Theatre is subversive or rebellious in some way as a commercial institution?

WT I would say I'm probably the most subversive person on the staff. I tried to be. I hope that I was very clear when I came on staff that I was interested in working with teachers and working with students to get them to be fully engaged citizens of the world that have a voice and use that voice for social change. I wasn't interested in just trucking in a bunch of young Black students that make a good photo op. That was not what I was doing. If those young Black students didn't understand how to parse the world they were living in, I wasn't doing my job. I think they sort of nodded and said "yes" to that because it sounded good at the time. I don't think they really realized what that was going to mean in the long run. But what it has been in the long run is that I have had a certain level of leeway around that—the leeway that a lot of my colleagues in positions like mine have not had. I also think that the Goodman was ready for that in some ways. They didn't know that they were ready for that, but I think that they were ready for that.

KYL Your work goes outside of the theatre. You are in and amongst the communities in the Chicagoland area.

WT Which is the difficult part about going back to the office after the pandemic because most of my work doesn't happen in the office. Most of my work happens in community or happens in schools or happens in the neighborhoods. That is a very different model from everybody else on the staff other than the folks that are in our department. We all teach both in our programs and outside of our programs. We believe very strongly that you don't just enter a community and say, "hey, we're the Goodman. Here's what we can do for you." You must build a level of trust, and that means showing up in the community, maybe 150 times before you ever say anything about partnering. That kind of presence requires you to be in the space with people, not always expecting people to come to your space.

KYL And you're in spaces with people who may have never stepped foot in the Goodman Theatre or any other theatre.

WT That's right. I guess the subversive part of the question you just asked me is that I don't care. I don't care if they ever come to the Goodman. That's not the job. That, I think, was a very different, very difficult delineation for folks at the theatre to understand. The difference between audience engagement and the engagement that I do is not about going to the community so people will come see *School Girls*. That's not the work that we're talking about. If the people that I work with don't ever come to the theatre, that needs to be okay. What they need to understand is how theatre can help them develop the voices that they need to make change in their communities.

KYL What I hear you denoting is that the Goodman Theatre is a theatre that has resources and access, so why not put that to use.

WT We are, in many ways, big and large and old. We have a huge spotlight, so why not shine that spotlight away from ourselves and help community-based organizations, help individuals in the community who are really trying to make a difference on the ground where they are. How do we help them, and not always expect everybody to come downtown and be with us?

KYL It was never just about conventional schools either. For example, you've worked in detention homes and schools for students with behavioral problems.

WT I was really lucky as a kid. I had a family that believed in education and believed in the arts, and I got a lot of exposure. But I had a lot of friends who didn't get that. I know that a lot of why I was happy in school, and did well, was not because my parents insisted that education was important, but because I was in band. Because I was in choir. Because I was in the extracurricular activities, the artistic extracurricular activities, because that's where I found my place. I was a great student in English. I was not a good student in math and science. But I tried because if I didn't do well in class, Mr. Marks wouldn't allow me to march with the band on Friday night football games. That artistic effort was my academic motivation. I want every student to have that.

KYL Who are some of the Black theatre artists today you believe are rebellious?

WT Christina Anderson—both in form and function. That voice, I think, is singular and unique. Kristiana Rae Colón is really crafting work that speaks directly to the moment in which we live. She is probably, in terms of artistic voices, the closest to Nina Simone saying an artist's duty is to reflect the times in which they live. Jeremy O. Harris. Folks will be talking about his work for a long time. It's great to go to the theatre and have a good time, but if you're not talking about what you saw, like a couple of weeks later, then I don't think it did what it was supposed to. I have a t-shirt that says, "Art should disturb the comfortable and comfort the disturbed." I think that's true. That's what his work does. You cannot sit and not examine some part of yourself when you watch his work. That's what makes people uncomfortable. Thomas Bradshaw, same thing. Robert O'Hara, same thing. You need to be disturbed when you walk out of that theatre after seeing the work. If you're not, I think they would be disappointed as playwrights. I think the other person who does that well, but more subtly is Ike Holter.

KYL What do you think the future of Black theatre and performance is? What are we looking for? What should we expect? What do we need to happen?

WT Let me just say, I am only speaking for me. Whenever a show gets to Broadway, whenever a show gets into a large regional theatre house, I am happy because of all the resources they can provide for a show, for that playwright, for those actors. But until we figure out a different funding model, for not-for-profit theatre, it disadvantages BIPOC theatres and Black theatres. Foundations will give money to Goodman to do Wilson's *Gem of the Ocean*, but they won't give it to Black Ensemble Theater (BET). They will give it to Steppenwolf or Long Wharf or to Roundabout in New York to do a new piece, but they won't give it to Definition Theatre Company, even though those companies are rooted and embedded in the community in a way that Goodman cannot be. That's problematic. Until that changes, the future is cloudy for Black theatre. We have to understand that the power of what we do is telling the stories of the people that live in those communities. I would hope that theatre generally, but especially Black theatre, moves more in the direction of the Public Works initiative at the Public Theatre where actors and a theatre company come in and embed themselves in a community and collect those stories, and work with those people in that community, as actors, as directors, as designers, as dramaturgs, as literary managers, as whatever is needed to put on a show. And put that show on for the community. That kind of work is as valued as the next Robert O'Hara premiere at the Public Theatre. I think Black theatre has an opportunity and a unique ability to do that more so than a Goodman or a Roundabout because Black theatre is rooted and lived in the Black community. Black Ensemble Theater is not downtown. Definition Theatre is not downtown. They are in the communities where people walk down the street to go to the theatre. If we can figure out how to make that kind of work as valuable. And unfortunately, what I mean when I say valuable is capitalism. As financially profitable and revenue generating as that other kind of work, then I don't think we have as bright a future as we could have.

Bibliography

11Alive, "Large Crowds Gathered Outside Ebenezer Baptist for John Lewis' Funeral," *YouTube*. Accessed July 30, 2020, https://www.youtube.com/watch?v=s8xxz6sLmFM&ab_channel=11Alive

"2019 boulevard des limites, boundaries." *Revolution They Wrote*. Accessed December 31, 2021. *A Public History of 35W*. University of Minnesota. https://35w.heritage.dash.umn.edu/

"About Us." *Revolution They Wrote*. Accessed December 31, 2021. https://revolutiontheywrote.com/about-us/

Adams, Tim. "Venus and Serena: How the 'Ghetto Cinderellas' Swept All before Them | Tim Adams." *The Guardian*. Accessed June 15, 2013, sec. Sport. https://www.theguardian.com/sport/blog/2013/jun/15/venus-serena-williams-film

Ahmed, Sara. "Orientations Matter." In *New Materialisms: Ontology, Agency, and Politics*, edited by Diana Coole and Samantha Frost, 234–57. Durham: Duke University Press, 2010.

Alexander, Michelle. *The New Jim Crow: Mass Incarceration in the Age of Colorblindness*. New York: The New Press, 2010.

Altheide, David L. "Media Hegemony: A Failure of Perspective." *Public Opinion Quarterly* 48, no. 2 (1984): 476–90. https://doi.org/10.1086/268844

Armstrong, Ann Elizabeth, and Joan Lipkin. "The Every 28 Hours Plays and after Orlando Networked, Rapid-Response, Collective Theatre Action—New Forms for a New Age." *Theatre Topics* 28, no. 2 (2018): 159–64.

Arnold, Wayne E. "Sarah Churchwell, Behold, America: A History of America First and the American Dream." *European Journal of American Studies*. Accessed September 23, 2020. https://journals.openedition.org/ejas/16324

Associated Press. "From Rep. John Lewis, Quotes in a Long Life of Activism," *Washington Post*. Accessed July 18, 2020, https://www.washingtonpost.com/national/from-rep-john-lewis-quotes-in-a-long-life-of-activism/2020/07/18/7ee684d8-c8b0-11ea-a825-8722004e4150_story.html

Badger, Emily. "Why Highways Have Become the Center for Civil Rights Protest." *The Washington Post*. Accessed July 13, 2016.

Bain, Kimberly. "On Black Breath." 2020. http://www.kimbain.com/

Banks, Daniel. "The Welcome Table: Casting for an Integrated Society." *Theatre Topics* 23, no. 1 (2013): 1–18. https://doi.org/10.1353/tt.2013.0011

Barone, Tom, and Elliot Eisner. *Arts Based Research*. Los Angeles: Sage, 2012.

Başar, Deniz. "söylenemeyenler." In Hevesle Beraberlik Arası Bir Şey - *Bir Kritik Kolektif Kitabı [Between Enthusiasm and Cooperation - A Critical Collective Book]*, compiled by Eylem Ejder and Handan Salta, 122–34. İstanbul, Turkey: Mitos Boyut Yayınları, October 2021.

Baudrillard, Jean. *America*. New York: Verso, 1989.

Baugh, John. "Linguistic Profiling." In *Black Linguistics: Language Society, and Politics in Africa and the Americas*. Oxford: Routledge, 2006, 35.

Benson, France-Luce. *Detained*. Los Angeles, 2020.

Berger, John. Ways of Seeing. *Pelican Book*. London: British Broadcasting Corporation, 1972.

Betancourt, David. "Christian Cooper Hopes America Can Change. Because He's Not Going to," *The Washington Post*. Accessed July 23, 2020, https://www.washingtonpost.com/arts-entertainment/2020/06/23/christian-cooper-central-park-birder-comics/

"The BiG SiSSY Show – The Message." *Revolution They Wrote*. Accessed December 31, 2021. https://revolutiontheywrote.com/the-big-sissy-show-the-message/

Bioh, Jocelyn. *School Girls; or the African Mean Girls Play*. New York: Oberon Books Limited, 2020.

Blake, Bill. *Theatre & the Digital*. New York: Palgrave MacMillan, 2014.

Boder, Rosalyn. "How to Get Verified on TikTok," *SpinUp*. Accessed April 12, 2021, https://spinnup.com/blog/how-to-get-verified-on-tiktok/

Bodroghkozy, Anne. *Equal Time: Television and the Civil Rights Movement*. Baltimore: University of Illinois Press, 2012.

Botella, Elena. "TikTok Admits It Suppressed Videos by Disabled, Queer, and Fat Creators." *Slate*. Accessed December 4, 2019. https://slate.com/technology/2019/12/tiktok-disabled-users-videos-suppressed.html

Brady, Loretta L.C. "Performance Review: The White Card." *Texas Theatre Journal* 15 (Fall 2018): 88–90.

Brady, Loretta L.C. "Connected World, Connected Profession: Increased Recognition of Opportunities for Local and Global Engagement by

Psychologists in Postcrisis Communities." *Consulting Psychology Journal: Practice and Research* 71, no. 1 (2019): 47–62.

Brady, Loretta, and Suzanne Delle. "Beyond Streaming: Safe Discomfort." Traumaturgy Podcast (podcast). July 30, 2020. n.d. https://www.traumaturgypodcast.com/podcast-1/episode/3d2d74ab/beyond-streaming-safe-discomfort.

Brooks, Daphne A. *Bodies in Dissent: Spectacular Performances of Race and Freedom, 1850–1910*. Durham: Duke University Press, 2006.

Brooks, Daphne A. *Liner Notes for the Revolution: The Intellectual Life of Black Feminist Sound*. Cambridge, MA: Belknap Press: An Imprint of Harvard University Press, 2021.

brown, adrienne maree. *Emergent Strategy: Shaping Change, Changing Worlds*. Chico, CA: AK Press, 2017.

brown, adrienne maree. *Pleasure Activism*. Chico, CA: AK Press, 2019

Buffone, Trevor. *Renegades: Digital Dance Cultures from Dubsmash to TikTok*. Oxford: Oxford University Press, 2021, 4.

Burton, India Nicole. 2021. Language, Communication, and Power between BIPOC and PWIs in the American Theatre. September 25. Accessed September 27, 2021. https://www.notes.nnpn.org/post/language-communication-and-power-between-bipocs-and-pwis-in-the-american-theater

"Buxton Train." *Revolution They Wrote*. Accessed December 31, 2021. https://revolutiontheywrote.com/buxton-train/

callender, s. e. *ineffable. A Play in Process*. Montreal: Fine Arts Reading Room, 2019.

Campbell-Stephens, Rosemary. "Global Majority: Decolonizing the Language and Reframing the Conversation about Race," 2020. https://www.leedsbeckett.ac.uk/-/media/files/schools/school-of-education/final-leeds-beckett-1102-global-majority.pdf

Campt, Tina M. *Listening to Images*. Durham: Duke University Press Books, 2017.

Carruthers, Charlene. *Unapologetic: A Black, Queer, and Feminist Mandate for Radical Movements*. Boston: Beacon Press, 2018.

Champaïgne, Naïka. "Y'all Remember the Play I Was Part of 'Ineffable'?" *Instagram*. Accessed June 27, 2020. https://www.instagram.com/p/CB8_vDOHnbe/

Chernow, Ron. *Alexander Hamilton*. New York: Penguin Press, 2004.

Childress, Alice. *Trouble in Mind.* New York: Theatre Communications Group, 2022. https://revolutiontheywrote.com/2019-boulevard-des-limites-boundaries/

"Civil Rights Veteran on Why She Opposes Renaming the Edmund Pettus Bridge." *Here and Now. WBUR.org.* Accessed.August 13, 2020. https://www.wbur.org/hereandnow/2020/08/13/edmund-pettus-bridge-renaming

Clarke, Cheryl. "Lesbianism: An Act of Resistance." In *This Bridge Called My Back: Writings by Radical Women of Color*, edited by Cherrie Morega and Gloria Anzaldua, 126–35. Albany: Suny Press, 1995.

Clement, Olivia. "The Public to Bring Free Performances of Lynn Nottage's *Sweat* to the Midwest," *Playbill.* Accessed August 2, 2018, https://playbill.com/article/the-public-to-bring-free-performances-of-lynn-nottages-sweat-to-the-midwest

Clinton, Bill. "Remarks on Signing of NAFTA," *Presidential Speeches*, UVA Miller Center. December 8, 1993.

Collins, Patricia Hill. *Another Kind of Public Education: Race, Schools, the Media, and Democratic Possibilities.* Boston: Beacon Press, 2009.

Colón, Kristiana Rae. "At Freedom Square, the Revolution Lives in Brave Relationships." *Truthout.* August 7, 2016.

Considine, Allison. "This Is Reading, This Is Home." *American Theatre Magazine.* July 26, 2017.

Crawley, Ashon T. *Blackpentecostal Breath: The Aesthetics of Possibility.* New York: American Literatures Initiative, 2016.

Crawley, Ashon T. *Blackpentecostal Breath: The Aesthetics of Possibility.* New York: Fordham University Press, 2016.

"Crybaby." *Revolution They Wrote.* Accessed December 31, 2021. https://revolutiontheywrote.com/crybaby/

"Dark Red." *Revolution They Wrote.* Accessed December 31, 2021. https://revolutiontheywrote.com/dark-red/

DeFrantz, Thomas F., and Anita Gonzalez, eds. *Black Performance Theory.* Durham and London: Duke University Press Books, 2014.

DeGregory, Crystal. "Congressman John Lewis Remembered in Selma, Alabama with Carriage Ride across Edmund Pettus Bridge." *The Atlanta Voice.* Accessed July 26, 2020. https://www.theatlantavoice.com/articles/congressman-john-lewis-remembered-in-selma-alabama-with-carriage-ride-across-edmund-pettus-bridge/

Delaronde, Karonhí: io and Jordan Engel. "Montreal in Mohawk." *The Decolonial Atlas.* Accessed February 4, 2015. https://decolonialatlas.wordpress.com/2015/02/04/montreal-in-mohawk/

Delgado, Richard, and Jean Stefancic. *Critical Race Theory: An Introduction*. New York: NYU Press, 2017.

Derysh, Igor. "How Decades of Racist Policies and 'White Mob Violence' Heightened Tensions in Minneapolis." *Salon*. Accessed June 8, 2020. https://www.salon.com/2020/06/08/decades-of-racist-policies-and-white-mob-violence-sparked-minneapolis-unrest-after-floyd-murder/

Deveare Smith, Anna. 2021. "We Were the Last of the Nice Negro Girls." February 9. Accessed February 2021, 2021. https://www.theatlantic.com/magazine/archive/2021/03/the-last-of-the-nice-negro-girls/617786/

Diaz-Marcano, Nelson. *World Classic*. New York, 2017.

Dillard, Cynthia. "When the Ground is Black, the Ground Is Fertile: Exploring Endarkened Feminist Epistemology and Healing Methodologies in the Spirit." *Handbook of Critical and Indigenous Methodologies* (2008): 277–92. https://www.doi.org/10.4135/9781483385686

Dolan, Jill. "Performance, Utopia, and the 'Utopian Performative.'" *Theatre Journal* 53, no. 3 (2001): 455–79. http://www.jstor.org/stable/25068953

Douglass, Frederick. *Narrative of the Life of Frederick Douglass: An American Slave*. Oxford: Oxford University Press, 1999.

"Drag Version of 'Steel Magnolias' on Hold after Licensing Issue." Accessed June 15, 2022. https://www.wect.com/story/15118202/actors-in-drag-closes-the-curtain-on-wilmington-play/

Drury, Jackie Sibblies. *Fairview: A Play*. New York: Theatre Communications Group, 2019.

Du Bois, W. E. B. *The Souls of Black Folk*. Edited with an introduction and notes by Brent Hayes Edwards. Oxford: Oxford University Press, 2007.

Dunne, Carey. "'No More Stolen Sisters': 12,000-mile Ride to Highlight Missing Indigenous Women." *The Guardian*. Accessed June 7, 2019. https://www.theguardian.com/us-news/2019/jun/07/indigenous-women-missing-murdered-activists-ride-north-america

Eidsheim, Nina Sun. *The Race of Sound: Listening, Timbre, and Vocality in African American Music*. Durham: Duke University Press Books, 2019.

Eisenhower, Dwight D. *At Ease: Stories I Tell to Friends*. New York: Doubleday, 1967.

Elam, Harry Justin and David Krasner. *African-American Performance and Theater History a Critical Reader*. Oxford [England]: Oxford University Press, 2001.

Elam, Jr., Harry J. *The Past as Present in the Drama of August Wilson*. Ann Arbor: University of Michigan Press, 2006.

Elam, Jr., Harry J., and Douglas A. Jones, Jr., eds. *The Methuen Drama Book of Post-Black Plays*. London: Methuen Drama, 2013.

Ellis, Justin. "Minneapolis Had This Coming." *The Atlantic*. Accessed July 1, 2020. https://www.theatlantic.com/ideas/archive/2020/06/minneapolis-long-overdue-crisis/612826/

"Enough Is Enough Report: A 150 Year Performance Review of the Minneapolis Police Department." *MPD150*. 2017. https://www.mpd150.com/wp-content/themes/mpd150/assets/mpd150_report.pdf

ESPN.Com. n.d. "Chris Evert: Women's 'Grunting' Getting out of Hand." Accessed December 11, 2020. https://www.espn.com/sports/tennis/news/story?id=4293867

Faver, Catherine A. "Rights, Responsibility, and Relationship: Motivations for Women's Social Activism." *Affilia Journal of Women and Social Work* 16, no. 3 (August 2001): 314–36. quoted in Gouin, Rachel. "An Antiracist Feminist Analysis for the Study of Learning in Social Struggle." *Adult Education Quarterly 59*, no. 2 (2009): 158–75.

Fleetwood, Nicole R. *On Racial Icons: Blackness and the Public Imagination*. First edition. New Brunswick, NJ: Rutgers University Press, 2015.

Foster, Susan Leigh. "Choreographies of Protest." *Theatre Journal* 55, no. 3 (2003): 395–412.

Fraser, Nancy. "Rethinking the Public Sphere: A Contribution to the Critique of Existing Democracy." *Social Text*, no. 25/26 (1990).

Frenkel, Sheera, Mike Isaac, Cecilia Kang, and Gabriel J. X. Dance. "Facebook Employees Stage Virtual Walkout to Protest Trump Posts." *The New York Times*. 6/1/20. Web. Accessed December 15, 2020. https://www.nytimes.com/2020/06/01/technology/facebook-employee-protest-trump.html

Gadelha, Kaciano Barbosa. "Friendship, Affect and Capitalism." In *Friendship as Social Justice Activism: Critical Solidarities in a Global Perspective*, edited by Niharika Banerjea, Debanuj DasGupta, Rohit K. Dasgupta, and Jaime M. Grant, 9–20. London, New York, Calcutta: Seagull Books, 2018.

Glasgow, Kenneth. "Marching Backwards for Freedom." *Common Dreams*. Accessed March 12, 2018. https://www.commondreams.org/views/2018/03/12/marching-backwards-freedom.

Gouin, Rachel. "An Antiracist Feminist Analysis for the Study of Learning in Social Struggle." *Adult Education Quarterly* 59, no. 2 (2009): 158–75.

Gramsci, Antonio. *Selections from the Prison Notebooks*. Edited by Quintin Hoare and Geoffrey Nowell Smith. Reprint, 1989 edition. London: International Publishers Co, 1971.

Granston, Nicole. "Playwright & Oscar Winner Tarell Alvin McCraney on Why 'Choir Boy' Sings to Your Heart." *Blackfilm.com*. Accessed January 20, 2019. https://www.Blackfilm.com/read/2019/01/playwright-oscar-winner-tarell-alvin-mccraney-on-why-choir-boy-sings-to-your-heart/

Green, Joshua. "Digital Blackface: The Repackaging of the Black Masculine Image," Electronic thesis, Miami University, 2006, https://etd.ohiolink.edu/

Guynn, Jessica. "Facebook Apologizes to Black Activist Who Was Censored for Calling out Racism," *USA Today*. Accessed August 3, 2017, https://www.usatoday.com/story/tech/2017/08/03/facebook-ijeoma-oluo-hate-speech/537682001/

Guzzetta, Juliet. "Oratory and the Public Sphere: Hearing Italy through Narrative Theater." *Spaziofilosofico Italia*, no. 2 (2011): 201–8.

Harris, Aleshea. *What to Send Up When It Goes Down*. New York: Samuel French, 2019.

Harris, E. Lynn. *Invisible Life: A Novel*. New York: Anchor, 1994.

Harris, Jeremy O. "Slave Play Playscript." *American Theatre* (July/August 2019): 42–67.

Harris, Jeremy O. "People Say I Wrote Slave Play for White People." *The Guardian*. November 2019. Accessed August 29, 2021. https://www.theguardian.com/stage/2019/nov/06/jeremy-o-harris-slave-play-interview

Hartman, Saidiya V. *Scenes of Subjection: Terror, Slavery, and Self-making in Nineteenth-century America*. 1997. Print. Race and American Culture.

Hartman, Saidiya V. "Venus in Two Acts." *Small Axe* 12, no. 2 (2008): 1–14.

Herman, Judith. *Trauma and Recovery: The Aftermath of Violence—from Domestic Abuse to Political Terror*. New York: Basic Books, 1992.

Hill, Errol. *The Theater of Black Americans: A Collection of Critical Essays*. New York, NY: Applause, 1987.

Holdren, Sara. "Theatre Review: Contemporary Northern Prep and Southern Gothic," in *Choir Boy* and Holiday, Billie. "Strange Fruit." April 20, 1939.

Holdren, Sara. "Theatre Review: Contemporary Northern Prep and Southern Gothic, in Choir Boy and Blue Ridge," *Vulture*, January 8, 2019, https://www.vulture.com/2019/01/theater-reviews-choir-boy-and-blue-ridge.html.

Holnes, Darrel Alejandro. n.d. Writer, Performer, *Educator*. Accessed 2020. https://www.darrelholnes.com/

hooks, bell. "Performance Practice as a Site of Opposition." In *Let's Get It On: The Politics of Black Performance*, edited by Catherine Ugwu, 210–19. Seattle: Bay View Press, 1995.

hooks, bell. and Cornel West. *Breaking Bread: Insurgent Black Intellectual Life*. New York: Routledge, 2017.

hooks, bell and George Yancy. "bell hooks: Buddhism, the Beats and Loving Blackness." *Opinionator. The New York Times*. Last modified December 10, 2015. https://opinionator.blogs.nytimes.com/author/bell-hooks/

Hughes, Langston. "Let America Be America Again." In *The Collected Poems of Langston Hughes*. New York: Vintage, 1994.

Humphrey, Jeff. "Questions Raised about NAACP Hate Mail Report." *KXLY*, and "Human Rights Advocate Finds Noose On Porch," *KXLY*, 6/10/2015.

Inc, Crowdcast. "Understanding Critical Race Theory & Education with Dr. David Childs." *Crowdcast*. Accessed June 15, 2022. https://www.crowdcast.io/e/understanding-critical

Incampo, Theresa. *"But What If Instead We Imagine Black Life": Femininity, Performance, and the Black Lives Matter Movement*. ProQuest Dissertations and Theses, 2018.

Isherwood, Charles. "Hoping the Songs Lead Him to Freedom." *New York Times*. Accessed July 2, 2013. https://www.nytimes.com/2013/07/03/theater/reviews/in-tarell-mccraneys-choir-boy-spirituals-are-solace.html

Jackson, Lauren Michele. "The Layered Deceptions of Jessica Krug, the Black-Studies Professor Who Hid That She Is White," *The New Yorker*. Accessed September 12, 2020, https://www.newyorker.com/culture/cultural-comment/the-layered-deceptions-of-jessica-krug-the-black-studies-professor-who-hid-that-she-is-white

Jackson, Lauren Michele. *When Cornrows Were in Vogue and Other Thoughts on Cultural Appropriation*. Boston: Beacon Press, 2019.

Jacobs-Jenkins, Brandon. "What to Send Up When It Goes Down: A Black Gaze." *American Theatre*. April. Accessed August 29, 2021. https://www.americantheatre.org/2019/04/05/what-to-send-up-when-it-goes-down-a-black-gaze/

Jacobs, Harriet. *Incidents in the Life of a Slave Girl*. 1861. Accessed via Project Gutenberg, uploaded February 11, 2004, https://www.gutenberg.org/files/11030/11030-h/11030-h.htm

Jackson, Lauren Michele. *When Cornrows Were in Vogue and Other Thoughts on Cultural Appropriation*. Boston: Beacon Press, 2019, 4.

Jeff, Humphrey, "Questions raised about NAACP hate mail report," *KXLY*, and "Human Rights Advocate Finds Noose on Porch," *KXLY*, 6/10/2015.

Johnson, E. Patrick. *Appropriating Blackness: Performance and the Politics of Authenticity*. Durham: Duke University Press, 2003.

Johnson, E. Patrick. *Sweet Tea: Black Gay Men of the South*. Chapel Hill: University of North Carolina Press, 2011.

Johnson, James Weldon. "Preface." In *The Book of American Negro Spirituals*, edited by James Weldon Johnson and J. Rosamond Johnson. New York: Da Capo Press, 2002.

Johnston, Chloe and Coya Paz Brownrigg. *Ensemble-made Chicago: A Guide to Devised Theater*. Evanston: Northwestern University Press, 2019.

"Journey to Free." *Revolution They Wrote*. Accessed December 31, 2021. https://revolutiontheywrote.com/journey-to-free/

Jones, Kenneth and Okun Tema. *Dismantling Racism: A Workbook for Social Change Groups*. Portland: Peace Development Fund, 2001.

Kelley, Elleza. "'Follow the Tree Flowers:' Fugitive Mapping in *Beloved*." *Antipode* 53, no. 1, (January 2021): 181–99.

Krug, Jessica A. "The Truth, and the Anti-Black Violence of My Lies," *Medium*. Accessed October 3, 2020, https://medium.com/@jessakrug/the-truth-and-the-anti-black-violence-of-my-lies-9a9621401f85

Lacoste, Yves. "An Illustration of Geographical Warfare: Bombing Dikes on the Red River, North Vietnam." *Antipode* 5, no. 2 (May 1973): 1–13.

Lamont Hill, Marc. *Nobody: Casualties of America's War on the Vulnerable, from Ferguson to Flint and Beyond*. New York: Atria Paperback, 2016.

Landy, Robert and David Montgomery. *Theatre for Change: Education, Social Action, and Therapy*. New York: Palgrave Macmillan, 2012.

Lerman, Liz. 2022. Critical Response Process. https://lizlerman.com/critical-response-process/

Levin, Josh. 2011. "Tennis: An Aural History." *Slate*. Accessed September 14, 2011. http://www.slate.com/articles/sports/sports_nut/2011/09/tennis_an_aural_history.html

Lorde, Audre. 2007. "The Master's Tools Will Never Dismantle the Master's House." 1984. *Sister Outsider: Essays and Speeches*. Berkeley, CA: Crossing Press.

"Mā Ma." *Revolution They Wrote*. Accessed December 31, 2021. https://revolutiontheywrote.com/ma-ma/

MasterClass. "How to Cast a Film: Understanding the Casting Process—2022." Accessed June 15, 2022. https://www.masterclass.com/articles/how-to-cast-a-film

McClay, Cache. "Why Black TikTok Creators Have Gone on Strike," *BBC News*. Accessed July 15, 2021, https://www.bbc.com/news/world-us-canada-57841055

McCraney, Tarell Alvin. *Choir Boy*. New York: Theatre Communications Group, 2016.

McGinley, Paige A. *Staging the Blues: From Tent Shows to Tourism*. Durham: Duke University Press, 2014.

McKittrick, Katherine. *Demonic Grounds: Black Women and the Cartographies of Struggle*. Minneapolis: University of Minnesota Press, 2006.

McKittrick, Katherine and Clyde Woods, ed. *Black Geographies and the Politics of Place*. Toronto: Between the Lines Press, 2007.

Miranda, Lin-Manuel. *In the Heights*. New York: Theatre Communications Group, 2013.

Mohanty, Chandra Talpade. *Feminism without Borders: Decolonizing Theory, Practicing Solidarity*. Durham: Duke University Press, 2003, 4, quoted in Gouin, Rachel. "An Antiracist Feminist Analysis for the Study of Learning in Social Struggle." *Adult Education Quarterly* 59, no. 2 (2009): 158–75.

Mohler, Courtney Elkin, Christina McMahon, and David Román. "Three Readings of Reading, Pennsylvania: Approaching Lynn Nottage's *Sweat* and Douglas Carter Beane's *Shows for Days*." *Theatre Journal* 68, no. 1 (March 2016): 79–94.

Montilla, Altagarcia. "How White Supremacy Lives in Our Schools," *Medium*, 2020. https://medium.com/@altagraciamontilla/how-white-supremacy-lives-in-our-schools-e541c5b3355

Montilla, Altagarcia. 2021. AM Consulting. https://altagraciamontilla.com/

Moosavi, Marjan. "In Conversation with Deniz Başar: 'Wine & Halva'—A Play That Tests The Limits Of Friendship Within Canadian Institutional Racism (Part I)." *The Theatre Times*. Accessed August 22, 2020. thetheatretimes.com/in-conversation-with-deniz-basar-winehalva-a-play-that-tests-the-limits-of-friendship-within-canadian-institutional-racism-part-i/

Moosavi, Marjan. "In Conversation with Deniz Başar: 'Wine & Halva'—A Play That Tests the Limits of Friendship within Canadian Institutional Racism (Part II)." *The Theatre Times*. Accessed July 6, 2020. thetheatretimes.com/in-conversation-with-deniz-basar-winehalva-a-play-that-tests-the-limits-of-friendship-within-canadian-institutional-racism-part-i/

Morrison, Romi Ron. "Residual Black Data." Filmed at Eyeo Festival 2019. https://vimeo.com/354276852

Morrison, Toni. "The Site of Memory." In *The Source of Self Regard: Selected Essays, Speeches, and Meditation*, 233–45. New York: Knopf, 2019.

Moten, Fred. *In The Break: The Aesthetics of the Black Radical Tradition*. Minneapolis: University of Minnesota Press, 2003.

Myers, Victoria. "Lynn Nottage on the Music and Images of Writing 'Sweat,'" *The Interval*. Accessed December 6, 2016. https://www.theintervalny.com/featurettes/2016/12/lynn-nottage-on-the-music-and-images-of-writing-sweat/

Nashrulla, Tasneem. "Rachel Dolezal's Brother Says She Warned: 'Don't Blow My Cover,'" *Buzzfeed News*. Accessed June 12, 2015, https://www.buzzfeednews.com/article/tasneemnashrulla/rachel-dolezals-brother-says-she-warned-dont-blow-my-cover#.ogrRQaZYy

National Fair Housing Alliance. *Fair Housing: The Case for Fair Housing*, 2017 Fair Housing Trends Report, 2017, 35.

Newberry, Christina. "How the TikTok Algorithm Works in 2021 (and How to Work with It)." Accessed August 23, 2021, https://blog.hootsuite.com/tiktok-algorithm/

Nora, Pierre. "Between Memory and History: Les Lieux de Mémoire." *Representations* 26. University of California: Spring 1989.

Nottage, Lynn. "Extracting Art from a Downfall." *The New York Times*. Accessed July 30, 2015. https://www.nytimes.com/interactive/2015/07/29/theater/20150802-sweat.html

Nottage, Lynn. *Sweat*. New York: Theatre Communications Group, 2018.

Nottage, Lynn. "This Is Reading." *Lynn Nottage*. Accessed June 17, 2022. http://www.lynnnottage.com/this-is-reading.html

Pappas, Vanessa and Kudzi Chikumbo, "A Message to Our Black community." Accessed September 2, 2020, https://newsroom.tiktok.com/en-us/a-message-to-our-black-community

Pappas, Vanessa and *Beloved*. New York: Knopf, 1987.

Pinkins, Tonya. "Racism Doesn't Have a Safe Word: An Interview with the Playwright." *American Theatre* (July/August 2019): 40–1.

Parham, Jason. "TikTok and the Evolution of Digital Blackface," *Wired Magazine*. Accessed August 4, 2020, https://www.wired.com/story/tiktok-evolution-digital-blackface/

Paulson, Michael. "A Black Actor in 'Virginia Woolf'? Not Happening, Albee Estate Says." *The New York Times*. Accessed May 21, 2017, sec. Theater. https://www.nytimes.com/2017/05/21/theater/a-black-actor-in-virginia-woolf-not-happening-albee-estate-says.html

Peluso, Nancy Lee. "Whose Woods Are These? Counter-mapping Forest Territories in Kalimantan, Indonesia." *Antipode* 27, no. 4 (October 1995): 383–406. https://doi.org/10.1111/j.1467-8330.1995.tb00286.x

Perry, Imani. *Looking for Lorraine: The Radiant and Radical Life of Lorraine Hansberry*. Boston: Beacon Press Books, 2018.

Peterson, Chris. "The Ridiculousness of the Hamilton Casting Controversy in 5 Images." *OnStage Blog*. Accessed June 15, 2022. https://www.onstageblog.com/columns/2016/3/30/the-ridiculousness-of-the-hamilton-casting-controversy-in-5-images

"Presidential Speeches." *Miller Center*. Accessed July 14, 2020. https://millercenter.org/the-presidency/presidential-speeches

"Protests Shut Down Part of I-35-W for Over an Hour." *MPR News*. Accessed December 4, 2014. https://www.mprnews.org/story/2014/12/04/protesters-close-i35w

Rankine, Claudia. "The Condition of Black Life Is One of Mourning." *The New York Times*. Accessed June 22, 2015, https://www.nytimes.com/2015/06/22/magazine/the-condition-of-black-life-is-one-of-mourning.html?searchResultPosition=1

Rankine, Claudia. "An Excerpt from Help." *The Paris Review* no. 235 (Winter 2020): 13–41.

Reagon, Bernice Johnson. *If You Don't Go, Don't Hinder Me: The African American Sacred Song Tradition*. Lincoln: University of Nebraska Press, 2001.

Redmond, Shana L. *Anthem: Social Movements and the Sound of Solidarity in the African Diaspora*. New York: New York University Press, 2014.

"Remembering Bloody Sunday: Thousands Gather in Selma for Commemoration Events." *WVUA 23*. Accessed March 5, 2018. https://www.youtube.com/watch?v=Sx3pQtymrr0&ab_channel=WVUA23

Robertson, Campbell. "Marking Davis's Confederate Inauguration." *The New York Times*. Accessed February 20, 2011. https://www.nytimes.com/2011/02/21/us/21davis.html

Romano, Aja. "'Arrest the Cops Who Killed Breonna Taylor': The Power and the Peril of a Catchphrase." *Vox*. Accessed August 10, 2020, https://www.vox.com/21327268/breonna-taylor-say-her-name-meme-hashtag

Romano, Aja, Allegra Frank, and Constance Grady. "Reckoning with Slave Play, the Most Controversial Show on Broadway." *Vox*. December 5, 2019. Accessed February 19, 2021. https://www.vox.com/culture/2019/12/5/20961826/slave-play-broadway-2019-review

Romano, John and James Baldwin, "Writing and Talking," *The New York Times*, September 23, 1979.

Rothstein, Richard. *The Color of Law: A Forgotten History of How Our Government Segregated America*. New York: Liveright, 2017.

Rovell, Darren. "Top Tennis Stars Have to Do the Grunt Work." *ESPN.Com*. Accessed August 30, 2005. https://www.espn.com/sports/tennis/usopen05/columns/story?columnist=rovell_darren&id=2147218

Samuels, Allison. "Rachel Dolezal's True Lies," *Vanity Fair*. Accessed July 19, 2015. https://www.vanityfair.com/news/2015/07/rachel-dolezal-new-interview-pictures-exclusive

Sedgman, Kirsty. *The Reasonable Audience: Theatre Etiquette, Behavior Policing, and the Live Performance Experience*. Switzerland: Palgrave McMillian, 2018.

"Serena Williams | Player Stats & More – WTA Official." n.d. Women's Tennis Association. Accessed January 31, 2021. www.wtatennis.com/players/230234/serena-williams

Sewell, Terri and John Lewis. "Editorial: John Lewis, Terri Sewell Defend Keeping Selma Bridge Named after Edmund Pettus." *Sewell.house.gov*. Accessed June 17, 2015. https://sewell.house.gov/media-center/in-the-news/alcom-john-lewis-terri-sewell-defend-keeping-selma-bridge-named-after

Sharpe, Christina Elizabeth. *In the Wake: On Blackness and Being*. Durham: Duke University Press, 2016.

Singh, Maanvi. "George Floyd Told Officers 'I Can't Breathe' More Than 20 Times, Transcripts Show." *The Guardian*. Accessed July 9, 2020, sec. US news. https://www.theguardian.com/us-news/2020/jul/08/george-floyd-police-killing-transcript-i-cant-breathe

Solon, Olivia. "Facebook Ignored Racial Bias Research, Employees Say," *NBC News*. Accessed July 23, 2020, https://www.nbcnews.com/tech/tech-news/facebook-management-ignored-internal-research-showing-racial-bias-current-former-n1234746

Sondel, Justin and Hannah Knowles. "George Floyd Died after Officers Didn't Step in. These Police Say They Did—and Paid a Price," *The Washington Post*. Accessed June 13, 2020, https://www.washingtonpost.com/nation/2020/06/10/police-culture-duty-to-intervene/

Sorin, Gretchen Sullivan. *Driving While Black*. http://www.dwbfilm.com/history

Sorin, Gretchen Sullivan. *Driving While Black: African American Travel and the Road to Civil Rights*. New York: Liveright, 2020.

Spillers, Hortense J. "Mama's Baby, Papa's Maybe: An American Grammar Book." *Diacritics* 17, no. 2 (1987): 65–81.

Sports Illustrated. "Rod Rockets into Orbit," August 27, 1962.

Tavernise, Sabrina. "Reading PA Knew It Was Poor. Now It Knows How Poor." *The New York Times*. Accessed September 26, 2011. https://www.nytimes.com/2011/09/27/us/reading-pa-tops-list-poverty-list-census-shows.html?searchResultPosition=1

Taylor, Diana. *The Archive and the Repertoire: Performing Cultural Memory in the Americas*. Durham: Duke University Press, 2003.

Taylor, Keeanga-Yamahtta. *From #BlackLivesMatter to Black Liberation*. Chicago: Haymarket Books, 2016.

Thomas, June. "Lynn Nottage on Her Broadway-Bound Play, *Sweat*, and Why She's Wary of 'Poverty Porn.'" *Slate Magazine*. Accessed December 6, 2016. https://slate.com/culture/2016/12/lynn-nottage-on-her-broadway-bound-play-sweat-and-why-shes-wary-of-poverty-porn.html

Thompson, Wanna. Twitter. Accessed November 28, 2020, https://twitter.com/WannasWorld/status/1059989652487069696

"This Is Reading," *Lynn Nottage*. Accessed June 17, 2022, http://www.lynnnottage.com/this-is-reading.html

"This Is Reading," *Project &*. Accessed June 17, 2022, https://projectand.org/project/this-is-reading/

"tldr; smh." *Revolution They Wrote*. Accessed December 31, 2021. https://revolutiontheywrote.com/tldr-smh/

Toll, Robert C. *Blacking Up: The Minstrel Show in Nineteenth Century America*. New York: Oxford University Press, 1974.

Twitter. "About Verified Accounts:" "Activists, Organizers, and Other Influential Individuals: Outside the Professional Categories Defined Above, People Who Are Using Twitter Effectively to Bring Awareness, Share Information, and Galvanize Community Members around a Cause, to Bring about Socioeconomic, Political, or Cultural Change, or to

Otherwise Foster Community, May Be Verified," https://help.twitter.com/en/managing-your-account/about-twitter-verified-accounts

Vanessa, Pappas and Kudzi Chikumbo. "A Message to Our Black Community." Accessed September 2, 2020, https://newsroom.tiktok.com/en-us/a-message-to-our-black-community.

Vazquez, Alexandra T. *Listening in Detail: Performances of Cuban Music*. Durham: Duke University Press Books, 2013.

"Voice of Belief Feat. Serena Williams—Nike News." n.d. Accessed December 11, 2020. https://news.nike.com/featured_video/voice-of-belief-serena-williams-just-do-it-film

Watkins, Mary and Helene Shulman. *Toward Psychologies of Liberation*. London: Palgrave McMillan, 2008.

"We Shall Overcome: The Story behind the Song." *The Kennedy Center*. https://www.kennedy-center.org/education/resources-for-educators/classroom-resources/media-and-interactives/media/music/story-behind-the-song/the-story-behind-the-song/we-shall-overcome/

Weatherford, Ashley. "The Rachel Dolezal Documentary Gave Us the Hair Tutorial We Didn't Ask for." Accessed April 27, 2018, https://www.thecut.com/2018/04/the-rachel-divide-netflix-rachel-dolezal-hair.html

Weingroff, Robert F. "U.S. Route 80 the Dixie Overland Highway." *U.S. Department of Transportation—Federal Highway Administration*, https://www.fhwa.dot.gov/infrastructure/us80.cfm

"White Actors Suing 'Hamilton' for Discrimination? Supreme Court Hears Warning—The Hollywood Reporter." Accessed June 15, 2022. https://www.hollywoodreporter.com/business/business-news/white-actors-suing-hamilton-discrimination-supreme-court-hears-warning-1195755/

Wilson, August. *Gem of the Ocean*. New York: Theatre Communications Group, 2007.

Winberry, John T. "'Lest We Forget': The Confederate Monument and the Southern Townscape." *Southeastern Geographer* 23, no. 2 (1983): 107–21.

Wong, Julia Carrie. "White Nationalists Are Openly Operating on Facebook. The Company Won't Act." Accessed November 21, 2019, https://www.theguardian.com/technology/2019/nov/21/facebook-white-nationalists-ban-vdare-red-ice

Yasharoff, Hannah. "Jimmy Fallon Addresses His TikTok Dance Segment with Addison Rae. Here's Why It Sparked Backlash," *USA Today*. Accessed March 30, 2021, https://www.usatoday.com/story/entertainment/

tv/2021/03/30/tiktok-dances-why-addison-rae-jimmy-fallon-clip-sparked-backlash/7058920002/

Young, Harvey. *Embodying Black Experience: Stillness, Critical Memory, and the Black Body*. Ann Arbor: University of Michigan Press, 2010.

Young, Sharon Pruitt. "Black TikTok Creators Are on Strike to Protest a Lack of Credit for Their Work," *NPR*. Accessed July 1, 2021. https://www.npr.org/2021/07/01/1011899328/black-tiktok-creators-are-on-strike-to-protest-a-lack-of-credit-for-their-work

Index